24.95

INVESTING FOR A LIFETIME
Paul Merriman's Guide
to Mutual Fund Strategies

INVESTING FOR A LIFETIME
Paul Merriman's Guide
to Mutual Fund Strategies

Paul Merriman

BUSINESS ONE IRWIN
Homewood, Illiinois 60430

This publication is designed to provide accurate and authoritative information in regard to the subject matter covered. It is sold with the understanding that neither the author nor the publisher is engaged in rendering legal, accounting, or other professional service. If legal advice or other expert assistance is required, the services of a competent professional person should be sought.

From a Declaration of Principles jointly adopted by a Committee of the American Bar Association and a Committee of Publishers.

Sponsoring editor: Amy Hollands
Project editor: Karen J. Nelson
Production manager: Mary Jo Parke
Printer: The Book Press, Inc.

Library of Congress Cataloging-in-Publication Data

Merriman, Paul A.
    Investing for a lifetime: Paul Merriman's guide to mutual fund strategies/Paul A. Merriman.
        p.   cm.
    Includes bibliographical references and index.
    ISBN 1-55623-485-6
    1. Mutual funds. 2. Investments. I. Title.
HG4530.M479 1992
332.63'27—dc20   91–28625

Printed in the United States of America

    3 4 5 6 7 8 9 0 BP 8 7 6 5 4 3 2

To Doll—whose love taught me that making money is not the only goal in life.
To Jeff and Julie—the best two kids a father could ever have.

ACKNOWLEDGMENTS

This book could not have been written without the expert assistance of Merle Dowd. Nor could it have been written without the editorial guidance of Amy Hollands. I would like to extend special thanks to Bill Donoghue and Sheldon Jacobs for their tremendously effective endorsement and support of the no-load fund industry. I also wish to express my thanks to Stan Lipstadt, Charlie Hooper, Marshall Schield, David Wright, and Ken Sleeper. All five are market timers I work with on a day-to-day basis. They have all been instrumental in helping me improve my knowledge and understanding of how market timing can make investing less risky and more profitable.

PREFACE

Investing for a lifetime! What does it mean? Your answers to the following questions can help you think through your needs and concerns about money:

1. How do you acquire capital for investing? Sorting through the many opportunities for investing your cash puts the cart before the horse unless you have a plan for saving or collecting the capital you need to invest.

2. Why do you invest? Your investment goals and objectives exert a powerful influence on how and where you put your money. And I expect the reasons you invest your money change at various ages.

3. Would you invest in the same stocks, bonds, mutual funds or other investments at age 25 as you would at 52? Probably not, and you should understand the reasons behind the differences, hence my plans for a lifetime of investing.

4. What about taxes and inflation? All investments are affected by both. It's not how much you earn, it's how much you keep, and taxes and inflation make up the difference.

As you ponder these and other questions that will affect your financial future, I encourage you to assume the role of a financial manager. I want you to take control of your money and put it to work for your benefit. My purpose in writing this book is to help you evaluate the risks, study potential returns, look at alternative costs, and set aside the time you will need to manage and monitor your investments. That may sound like a tall order, but once you understand my simple, limited-risk plan that aims to help you achieve financial security, you can manage your money in less than one hour per month.

Consider this book as a guide to help you find your way through the maze of money management—a broader term than *investing.* I expect to guide you to the investment that offers the:

Highest return.
Lowest risk.
Highest liquidity.
Least cost.

Unfortunately, such an ideal single investment doesn't exist, but you can trade off one trait against the others. Finding the right mix of investments will help you reach your lifetime financial goals.

I have included basic information to help you understand the implications of your actions before making decisions. Once you gain confidence, you will begin earning more money from your money than you ever thought possible. Portions are pragmatic, such as a plan to acquire the capital you need to get you started on the road to wealth accumulation. Other portions are subjective, such as the need to wring emotion—your emotion—out of investment decision making. My aim is to develop you into a seasoned, unemotional, disciplined investor.

To help you embark on a sound plan for managing your money profitably, you may need to discard some distracting baggage you may have picked up along the way. Clearing the slate can be a catharsis that will prepare you for the positive program I expect you to adopt for the rest of your life. But exercise caution; understanding the pitfalls that can reduce the effectiveness of your program is critical to your success. The plan of this book is in three parts:

Part one—Look closely at yourself. Do you see or recognize any of the key characteristics that keep many investors from achieving their potential. Emotion and an overly-cautious approach to risk can doom your long-range program if you let them.

Part two—Examine the six risks that affect any investment program. I describe in detail one or more defensive strategies for dealing with each of the six risks every investor faces.

Part three—Build an odds-on minimum-risk investment plan to achieve your objectives. No generalities; you will find specific answers with names and strategies that you can adopt as your own.

Positive Planning Steps You Can Take

1. Find yourself as an investor. Are you comfortable managing money, either yours or others'? Can you sift through masses of conflicting information to find the action most likely to succeed for you? Or are you emotionally involved with gurus, rumors, tips, and pseudoscientific mumbo jumbo that inhibit rational investing? Your mind-set is critically important when selecting investment opportunities.

2. Evaluate your interest and capability for managing your own money. You may prefer to turn the job over to someone else for a variety of reasons. You can ask yourself, "If I expect to prosper from managing my own money, how good is my track record?"

3. Find reliable professionals you trust. Some of the most available, brokers and financial planners masquerading as brokers, may be poor choices for one overriding reason—your goals and their goals are in conflict. You'll understand why I take a dim view of certain professionals when you read Chapter 8. I am often ashamed of our industry, and the following analogy explains what can happen. Remember your emotions during courtship? Promises of great things to come, some openly outrageous, are accepted on faith with hope for the future. After the courtship comes the honeymoon—and then reality. The financial services industry is a master of the courtship. Salespersons may tell lies, omit important information on risk and liquidity, forecast success—and many investors take it all in like a promise on a moonlight night. Instead of falling for get-rich-quick promises, you need to seek out those professionals who can help you.

4. Access the information you need. Newsletters and major sections of magazines trumpet new and promising financial opportunities regularly. *The Wall Street Journal* and *Investor's Business Daily* pump out more information than most of us can even read let alone act on every day. With our promise of a program that requires no more than one hour per month, you will learn to access information quickly and effectively.

5. Evaluate strategies. Are you patient enough for a buy-and-hold strategy to work for you? Some minimum-risk strate-

gies may appear to require more daring but actually are less risky overall than supposedly conservative programs. Some strategies work for some investors and not for others. Or some strategies work better within certain age limits than others. No strategy works equally well for everybody, so helping you to find a strategy that works for you within your risk tolerance is one of my major goals.

6. Recognize and understand how various investments have performed historically because, "Those who ignore the lessons of history are doomed to repeat them." Don't expect long-term results to suddenly change. Ibbotson Associates' monumental study of Treasury bills and bonds, major and small stocks, and inflation provide a solid base for the comparison of performance between financial instruments.

7. Understand the advantages of investing in mutual funds. During the 1980s, capital invested in mutual funds increased 10-fold, from $100 billion at the beginning of 1980 to $1 trillion at the end of 1989, according to the Investment Company Institute, a mutual fund trade association. Mutual funds' capital increased two ways—partly from the increase in the value of portfolio holdings and partly from the addition of new money to buy more shares. Since mutual funds are key elements in my program of Investing for a Lifetime, you need to understand why they afford a better instrument than individual issues of stocks or bonds.

That's the program. You can skip to Chapter 11 to put your long-term investing program into action today. But you'll feel better about what you're doing if you read the other chapters first.

Finally, I make an offer never before made in any book. Many of you may find it difficult to maintain the simple discipline that is the key to your success with this book. To help you keep the faith, I extend a special offer—a free annual update on the options spelled out in Chapter 11. All you need to do is send me a stamped, self-addressed business envelope each year, and the updates are yours free.

And now you're off on an exciting adventure.

Paul A. Merriman

CONTENTS

INVESTING FOR A LIFETIME
Paul Merriman's Guide
to Mutual Fund Strategies

CHAPTER 1

WHAT KIND OF INVESTOR
ARE YOU?

Investing for a lifetime! What does it mean? Would you invest in the same instruments at age 25 as you would at 52? Or 65? Probably not. Where and how do you acquire the capital to invest? Why do you invest; that is, what are your objectives? What about taxes? How do they affect your strategies?

Your answers to these and other questions will help you shape your financial future. To build the best life possible for you and your family, you need to assume the role of money manager and develop your money management skills. You already manage your money—one way or another—even if you default and do nothing. So, why not ask yourself, "What kind of a job am I doing as a money manager?"

As a first step, ask yourself this question, "Am I managing my lifetime earnings effectively? Am I getting the maximum living value out of my earnings?" If you earn an average $50,000 per year for 40 years, that's $2 million. Maybe you didn't earn $50,000 last year, but inflation is pushing many beyond that range today. Many more people will move to those earning levels at earlier ages in the years ahead as inflation continues. Wouldn't you agree that with $2 million to manage, you would spend some time and devote considerable effort to the task? If

$200,000 were to drop into your lap from a relative's estate, would you deposit it in your local bank's savings account and forget it? Probably not. But $200,000 is 10 percent of your life's earnings, about what $2 million would earn if you had it all in one year. To see how managing your money fits into an overall plan, look briefly at how a sound financial plan is put together:

FINANCIAL PLANNING

Financial planners consider five key activities to be essential elements of a financial plan. Investing is the third or middle element.

1. Acquiring the capital to invest is the tough part of your financial plan. Most of us acquire capital by spending less than we earn. You may acquire capital by inheritance, lottery winnings or a big strike at a casino—but you cannot count on these sources.

2. Managing risk with insurance protects against catastrophes and enables you to focus on positive objectives.

3. Investing is the fascinating and compelling part of any financial plan. Investing is where the continuing action is. A friend taught personal financial planning at the University of Washington for a number of years. Each student or couple was asked to develop a personal balance sheet and a prioritized list of financial objectives. Later, he reviewed each student's or couple's balance sheet and objectives with them privately. Fully one third of the class was so heavily in debt they could not under any circumstances consider investing. Their best money management decision would have been to pay off the balances due on their bank credit cards. Yet, they found the investing portion of the class to be the most exciting. They were like the wide receiver in football who drops a pass he should have caught, and the announcer comments, "He tried to run with the ball before he caught it."

4. Retirement planning is a key objective for older persons, particularly those whose children have graduated from college. Most individuals and couples acquire assets to supplement Social Security and pension benefits after the kids gradu-

TABLE 1A
Effect of Time and Compound Interest on Wealth Accumulation

Initial Deposit at Age 26—$2,000

Age	Total at Beginning of Year	Interest at 10%	Total at End of Year	Total at Beginning of Year	Interest at 12%	Total at End of Year
26	$2,000	$200	$2,200	$2,000	$240	$2,240
27	2,200	220	2,420	2,240	269	2,509
28	2,420	242	2,662	2,509	301	2,810
29	2,662	266	2,928	2,810	337	3,147
30	2,928	293	3,221	3,147	378	3,525
31	3,221	322	3,543	3,525	423	3,948
32	3,543	354	3,897	3,948	474	4,421
33	3,897	390	4,287	4,421	531	4,952
34	4,287	429	4,716	4,952	594	5,546
35	4,716	472	5,187	5,546	666	6,212
36	5,187	519	5,706	6,212	745	6,957
37	5,706	571	6,277	6,957	835	7,792
38	6,277	628	6,905	7,792	935	8,727
39	6,905	690	7,595	8,727	1,047	9,774
40	7,595	759	8,354	9,774	1,173	10,947
41	8,354	835	9,190	10,947	1,314	12,261
42	9,190	919	10,109	12,261	1,471	13,732
43	10,109	1,011	11,120	13,732	1,648	15,380
44	11,120	1,112	12,232	15,380	1,846	17,226
45	12,232	1,223	13,455	17,226	2,067	19,293
46	13,455	1,345	14,800	19,293	2,315	21,608
47	14,800	1,480	16,281	21,608	2,593	24,201
48	16,281	1,628	17,909	24,201	2,904	27,105
49	17,909	1,791	19,699	27,105	3,253	30,357
50	19,699	1,970	21,669	30,357	3,643	34,000
51	21,669	2,167	23,836	34,000	4,080	38,080
52	23,836	2,384	26,220	38,080	4,570	42,650
53	26,220	2,622	28,842	42,650	5,118	47,768
54	28,842	2,884	31,726	47,768	5,732	53,500
55	31,726	3,173	34,899	53,500	6,420	59,920
56	34,899	3,490	38,389	59,920	7,190	67,110
57	38,389	3,839	42,228	67,110	8,053	75,163
58	42,228	4,223	46,450	75,163	9,020	84,183
59	46,450	4,645	51,095	84,183	10,102	94,285
60	51,095	5,110	56,205	94,285	11,314	105,599
61	56,205	5,620	61,825	105,599	12,672	118,271
62	61,825	6,183	68,008	118,271	14,193	132,464
63	68,008	6,801	74,809	132,464	15,896	148,359
64	74,809	7,481	82,290	148,359	17,803	166,162
65	82,290	8,229	90,519	166,162	19,939	186,102

TABLE 1B
Effect of Starting Time on Value of IRA at Retirement

Year No.	Annual Deposit	Total at Beginning of Year	Interest at 10%	Total at End of Year	Total at Beginning of Year
1	$2,000	$2,000	$200	$2,200	
2	2,000	4,200	420	4,620	
3	2,000	6,620	662	7,282	
4	2,000	9,282	928	10,210	
5	2,000	12,210	1,221	13,431	
6	2,000	15,431	1,543	16,974	
7	2,000	18,974	1,897	20,872	
8	2,000	22,872	2,287	25,159	
9	2,000	27,159	2,716	29,875	
10	2,000	31,875	3,187	35,062	
11	2,000	37,062	3,706	40,769	$2,000
12	2,000	42,769	4,277	47,045	4,200
13	2,000	49,045	4,905	53,950	6,620
14	2,000	55,950	5,595	61,545	9,282
15	2,000	63,545	6,354	69,899	12,210
16	2,000	71,899	7,190	79,089	15,431
17	2,000	81,089	8,109	89,198	18,974
18	2,000	91,198	9,120	100,318	22,872
19	2,000	102,318	10,232	112,550	27,159
20	2,000	114,550	11,455	126,005	31,875
21	2,000	128,005	12,800	140,805	37,062
22	2,000	142,805	14,281	157,086	42,769
23	2,000	159,086	15,909	174,995	49,045
24	2,000	176,995	17,699	194,694	55,950
25	2,000	196,694	19,669	216,364	63,545
26	2,000	218,364	21,836	240,200	71,899
27	2,000	242,200	24,220	266,420	81,089
28	2,000	268,420	26,842	295,262	91,198
29	2,000	297,262	29,726	326,988	102,318
30	2,000	328,988	32,899	361,887	114,550
31	2,000	363,887	36,389	400,276	128,005
32	2,000	402,276	40,228	442,503	142,805
33	2,000	444,503	44,450	488,953	159,086
34	2,000	490,953	49,095	540,049	176,995
35	2,000	542,049	54,205	596,254	196,694
36	2,000	598,254	59,825	658,079	218,364
37	2,000	660,079	66,008	726,087	242,200
38	2,000	728,087	72,809	800,896	268,420
39	2,000	802,896	80,290	883,185	297,262
40	2,000	885,185	88,519	973,704	328,988

TABLE 1B *(continued)*

Interest at 10%	Total at End of Year	Total at Beginning of Year	Interest at 10%	Total at End of Year
$200	$2,200			
420	4,620			
662	7,282			
928	10,210			
1,221	13,431			
1,543	16,974			
1,897	20,872			
2,287	25,159			
2,716	29,875			
3,187	35,062			
3,706	40,769	$2,000	$200	$2,200
4,277	47,045	4,200	420	4,620
4,905	53,950	6,620	662	7,282
5,595	61,545	9,282	928	10,210
6,354	69,899	12,210	1,221	13,431
7,190	79,089	15,431	1,543	16,974
8,109	89,198	18,974	1,897	20,872
9,120	100,318	22,872	2,287	25,159
10,232	112,550	27,159	2,716	29,875
11,455	126,005	31,875	3,187	35,062
12,800	140,805	37,062	3,706	40,769
14,281	157,086	42,769	4,277	47,045
15,909	174,995	49,045	4,905	53,950
17,699	194,694	55,950	5,595	61,545
19,669	216,364	63,545	6,354	69,899
21,836	240,200	71,899	7,190	79,089
24,220	266,420	81,089	8,109	89,198
26,842	295,262	91,198	9,120	100,318
29,726	326,988	102,318	10,232	112,550
32,899	361,887	114,550	11,455	126,005

ate. My friend calls this the recovery period. I hope you will extend that investment period by starting earlier. Put the power of compound interest to work for you over a longer period to rev up your investment program. Table 1A explores the potential for building a retirement nest egg from an early start with a single investment of $2,000 in an IRA. Table 1A shows you something else—how much more money an improvement of 2 percent from 10 percent to 12 percent in earning rate makes over a 40-year compounding period—$90,519 to $186,102. Table 1B shows the penalty you pay for waiting. A 10 percent rate of return is about average from 1926 through 1990 (see Chapter 2). You can expect to do better than 10 percent using the tactics you will discover later in this book.

   5. Estate planning arranges for the orderly conveyance of your property and personal effects to heirs at death.

   As a money manager, you can skip steps 2, 4, and 5 for now, as I deal with these later in various scenarios. You need to concentrate on acquiring capital to invest and learning how to make it work for you—by managing it effectively.

RATING YOUR MONEY MANAGEMENT SKILLS

Let's see how you rate as a money manager, using Chart 1A. A surprising variety of investment opportunities compete for your attention—and your money. Each opportunity carries a mixed bag of characteristics—risks, yields, returns, cost, and liquidity. How would you pick one over another? Using only your present knowledge, mark your score on the work sheet. But first, a few guidelines:

   At the top of five columns are those characteristics you should consider before investing. Various investment possibilities are listed down the left side. Score each type of investment for each characteristic from 1 through 5 to indicate your ranking. A 1 score would indicate an investment is best, highly desirable, or least bad for that characteristic. A 5 score is worst or least desirable. After scoring each investment opportunity for each characteristic, add the numbers across for a total score. Try to isolate your scoring for each characteristic from any

CHART 1A
Risks and Benefits Ratings of Investment Opportunities

	Risk	Yield	Appre-ciation	Cost	Liquidity	Score
Bank/S&L savings account	2	5	5	1	1	14
Certificate of deposit	2	5	5	1	3	16
EE bond	1	5	4	1	1	12
U.S. Treasury bond	1	5	4	2	1	13
Corporate bonds	2	3	3	2	2	12
Common stocks, listed	4	3	2	3	2	14
Common stocks, OTC	4	3	2	3	2	14
Preferred stocks	3	3	3	4	3	16
Real estate	3	2	3	4	5	18
Stock options	4	2	2	3	1	12
Futures options	4	1	2	3	1	11
Commodities	5	2	2	3	1	13
Mutual funds, load	3	2	3	2	3	13
Mutual Funds, no-load	3	2	3	1	3	12
Mutual Funds, no-load with timing	3	2	3	1	3	12
Gold	3	5	3	3	3	17
Limited partnerships	4	3	3	3	4	17
Insurance, cash value	2	3	3	3	5	15
Insurance, tax-deferred annuity	2	3	3	3	4	15

subconscious effect of other characteristics. For example, when scoring an investment for yield, forget about risks, costs or any of the other characteristics. An explanation will help.

1. How do you perceive the *risk* of each investment opportunity? An insured bank savings account would score a 1 because it incurs no credit risk; you can expect to get all of your money back with interest. Commodities and options often leave investors with an empty wallet, so they deserve a 5.

2. Interest or dividends you can expect from the investment are distinct from growth or appreciation. Interest on a savings account is pure *yield* because there is no change in value of the capital or principal. As an example of how to score each investment opportunity, consider interest payable on bank savings accounts. Rates tend to be low, possibly in the range of 4 1/2 to 5 1/2 percent, but not as low as the yield on some growth stocks. A score of 3 might be appropriate. Scores represent your best judgment; there are no right or wrong answers.

3. *Appreciation* represents your evaluation of the investment's potential for growth. A bank savings account offers no growth potential, so it scores a 5.

4. *Cost* is either nothing, as in the case of a bank savings account, or substantial, as in the case of a limited partnership. Commissions on stock or load mutual funds are costs.

5. *Liquidity* is a measure of how quickly you can turn your investment into cash without giving up part of its value or influencing its price in the market. A bank savings account can be converted to cash by a withdrawal any day the bank is open. There is no delay and no cost, so it would score a 1. Where each security trades on a secondary market, such as the various exchanges, affects liquidity and must be judged in scorings.

When you have finished, compare the total scores for each investment. A high score indicates an investment may be less desirable than an investment with a low score. You should not be surprised if your score for mutual funds ends up on the low end with commodities and options at the opposite end of the spectrum.

To see how you rate as a money manager, check your scores with our ratings on the same work sheet in the Appendix. Don't be too concerned if your scores differ from ours. Remember—these are judgments; your scores represent your current perceptions. Your perceptions of various investments flow from your current knowledge and feelings, possibly based on good or bad experiences. Don't peek at our scores in the Appendix until you have worked out the chart on your own. If your ratings and scores differ, try to ascertain why. As noted earlier, there are no right or wrong answers. Appropriate investments can be tailored to your goals using skills you are developing. The next step in developing your investment skills for managing money is . . .

REMOVING EMOTION FROM INVESTING

If you expect to become an effective money manager, you must eliminate emotion from your investment decisions. Learn to use steely discipline based on facts and probabilities—not how you feel. Suppose you decide to invest in a stock or mutual fund. If you feel good about it, are confident your reasoning is sound and expect a favorable outcome, you have probably done the wrong thing. Why? Because you feel comfortable following the lead of others. A contrarian, an investor who buys when others are selling and vice versa, profits from the discipline that counters the emotional reactions of most investors.

Probably the height of emotional investing is what I call *recreational investing*—having fun and getting one's kicks from the risks of brinksmanship. Recreational investors love to jump into and out of the market on hunches, to match wits with brokers. Recreational investors may get their jollies from jousting with Wall Street pros, taking fliers based on intuition or a tip heard at lunch, or developing their own secret system for beating the market. Money made or lost is simply a way of keeping score. Having fun investing differs little from the fun weekend gamblers experience when they take a fling in Las Vegas or Atlantic City. They enter the casino knowing deep inside they will likely lose because house odds are stacked against them. But gambling is fun as long as they lose only their limit. They enjoy the inner tension of shooting craps or looking at and waiting intently for those three wheels to stop at a winning combination. Gambling is highly emotional; it is not disciplined or intellectual. Recreational investing, despite its appeal to a few, tends to be counterproductive. Here is a typical example.

A successful dentist told me about his flier into a commodity pool. He is conservative—button-down Oxford shirts, sincere gray suits—but with a Walter Mitty desire to break out of his constrained image. He had already set aside money for his children's education and set them up with IRAs to encourage saving for retirement. He told me, "I decided to put $35,000 into this commodity fund because I could afford it and was willing to lose $35,000 if it didn't work out. I figured it would be fun to do something different—even daring. So I put $35,000 into this commodity pool that appeared to have a good track record."

When I talked with him, his $35,000 had shrunk to $23,000. He was now feeling very differently about losing $35,000—even $12,000. I asked him, "Ken, how long are you going to live? Another 30 years?"

"Sure."

"Well, you're not talking about losing $35,000. You're really talking about losing the compounded earnings from $35,000. Assume a minimal 10 percent per year. If the $35,000 stops working for you, you're looking at a loss of more than $610,000 before taxes over the next 30 years." Ken decided he had tasted enough high-risk pie and pulled out to salvage his $23,000.

A bit of introspection may help you find yourself as an investor. In your role of money manager have you experienced one or more of these emotional reactions?

• Putting things off, or procrastinating. Most of us procrastinate to avoid a wrong decision that could produce unfortunate results. There's also another reason. If you don't commit to some plan, then you can't be held accountable if you fail. Even something as simple as deciding how many dollars to spend for food, paper products, and sundries at the supermarket can be a turnoff. If you decide, "I'll spend $400 at the market this month," that's a commitment. If you spend $500, you've overspent your budget. If your wife or husband asks, "How come you spent $100 more than you said you would?" an argument could erupt.

But if you set no goal, then no one can fault you if you miss. A reluctance to weigh options, set goals, and then take decisive action and stick to those decisions underlies most persons' problems with money. Handling money is highly emotional for many people.

• The gut-wrenching agony of watching a roller-coaster stock market drop precipitously one day only to rebound another. Responding emotionally to these ups and downs can weaken your resolve to gain more from your money than bank interest. Like President Truman said, "If you can't stand the heat, get out of the kitchen." Rather than drop out of investing, understand how it functions and then learn to beat it.

A start to understanding the market is to recognize that greed, fear and hope, all powerful emotions, drive the market. The stock market and, to a lesser extent, the bond market react emotionally, almost as if they felt the surging passions of a real person. Cold, calculating logic and steely-eyed discipline seldom support most small investors' actions. When you react emotionally to the actions of an emotional market, you lose your cool. The three basic emotions constantly tug you in one direction or another, sometimes in combination. Think of greed, fear, and hope at the corners of a triangle, as in Chart 1B. Sometimes hope controls your actions as you look forward to something positive happening. Greed may take over as you see the market pushing to new highs. At another corner of the triangle fear grips you, and you may wake in the middle of the night wondering what to do if the market begins falling.

Chart 1C maps the progression of these three basic emotions over a typical cycle of the market. Pick up the action from the first bottom of the diagram and follow the progression.

1. When stocks are down, few people buy. They, and you, are afraid—one of your three basic emotions. You are afraid to take a position in the market because it might continue to move even lower. Your friends and associates reinforce your fears by commenting that only a fool would invest in stocks with the market heading south.

2. As time slips by, the index bottoms out and begins moving up. Your broker calls suggesting now would be a good time to get into the market. Your reply, "Maybe. I think I'll wait a

CHART 1B
Emotional Triangle

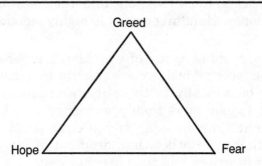

bit—see how the market reacts. I'll let you know later." Fear is still in control. As the market continues to move up, your fear subsides a bit.

When your broker calls again, you may reply, "Yes, things are looking better, but I would like to wait—see how the market reacts to the changes in (fill in your own excuse—Middle-East tensions, rising interest rates, mixed corporate earnings, or whatever)." Again you procrastinate. But hope begins to edge fear aside.

3. As time passes, the market continues climbing. Excitement grows, as you and your friends discuss the overall market and possible investment opportunities. Hope gradually replaces fear. Interest in the market accelerates. Your friends wonder how much higher the market will go. The volume of trades increases, and the market rises steadily. Some even believe stocks will continue rising forever—that bear markets are passe. You notice more and more of your friends and associates are eagerly buying into the market, a consensus that fosters greed. You want to get your share. The heady rise appears to make it all so simple. "Invest today and gain 50 percent by year's end!" You discard any thoughts of a steady-as-you-go, conservative approach. Now is the time for action—not caution. So you buy shares in a high-flying stock suggested by your broker. What you buy is not important; you are IN the market. Emotionally you are in the grip of that demon greed. Fear is long gone.

4. Gains in the market begin slowing. Then the market

CHART 1C
Investment Emotional Cycle

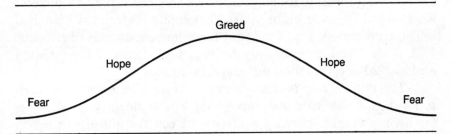

tips over and begins to slide down, ever so slowly at first, but definitely down. As the market drops 5 or 10 percent, you begin to be concerned. Hope reappears, but now you hope that the market will reverse its downward path and regain the high ground. You are no longer hoping for bigger and better things; instead, you are hoping the market will simply return to the levels where you invested. "I'll get out when I break even," you promise yourself.

5. But the market continues sliding, even picking up speed on the down side. Hope fades for a reversal and gradually changes to a fear that the market might not regain its former position. Instead of reversing direction, prices continue dropping and fears reappear. You begin waking up at night engaging in a continuing round of negative self-talk. Near the bottom, your fear of losing everything overpowers logic. You forget the market's reversal after the last bottom. You sell out into a declining market to salvage what you can of your investment. By buying near the top and selling near the bottom, you have obviously done exactly opposite what you should have done— all because you became emotionally involved in the market.

Replacing emotion with discipline will help you learn to cope with and profit from the emotional ups and downs of the market. Instead of reacting to fear, greed, and hope, you will act with confidence born of logic and discipline.

Successful money managers use the same discipline and tenacity as successful dieters. Let me tell you about my diet because it relates directly to the problem of controlling emotion in investing. I've been on a diet since I was in the fifth grade. I have a complete library of diet books, starting with the Air Force diet and running through the latest from Dr. Pritikin's son. I own a lifetime membership in a health club, but I haven't worked out for over eight years. When the restaurant attached to the club closed, I quit going. I have lost thousands of pounds, 1, 2, 5, or 10 at a time, only to gain them back. I have fasted and lost 20 pounds, then put them on again.

The bottom line is that every one of us who is smart enough to read and has ever been on a diet knows dozens of formulas for losing weight. Dieting and weight control add up to a $33 billion-a-year industry. But all of the books and seminars can be replaced by a single 3-by-5 note card. On one side is your diet plan. On the other is your exercise plan. All you need besides the note card are willpower and discipline.

It is the same with investing. The industry tries to be sophisticated and complicates investing by inventing fancy products. You're less likely to be successful if you try to be sophisticated because you will understand less about what you're doing. Discipline is the important and irreplaceable element you need to be a successful investor.

I've learned something about investing from dieting. I have learned to simply cut out things that are harmful to my physical or financial health.

1. I don't eat red meat, and I don't buy penny stocks.

2. I don't eat dairy products, and I don't buy options.

3. I don't eat eggs, and I don't buy individual stocks.

By cutting things out, I have become a more successful dieter. And a better investor.

CAN YOU MANAGE YOUR MONEY YOURSELF?

If you were totally satisfied with your investment program and your skills as a money manager, you probably wouldn't be reading this book. But you must decide what you really want and whether you can achieve your goals on your own. Your next step is to look at your record.

Examine the following five questions before deciding whether you might or might not succeed at managing your own money:

Question 1—Is managing your money high on your list of priorities? That is, have you made investing one or your top priority personal interests?

Thomas Porter, a senior vice president of Security Pacific Bank Washington with responsibilities for overseeing the bank's trust department and promoting financial planning among the bank's clients, conducts seminars as a key marketing tool.

Tom asks attendees at his seminars to list their 20 most important and interesting activities. He wants to know about the things his listeners really like doing—activities high on their list of priorities. Activities might include playing tennis or golf, traveling, dining out, working, jogging, working out at the gym, playing the piano, camping with the kids, and so on.

To help you decide whether to manage your own investments or not, make your own list of activities you enjoy. Don't rush. Over several days your subconscious mind will float ideas to the surface that you might not remember at a single session. After you note all of the things you enjoy doing, arrange them in order of their importance to you with the most important at the top. Tom Porter insists that unless managing money is among the top five activities you enjoy, you should probably rethink your decision about managing your own money. We tend to do better at activities we enjoy. Managing money is no different and is much like exercise. We all know we need it, but unless it is fun, we don't exercise regularly.

Excellent books on how to manage money appear regularly. Most are filled with sound advice. I think about these books the same way I think about the Canadian Air Force exercise program. Reading the Canadian Air Force book about exercise may be interesting, but you don't build your personal fitness by reading the book. You must do the exercises, do them regularly, and stick with them for months or years to gain long-term benefits. You won't build your personal fortune simply by reading books. You must resolve to follow through and get involved in managing your money. Using the strategies you will discover in the following chapters, you can manage your money effectively without a total commitment and far easier than any other system you may know about. Then you can spend your energy on pursuits that are more fun.

Question 2—Do you have the time? You're busy. Isn't

everyone? Maybe you are too busy to devote the time needed to manage your money, learn about investment opportunities and research specific moves for their impact on your portfolio. How much time do you now spend monitoring where your money goes, learning how to minimize your income taxes, picking the right place to invest your money, or checking your personal money plan to see how it is progressing? Obviously, you don't spend full time managing your money. Few people do. Acknowledging that management of your money will continue to be a part-time activity is OK. But ask yourself, "If I expect to get more income and growth from my capital, how much time must I spend?" And the follow-up question, "Do I want to spend that much time poring over statistics, attending seminars, analyzing alternatives, and then acting?" My objective is for you to oversee the management of your investments and to spend no more than TWELVE HOURS A YEAR doing it.

Many part-time personal money managers do surprisingly well for themselves. They are not consumed with a passion for making money that soaks up hours of personal time. Yet they carve enough time out of their busy schedules to keep abreast of developments. When the time comes for action, they act. Savvy part-time money managers do well because they eliminate nonessentials. They learn to find good sources of advice. Since all of us have the same 24 hours every day, these successful part-time money managers willingly give up something else in order to have time for their financial affairs. It's a matter of setting priorities and spending quality time on those activities likely to affect you the most. If you follow one of my strategies, you can count on spending no more than TWELVE HOURS A YEAR.

Question 3—How well have your investments fared in the past? If you keep slipping yourself "do better" notes, ask yourself why. Are you asking, "How come my investment portfolio is not keeping up with the S&P 500 index?" The Standard & Poor's 500 is a good average, but it is still average. Most of us are not satisfied with just average. Or you may be asking, "How come my money is not growing faster?" Faster than what?

You may be saying to yourself, "I think I'm doing OK or even pretty good." If you really know how your investments have been doing, you are one of a limited minority. Few individuals keep detailed records or update them regularly. Further, my experience indicates that most investors are not totally honest with themselves. They may have a selective memory that recalls the winners and conveniently forgets the losers when reviewing their investments anecdotally. Or they honestly don't recognize a loss.

Question 4—Can you make a decision and act on it? Honest appraisals of individual investment records disclose few portfolios that beat the market. The answer to subpar performance most often points to investors' inability or unwillingness to take action. This hesitancy to act in a timely manner is an emotional reaction rather than the discipline I want you to apply. Two common scenarios tend to plague investors alternatively:

• **Bull market action.** The market appears to be headed up; the bull is rampaging! But you wait. If you are holding stocks or mutual fund shares, you wait because you believe the market will go still higher. Remember the summer of 1987? Robert Prector, the most quoted guru at the time, in his newsletter about waves predicted the Dow Jones Industrial Average would reach 3,600. That's when you tell yourself you will sell—at 3,599 to avoid the rush at the century mark. If you are waiting to buy, you look for a pull back to buy on dips. Either way, nothing happens because you believe the time is not right to act—your actions are dictated by how you feel. That emotional response gets in your way time and time again.

• **Bear market action.** The market pulls back, but you don't sell because you hope it will resume its upward course. You don't buy either if you have been waiting for a lower price because now you believe prices will go even lower. Again, nothing happens, as you continue to wait for a better deal.

If your past performance has suffered because of your gut feelings for the market, what do you expect to do differently in the future? When will a cheetah change its spots? Will you suddenly gain the confidence and discipline you lack and move decisively? Not likely. At least not without a major change in your conditioning, attitude, and emotional response to market fluctuations.

Question 5—Can you tolerate the risks of being in the stock market? You are eager to gain the rewards, but do the risks trouble you? I have talked with thousands of investors over the years. Many appear venturesome and say they are willing to accept relatively aggressive levels of risk. This expressed level of aggressiveness rises during bull markets. But when the time comes to act, many freeze; they are too paralyzed to act and end up putting their money into certificates of deposit.

Some time ago I asked subscribers to the *Fund Exchange*, my own monthly newsletter, to comment on their risk tolerance and investment philosophy. The results were unexpected.

I asked: "How much money are you willing to lose on an individual trade? 0 percent, 10 percent, 15 percent, 20 percent, 25 percent, other percent?" About 70 percent of the respondents indicated a willingness to lose no more than 5 to 15 percent on a trade. This was consistent with a previous indication that most subscribers thought of themselves as mildly aggressive.

A surprising 15 percent indicated they were unwilling to accept any loss on a transaction. This response shocked me because I clearly point out to my subscribers that trades recommended by our timing strategies have been profitable 60 percent of the time and have led to losses 40 percent of the time on average. The 15 percent who cannot accept any loss should not be using our newsletter and should not be in the stock market.

Investing is never without risk. Even the so-called riskless investments, such as Treasury bills, insured certificates of deposit, and Series EE savings bonds, come with risks that may not be fully recognized. Interest-rate risk affects all U.S. Treasury bills, notes, and bonds. More on this basic risk later. Choosing is not without some risk, and the answer to minimum risk may be a sensible selection from among low-risk alternatives.

That said, you and I both recognize that investments involving risks that keep us tossing and turning at night are no good either. Some investors exhibit a high tolerance for risk and can sleep through the ups and downs of a volatile market with little inner turmoil. A high tolerance to risks does not necessarily make a successful investor. But tolerance to risks permits an investor to embark on a more venturesome route that will likely result in better long-term performance. A lengthy time line is the key. Venturesome investments allow time to iron out the up-and-down wrinkles.

Investors with a lower risk threshold need to proceed cautiously, but refusing to accept any risk can be less fulfilling than a willingness to accept a minimum level of risk. To be a successful investor, you must identify your risk tolerance; I will be tailoring specific strategies to suit investors with different levels of risk tolerance.

HOW TO EVALUATE YOUR RISK TOLERANCE

William E. Donoghue, originator of the *Money Fund Report* and *Donoghue's MoneyLetter*, developed a test for risk tolerance. It is reproduced in Chart 1D with his permission. Taking this test can help you define your ability to recognize different levels of risk and to live with them.

Your age will likely affect your reaction to risk and your comfort zone. The younger you are, the more risk you may be willing to accept in order to gain a higher total return. While I hope you will eliminate emotion from your investment planning as much as possible, tolerating risk is mostly emotional.

Learning to live with risks, and there are many in investing, begins with recognizing what they are and how you can cope with them. Now it's time to move ahead—time to make some important decisions.

DECISION TIME

Have you found yourself playing a role in one of these scenarios?

• Is my money working efficiently? Take a cold, hard look at where your money is and how it is doing; that is, how much it is earning or appreciating. For example, your money market account (MMA) at your local bank pays interest, and it allows you to write up to three checks each month. But is the interest paying you enough to keep you even with inflation after taxes?

CHART 1D
How to Find Your Risk Tolerance

When responding to each scenario, be candid—don't fool yourself.

Question 1
Your investment loses 15 percent of its value in a market correction a month after you buy it. Assuming none of the fundamentals has changed, do you:
a. ☐   Sit tight and wait for it to go back up.
b. ☐   Sell it to prevent further sleepless nights if it continues to decline.
c. ☒   Buy more—if it looked good at its original price, it looks even better now.

Question 2
A month after you purchase it, the value of your investment suddenly skyrockets by 40%. Assuming you can't find any further information, do you:
a. ☒ Sell it.
b. ☐ Hold it, expecting further gain.
c. ☐ Buy more—it will probalby go higher.

Question 3
Which would you have rather done:
a. ☒ Invested in an aggressive growth fund, only to see the aggressive growth fund you were thinking about double in value in six months.
b. ☐ Invested in a money-market fund, only to see the aggressivbe growth fund you were thinking about double in value in six months.

Question 4
Would you feel better if:
a. ☒ You doubled your money in an equity investment
b. ☐ Your money market fund investment saved you from losing half your money in a market slide.

Question 5
Which situation would make you feel happiest?
a. ☐ You win $100,000 in a publisher's contest.
b. ☐ You inherit $100,000 from a rich relative.
c. ☐ You earn $100,000 by risking $2,000 in the options markets.
d. ☒ Any of the above. You're happy with the $100,000 no matter how it ended up in your wallet.

Question 6
The apartment building where you live is being converted to condominiums. You can either buy your unit for $80,000 or sell the option for $20,000. The market value of the condo is $120,000. You know that if you buy the condo, it might take six months to sell. The monthly carrying cost is $1,200, and you'd have to borrow the down payment for a mortgage. You don't want to live in the building. What do you do?
a. ☐ Take the $20,000.
b. ☒ Buy the unit and then sell it on the open market.

CHART 1D (continued)

Question 7
You inherit your uncle's $100,000 house, free of any mortage. Although the house is in a fashionable neighborhood and can be expected to appreciate at a rate faster than inflation, it has deteriorated badly. It would net $1,000 monthly if rented as is and $1,500 per month if renovated. The renovations could be financed by a mortgage on the property. You would:
a. ☐ Sell the house.
b. ☐ Rent it as is.
c. ☒ Renovate it and then rent it.

Question 8
You work for a small but thriving privately held electronics company. The company is raising money by selling stocks to its employees. Management plans to take the company public, but not for four or more years. If you buy the stock, you will not be allowed to sell until shares are traded publicly. In the meantime, the stock will pay no dividends. But when the company goes public, the shares could trade for 10 to 20 times what you paid for them. How much of an investment would you make?
a. ☐ None at all.
b. ☐ One month's salary.
c. ☒ Three months' salary.
d. ☐ Six months' salary.

Question 9—
Your long time friend and neighbor, an experienced petroleum geologist, is assembling a group of investors (of which he is one) to fund an exploratory oil well that could pay back 50 to 100 times its investment if successful. If the well is dry, the entire investment is worthless. Your friend estimates that the chance of success is only 20%. How much would you invest?
a. ☐ Nothing at all.
b. ☒ One month's salary.
c. ☐ Three months' salary.
d. ☐ Six months' salary.

Question 10
You learn that several commercial building developers are looking seriously at undeveloped land in a certain location. You are offered an option to buy a choice parcel of that land. The cost is about two months' salary, and you calculate the gain to be 10 months' salary. Do you:
a. ☒ Purchase the option.
b. ☐ Let it slide—it's not for you.

Question 11
You are on a TV game show and can choose one of the following. Which would you take?
a. ☐ $1,000 in cash.
b. ☐ A 50% chance at winning $4,000.
c. ☐ A 20% chance at winning $10,000.
d. ☒ A 5% chance at winning $100,000.

CHART 1D *(continued)*

Question 12
Inflation is returning. Hard assets such as precious metals, collectibles, and real estate are expected to keep pace with inflation. Your assets are now all in long-term bonds. What would you do?
a. ☒ Hold the bonds.
b. ☐ Sell the bonds and put half the proceeds into money funds and the other half into hard assets.
c. ☐ Sell the bonds and put the total proceeds into hard assets.
d. ☐ Sell the bonds, put all the money into hard assets, and borrow additional money to buy more.

Question 13
You've lost $500 at the blackjack table in Atlantic City. How much more are you prepared to lose to win back the $500?
a. ☐ Nothing. You quit now.
b. ☒ $100.
c. ☐ $250.
d. ☐ $500.
e. ☐ More than $500.

Scoring

Total your score, using the point system listed below for each answer you gave.

1. a-3, b-1, c-4
2. a-1, b-3, c-4
3. a-1, b-3
4. a-2, b-1
5. a-2, b-1, c-4, d-1
6. a-1, b-2
7. a-1, b-2, c-3

8. a-1, b-2, c-4, d-6
9. a-1, b-3, c-6, d-9
10. a-3, b-1
11. a-1, b-3, c-5, d-9
12. a-1, b-2, c-3, d-4
13. a-1, b-2, c-4, d-6, e-8

Your risk tolerance if you score:

Below 21: You are a conservative investor who's allergic to risk. Stick with sober, conservative investments until you develop the confidence or desire to take on more risk. *One caution:* During a bull market, aggressive growth funds offer opportunities that may be too good to pass up.

21–35: You are an active investor who's willing to take calculated, prudent risks to achieve greater financial gain. Your investment universe is more diverse.

36 and over: You're a venturesome, assertive investor. The choices that are available to you promise dynamic opportunities. Remember, though, that the search for more return carries an extra measure of volatility.

Source: Used by permission of William E. Donoghue, publisher of *Donoghue's Moneyletter*, Box 411, Holliston, MA 01746.

Maybe you haven't run through the numbers. Yet a nagging thought keeps popping up in the back of your mind that seems to be saying, "Something is not right here." Addressing these concerns begins in the following chapter.

• What if you had a sudden windfall? A sudden change in fortune could dump you into the middle of a different world you may not be prepared to cope with. Suppose—

1. You inherit a lump sum, possibly including a portfolio of stocks, bonds, real estate, and other assets from your father's living trust. You knew it was coming—eventually. But eventually is now! The trustee just delivered the certificates and they are in your name.

2. A headhunter you thought was just kidding has found you a challenging new job that will double your take-home pay and you take it. As part of the move, you receive a lump sum distribution from your former company's 401(k) plan. Unless you do something within 60 days, it will be taxable this year.

3. You retire. As you wind down your affairs, the company sends you a statement of your benefits from its profit sharing plan. You will receive a check for the lump sum you have accumulated over the years. Like the 401(k) distribution, you must do something right away or face a whopping tax bill.

• Restless and dissatisfied, you have been planning to leave the stability of your job and start your own business. The timing of when you make your move, if you do, may depend on where the money will be coming from. Most small, new businesses depend on the owner's savings for start-up capital. Bank financing may be available later, but up front it's your money on the line. Have you acquired the cash you'll need? A favorite line of successful entrepreneurs is, "I needed twice as much cash to build my business as I ever expected I would."

• Less dramatic, possibly, but still traumatic is the not-so-sudden realization that college expenses for your three children will equal your gross income for the next two years by the time all three of them don that square-top hat with the tassel.

• Can you afford to retire? Financial planners typically advise about-to-be retirees they should expect to live on about 65 to 70 percent of the income they had been accustomed to while working. Sound like a downgrade? It does to many, but usually only after they have pulled the plug. By that time, it's too late to take constructive steps to generate more savings that would, in turn, throw off more income to supplement pension and Social Security benefits. Some expenses are lower in retirement, but most retirees expect to spend big chunks of their cash to travel, now that they have the time. Like the three-legged stool, retirement depends on three supports—Social Security benefits, company pension payments, and income from investments. Unless you supplement Social Security and pension benefits with income from an investment portfolio acquired along the way, your golden years could be tarnished—slim living when you should be reveling in those fun activities you postponed for so long.

MANAGING YOUR MONEY

Picture your family as a small business. Managing its finances uses the same techniques entrepreneurs and small-business managers use.

Your success in managing your money relates directly to your attitude. When you manage your money as a small business you hope it will become a growing and booming "company." Starting small is no handicap. Most businesses start small, and your investments, like a small business, can expand and grow with time. Key elements in managing the small business that is your family include:

1. Management skills. Managing a small business calls for all of the skills noted in every textbook on management—making a quality product, controlling costs, marketing innovatively, maintaining a positive cash flow, even sweeping the floors when everyone else has gone home. Your salary represents the successful sale of your skills, experience, and talent. Unless costs (day-to-day spending) are controlled, no amount of income will enable you and your family to acquire the goods and services you all want or do those things that interest you the most. You acquire capital to get started in your business and provide a hedge against uncertainty for your family by spending less than you earn. The difference goes into savings.

2. Cash flow. Every small business faces the problem of cash flow. The money needs to be there. As a sign on a business friend's office wall reminds him, "Cash flow is the name of the game." The dollars that flow into and out of the family's bank account are certainly numerous enough to deserve more planning than scribbles on the backs of old envelopes.

3. Goals. Who says you can't be a millionaire? Possibly several times over? Most people settle for goals that are too modest. Think big! If your goal is small, that is all you will ever accomplish. As Abraham Lincoln said, "Whether you think you can or you can't—you're right!"

Goals may sound or appear vague and without much substance. Instead, think of goals as those things you want. Ask yourself, "What do I want?" Not just what do you want, but what do you REALLY want? Here is where effective action begins, where you define your priorities clearly and precisely. Recognizing your goals is a critical first step. Write them down. Committing goals to paper crystalizes your thinking—burns them into your subconscious.

There are the usual wants—college for your kids, a new business of your own with a chance to be your own boss, a financially secure retirement. No surprises there. But why not think beyond those plain vanilla wants or goals? Make your goal a giant step; dare to dream!

Maybe you would really like to retire at 55, trade in your house for a tall-masted sailboat, and sail it around the world. Not exactly original, but wouldn't it be fun?

How about taking a three-year sabbatical while you're young enough to enjoy it to travel, study, or dig up old bones in the Middle East.

Maybe a change in careers would supercharge your energy bank. Tom Clancy switched from selling insurance to becoming a world class writer and hit it big with *The Hunt for Red October*. How about playing a modern Hemingway and captaining your own fishing charter boat off Florida's keys. While changing careers is a shot of large-bore caliber, actually putting your plan into action will most likely depend on how you manage your money and your investments now. If you don't have the cash as a backup, changing careers can be risky, even disastrous. The second half of the small-businessperson's lament that indicated twice as much money was needed is, "It took me twice as long as I ever figured it would."

CONCLUSION

When you manage your money, you are actually managing your life—it's as simple as that. You develop skills and learn to avoid common mistakes. Separating your own feelings from investing and applying discipline are the keys to my low-risk approach to earning more money. How you appraise and respond to risks at different stages of your life will affect your success in investing. Risks are unavoidable, but understanding risks and learning to cope with specific risks are the essential steps to success, as you will discover in the following chapters.

CHAPTER 2

INFLATION RISK—HOW IT AFFECTS YOUR INVESTMENTS

Inflation will probably always be with us. We can't avoid it, and we have little control over it. Nevertheless, inflation represents a threat to our financial well being that we must learn to live with by adjusting our spending and investing strategies. You need to:

• Understand how inflation affects different investment opportunities.

• Recognize the concept of real rate of return (RRR), which is the after-inflation, after-tax return from investments.

• Realize that wealth building can occur only if investment returns exceed inflation and taxes.

• Develop and refine your objectives to be able to adjust to the impact of inflation.

INFLATION RISK—WHAT IS IT?

Inflation risk is the uncertainty about the future buying power of your dollars. Inflation in Germany after World War I is a horrible example. There, printing presses rolled so fast and furiously that, near the end, paper money was printed on only one side and wheelbarrows full of currency were needed to buy bread and other staples. Workers were paid twice daily to permit spending wages before prices went up again. Nothing as wild as inflation in Germany has yet affected the United States, but inflation cannot and must not be neglected or forgotten. Inflation affects the buying power of your capital as well as earnings from that capital over time. You need to separate the concept of investing strictly for dollars and think in terms of investing for total purchasing power.

Inflation risk is distinct from other risks I will address later, such as stock risk, market risk, interest-rate risk and others. If you recognize how forcefully inflation affects your savings, earnings, and investments, you can adjust your strategies to minimize its effect.

If you decided to stash cash under your mattress, for example, its value in terms of purchasing power would decline by the rate of inflation. Suppose you withdrew $100 from your savings account and hid the currency in a teapot. On that day your $100 in cash would buy $100 worth of goods and services at that day's prices. If you assume an inflation rate of 5 percent, you can see what happens to the purchasing power of your $100. (The actual inflation rate for 1990, according to the U.S. Bureau of Labor Statistics, was a tick over 6 percent. But a 5 percent rate is easy to work with and is close to the long-term rate.) At the end of one year, your $100 in cash would purchase only $95 worth of goods and services. The price of gasoline would likely be higher, food at the supermarket would cost more, medical costs would certainly be higher, and most of the other things you buy or services you pay for would be priced higher. So your $100 cash would lose $5 in terms of purchasing power. Only if your $100 were invested in some vehicle or instrument that returns 5 percent, instead of hidden in a teapot, would you break even. Invested at a 5 percent rate, your $100 will have grown to $105 after one year—enough to pay the higher prices for the same bag of goods and services your $100 would buy today.

Unfortunately, this simplistic scenario neglects the effect of taxes. Your marginal tax rate is the percent of tax you pay on the next dollar of income earned. Be sure you distinguish marginal tax rate from average tax rate. To find your average tax rate, divide your total tax by your taxable income. Your average tax rate may include some income taxed at 15 percent, another chunk at 28 percent, and possibly a final chunk at 31 percent.

If your marginal tax bracket is 28 percent (federal only), payable on taxable income between $34,000 and $82,150 for married couples filing jointly (1991 rates), you would be liable for a tax of $1.40 on earnings of $5, leaving $3.60 to pay the higher prices for goods and services. With the annual inflation rate running at 5 percent, you sustain a loss of $1.40 in purchasing power.

CHART 2A
Real Rate of Return

___

Assume: Annual inflation rate   = 5%
          Marginal tax bracket   = 28%

Bank money market account earns 5%

Interest paid on $100	$5.00
Federal income tax ($5.00 x .28)	(1.40)
Net after tax	3.60
Annual inflation loss	(5.00)
Real rate of return	($1.40)

Loss [(1.40) ÷ 5] = − 28%

To break even @ 5% inflation rate and 28% federal tax rate, equate after-tax return to 5%, then divide by .72 (1 − .28)

$$\frac{5\% \text{ inflation}}{.72} = 6.94\%$$ Must earn at least 6.94% on investment to break even

State tax = net 8%
5% x (1 − .36) = 5% x .64 = 3.20%

With a state tax of net 8%, break-even is higher

$$\frac{5\% \text{ inflation}}{1 - (.28 + .08)} = \frac{5\%}{.64} = 7.81\%$$

___

Chart 2A recaps the arithmetic of this example for federal taxes only. As you will note from the chart, you would need to earn a gross return of 6.94 percent to break even with an inflation rate of 5 percent. You calculate this gross rate by dividing the 5 percent inflation rate by 1 – .28 or .72 (5 divided by .72 = 6.94 percent). Out of this gross income, you would pay 1.94 percent for taxes at the rate of 28 percent, leaving 5 percent to pay for goods whose prices are inflated at the rate of 5 percent.

State income taxes worsen this equation by increasing your loss or requiring a higher gross return to break even. Continuing the example, if your state and/or local taxes add a net 8 percent to your 28 percent marginal tax rate at the federal level for a total tax bite of 36 percent, your after-tax return drops to $3.20 for a loss of $1.80 in purchasing power. To break even with a 5 percent inflation rate and an overall federal and state marginal tax rate of 36 percent, your $100 investment would need to earn a gross return of 7.81 percent (5 divided by .64 = 7.81 percent).

REAL RATE OF RETURN

Real rate of return (RRR) on investments is the after-inflation, after-taxes rate. In the example detailed in Chart 2A, your RRR is negative unless your investment earns at least 6.94 percent in the case of a federal tax rate equal to 28 percent or 7.81 percent when federal and state taxes total 36 percent. Under the assumed example conditions, earnings less than 6.94 percent or 8.06 percent guarantee a loss of purchasing power. I don't mean to alarm you with these numbers, but unless you factor inflation risk into your investment planning, you could be building in a loss without recognizing long-term effects on your wealth. The 28-percent federal tax and 8 percent state tax are examples only; you can and should figure your own results. Chart 2B shows how you can relate investment returns to real rates of return. See Table 2A for calculations.

Numerous critics fault the consumer price index (CPI) as a measure of inflation, and I agree. Like many averages, it fails to fit any one person exactly. I believe the CPI understates the actual inflation rate affecting most middle- to upper-class indi-

CHART 2B
Gross Returns and Real Rates of Return

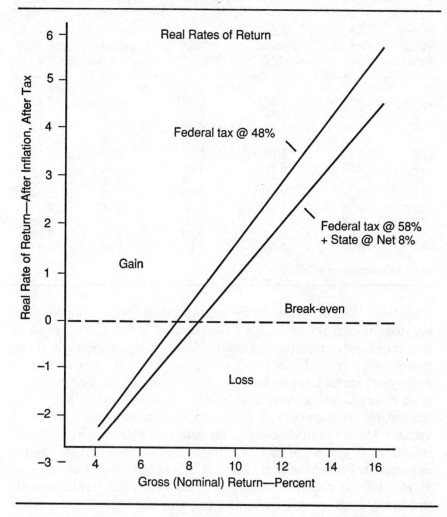

viduals and families. The CPI concentrates on the consumption patterns of urban workers who may earn less than middle- to upper-class consumers. As a result, CPI numbers reflect basic purchases of food, housing, clothing, and transportation. If the numbers are understated, the ramifications of neglecting inflation risk in investment planning can be more disastrous than indicated using the published CPI rates.

Money is an unreliable monitor of wealth and capital accu-

TABLE 2A
Computing After-inflation, After-tax Returns

Gross Return	28% Federal Tax	After Federal Tax @ 28%	Inflation Rate = 5%	After-tax After Inflation	After State Tax—Net 8%
4%	1.12%	2.88%	5.00%	−2.12%	−2.44%
5	1.40	3.60	5.00	−1.40	−1.80
6	1.68	4.32	5.00	−0.68	−1.16
7	1.96	5.04	5.00	0.40	−0.52
8	2.24	5.76	5.00	0.76	0.12
9	2.52	6.48	5.00	1.48	0.76
10	2.80	7.20	5.00	2.20	1.40
11	3.08	7.92	5.00	2.92	2.04
12	3.36	8.64	5.00	3.64	2.68
13	3.64	9.36	5.00	4.36	3.32
14	3.92	10.08	5.00	5.08	3.96
15	4.20	10.80	5.00	5.80	4.60

Graphical presentation in Chart 2B.

mulation. Wealth needs to be evaluated in terms of goods and services it can be exchanged for. Money is only a convenient but inaccurate method of keeping score. One of money's three major roles is to be a store of value. That is, if you collect money, it should represent a collection of goods and services that changes value only minimally. (Money's other two roles are to act as a means of exchange and to present a scale of value.) Money is ineffective in its role as a store of value due to inflation. If you were to store liquid dollars in a bucket, as an example, inflation could be likened to a steady leak from a hole. If you fail to continue filling the bucket, your liquid wealth gradually leaks away. Unless you add to the bucket faster than the leak drains it away, you will never increase the volume of water in the bucket.

Don't be confused by the connection between inflation and rising prices. Actually, the value of the dollar decreases as inflation continues. As the federal government increases the number of dollars in circulation, measured by aggregates M1, M2, and M3, the buying power of those dollars declines with resulting markups in prices to compensate. Thus, inflation is really the declining value of the dollar in goods and services rather than increasing prices. The perception is one of cause and effect. The value of dollars does not decline because prices increase; rather, prices increase because the value of the dollar declines.

Building your personal wealth without considering inflation risk represents a head-in-the-sand attitude. You need to think in terms of a positive real rate of return. As in this example. Refer to Chart 2A and note the 6.94 percent break-even rate (federal income taxes only), analogous to a RRR of zero or break even. If your investment yielded 7.94, your RRR would be a positive 1 percent; that is, you are filling the bucket 1 percent faster than taxes and inflation are draining it. If your investment were to yield 8.94 percent, your RRR would be a positive 2 percent—double the RRR for an investment yielding only 1 percentage point less at 7.94 percent in gross return. Thus, increasing total return by a relatively small 1 percentage point doubles your rate of wealth accumulation once you pass break-even. Failure to recognize the leveraging effect of earnings in excess of break-even could leave you mired in nonproductive investments.

If you were to ask a money manager, "What are your goals for a conservative after-inflation, after-tax return?" he or she would likely reply, "From 1 to 3 percent." These small numbers are quite different from the gross returns promised or advertised. Understanding and accepting the concept of real rate of return is crucial to my plans for helping you build your real wealth. Anything less than a positive RRR amounts to a loss. So how do you get started?

WHAT'S YOUR RRR?

You can't plan a move to reach some objective until you know where you start from. A friend told me a story about his son, who was a member of a Boy Scout Explorer post for search and rescue. As part of the training, the 17-year-old was taken deep into dense woods at night equipped with a tent, sleeping bag, minimal food, map, and compass. At sunup, his task was to find his way back to camp. The first thing the boy had to do was look for landmarks, such as a hilltop or microwave tower, that would fix his position on the map. Once he located his position, he could use the compass and map to find a path to a road and back to camp. He couldn't begin hiking until he knew where he was and could project a course on the map to the camp.

You can do the same; stop and calculate where you stand now. How are your current investments doing in terms of inflation and taxes? Rather than look at gross performance figures, I strongly recommend taking time to calculate the RRR from each of your investments. At year end, your collection of Form 1099s from banks, mutual funds, and companies whose stock or bonds you own will provide the raw data you need. But you need not wait for year end. Current data are available from quarterly reports, closing prices of stocks from newspaper sources, queries to brokers about bond values, and mutual fund confirmations.

1. Begin by calculating your marginal tax rate for both federal and state taxes. If you live in a city or metropolitan area that exacts a third local tax, figure that in as well. Use your marginal tax rate in these calculations because your salary, pension benefits or other income sources are likely to push you into a bracket higher than the minimum. Figuring your tax rate at the minimum and paying higher taxes on your incremental or marginal income is just another way of avoiding reality.

2. Figure your real rate of return on each investment by deducting taxes from earnings. In the example in Chart 2A, federal income taxes at 28 percent reduced the $5 of after-tax earnings to $3.60. Deduct the most recent number for annual inflation. You may see two numbers in media reports. First is an annualized rate. If a monthly rate is reported as an increase of 0.5 percent, the rate may be annualized to 6 percent by simply multiplying the monthly rate by 12, a method that fails to consider compounding. Second, since the inflation rate usually changes from month to month, an annualized rate can be deceptive. Better is the actual increase reported over the past 12 months. If, as I assume in Chart 2A, the inflation rate is 5 percent over 12 months, your RRR for that example drops to a negative 1.4 percent. Deduct the actual 12-month inflation rate from after-tax returns on each investment.

3. Evaluate how each investment did on the basis of real rate of return. If you kept savings in a bank money market account, your gross return may have been 5 1/2 percent. Even in states with no income tax, this gross rate represents a losing RRR if the inflation rate averages 5 percent. When evaluating mutual fund returns, look at total return—dividends received and capital gains distributed plus any change in net asset value.

During 1990, for example, most junk bond funds reported yields (interest from bonds paid out as dividends) between 14 and 16 percent, but total returns were negative by 6 to 10 percent. Negative total returns reflect the sharp declines of junk bond prices, as defaults and news of possible defaults

TABLE 2B
Compiling RRR on Mutual Fund Returns

Fund XYZ—Real Rate of Return		
	1/1/91	*12/31/91*
NAV	11.52	9.63
Dividends		2.20
Capital gains distributed		.06
Taxable distributions		2.26
Tax—Federal @ 28%		.63
Net after tax		1.63
NAV—Beginning of year		11.52
—End of year		9.63
Gain (Loss)		(1.89)
Total return		(.26)
Gain (loss) for year		

$$\frac{(.26)}{11.52} = (2.3\%)$$

Net income after tax	1.63
Inflation loss @ 5% (9.63 x .05)	(.48)
Total return before inflation	(.26)
Inflation effect	(.48)
	(.74)
Total	

Gain (loss) after inflation $\dfrac{(.74)}{11.52} = (6.25\%)$ RRR increased. When figuring RRR for negative total returns, as in the case of junk bond funds, deduct taxes on distributed dividends and/or capital gains plus inflation. The RRR for junk bonds with dividends paid and total return negative could be as much as double the reported negative total return. Total returns for a few top stock funds, on the other hand, were in the 10 percent range for all of 1990 while dividends and capital gains paid (yield) ranged from 4 to 6 percent. You would, of course, calculate deductions for taxes on dividends and realized gains only and not on the unrealized gains.

Table 2B shows examples of how to compute RRR for junk bond funds, stock funds, and bond funds with differences between total return and taxed yields. Stocks may report an increase in value worth more in total return than dividends paid. Even if you did not sell shares of stock, compute the unrealized gain or loss for the full year and add dividends, if any, adjusted for taxes.

Many growth stocks pay no dividends. Your only return will be the change in share values—up or down. Because no dividends were distributed, no taxes would be due; RRR would equal share value gain or loss less inflation. Thus, what you see on Form 1099 may not be the whole story. For consistency, base any calculations on total return rather than actual yield, but deduct taxes only on any income actually received, including the value of any dividends reinvested in additional shares.

How did your investments fare? I suggest you list each investment, from a bank savings account to stocks, mutual funds, and others, as individual line items. Then total real rates of return and divide by total dollars invested to calculate one overall figure—an all-inclusive RRR.

LONG-TERM INVESTMENT RESULTS

An analysis of your personal investment results in terms of real rate of return may surprise—or even shock you. If so, consider the bottom-line results as a wake-up call. Your next question is—what has been the long-term story on inflation? And which investments have fared best under inflationary conditions?

CHART 2C
Inflation Index

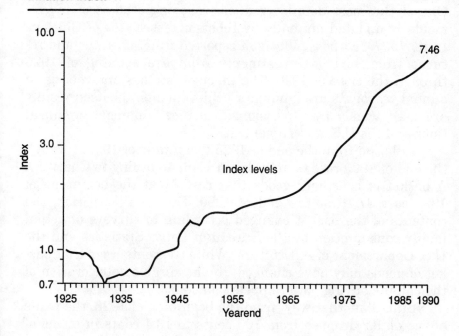

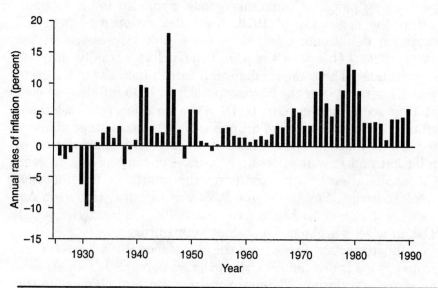

Inflation

One of the most detailed and far-reaching studies of investments is updated annually by Ibbotson Associates of Chicago. In its *1991 Yearbook*, Ibbotson reported inflation rates and returns from various investments from the opening of 1926 through the close of 1990. The Ibbotson studies and reports in annual *yearbooks* are landmark achievements. Ibbotson results are used widely by professionals in most financial organizations and the U.S. government.

Inflation from the end of 1925 (beginning of 1926) through the end of 1990 rose to an index of 7.46, according to Chart 2C. A basket of consumer goods that cost $1 at the beginning of 1926 cost $7.46 at the end of 1990. During that period, the contents of the basket changed according to surveys of actual family consumption by the Bureau of Labor Statistics and the U.S. Department of Agriculture. While the contents of that basket of goods may have changed, the inexorable deterioration of the dollar's buying power appears obvious.

Stated another way, from the beginning of 1926, the value of the dollar dropped from 100 cents to 13.4 cents in terms of purchasing power of consumer goods. From an index value of 1.0 at the beginning of 1926, the index dropped to near 0.7 during a deflationary period in the Great Depression in the early 1930s. This was the last time prices actually dropped significantly. The compound annual rate of increase in inflation was 3.1 percent over the 65-year period. In 1945 inflation peaked at 17 percent for the year. In 1979 the inflation rate rose to an official 13.3 percent before dropping back to an average of about 5 percent in the 1980s. For a more detailed appreciation of inflation and how it affects our lives, I encourage you to read the explanations that accompany the charts in the *Ibbotson 1991 Yearbook, Stocks, Bonds, Bills and Inflation* (Ibbotson Associates, 8 South Michigan Ave., Suite 700, Chicago, IL 60603). The *handbook* is expensive; ask at your library.

Ibbotson Associates uses the nonseasonally adjusted Consumer Price Index for All Urban Consumers (CPI-U NSA) as a measure of inflation. The percentages represent changes in the rate of change of consumer prices.

CHART 2D
Wealth Indexes of Investments in the U.S. Capital Markets

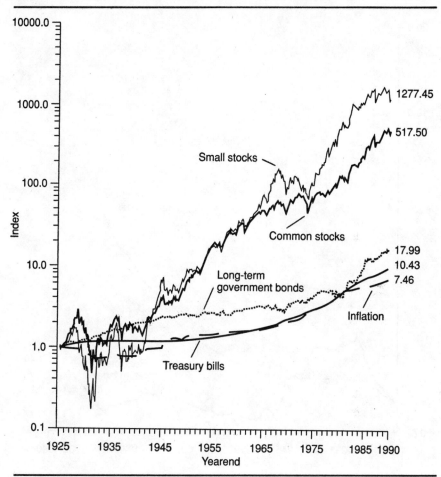

Capital Market Indexes

Various investments are charted as indexes in Chart 2D and are related to inflation over the same 65-year period.

Treasury bills as indexed increased to 10.43 during the period, as shown in Chart 2E. That is, $1 invested in T-bills at the beginning of 1926 would have grown to a value of $10.43 by the end of 1990 for a compound annual rate of growth of 3.7 percent. The increase over inflation (index of 7.46) was a margin

CHART 2E
U.S. Treasury Bills

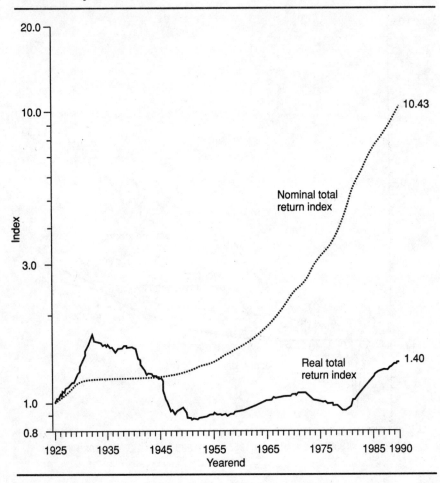

of 2.97 (10.43 − 7.46). This margin is not adjusted for income taxes, as rates, both federal and in many states, have changed radically over that period.

Long-term government bonds grew to an indexed value of 17.99, meaning that $1 invested in long-term government bonds at the beginning of 1926 grew to a value of $17.99, as shown in Chart 2F. Long-term bonds had an average maturity of about 20 years. The annual compound rate of return was 4.5 percent. However, the capital appreciation portion of long-term govern-

CHART 2F
Long-Term Government Bonds

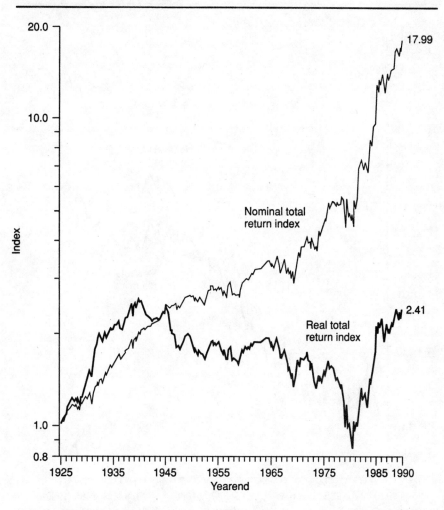

ment bonds' total return was only $0.72, indicating the increase resulted almost entirely from the income portion—interest.

Not shown on Chart 2F is the index for intermediate-term government bonds, those with 5-year maturities. The intermediate-term bond index rose to 23.61 for an average compound total rate of return of 5.0 percent. The higher rate for intermediate-term bonds appears to have resulted from their shorter

CHART 2G
Common Stocks

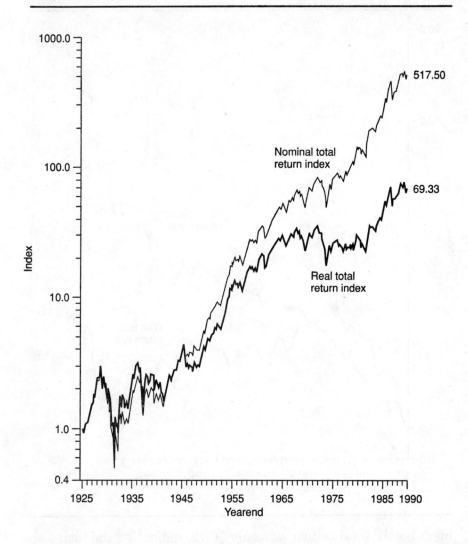

maturities that permitted the money retrieved from matured bonds to be reinvested at higher rates during periods of rising interest rates.

Common stocks' performance was based on the stocks included in the Standard & Poor's 500 index, although the composition of that index differed considerably over the 65-year period. Total returns for common stocks jumped to $517.50 for every $1 invested at the beginning of 1926, as shown in Chart 2G, for an annual compound rate of increase of 10.1 percent.

Small-company stocks were the stars of the study, as they rose to an index value of 1,277.45, as shown in Chart 2H, 122 times more than the index for T-bills. Small-company stocks grew at an annual compound rate of 11.6 percent. Gains in the values of small company stocks over the period were highly volatile, lagging the performance of the S&P 500 at times and outperforming the larger capitalization stocks in other periods. Major gains in small-company stocks occurred from 1974 through 1983, but, except for a spurt during 1988, gains lagged until early 1991.

INFLATION-ADJUSTED RESULTS

Reducing gross results by the effect of inflation paints a sharply different picture of realistic values between the investment opportunities studied. Due mainly to inflation, attempting to generate a positive real rate of return from fixed-income securities can be difficult to impossible.

Treasury bill results adjusted for inflation are shown graphically in Chart 2E. The huge difference between the nominal return from Treasury bills at an index of 10.43 and the inflation-adjusted or real total return index of 1.40 highlights the problem—little margin left for taxes. U.S. Treasury bills are considered to be as close to a risk-free investment as you can get. They are direct obligations of the U.S. government and, thus, eliminate credit risk. They typically run for short periods, 3 and 6 months, although 12-month T-bills are available. Short maturities of T-bills limit interest rate risks to minimal levels.

Ibbotson made no attempt to study the effect of personal income taxes on the inflation-adjusted index. Such a study is complicated by the many changes in the tax laws over the 65-year period and the substantial differences in individual tax brackets in the years before 1991. Using the example in Table 2A, you can figure the RRR for your tax bracket after allowing for current inflation rates.

CHART 2H
Small Stocks

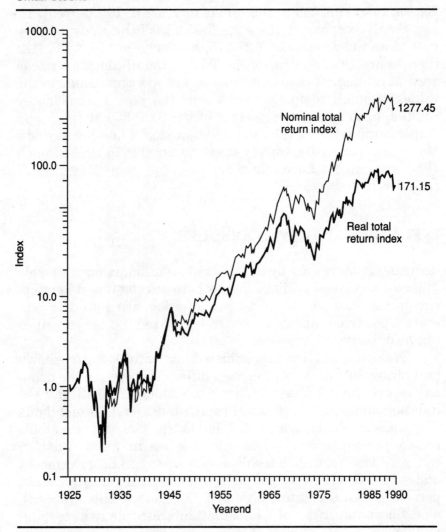

Long-term government bond results adjusted for inflation are shown in Chart 2F. Both the gross return of the index at 17.99 and the inflation-adjusted real total return index of 2.41 are higher than similar returns for T-bills. Further, the difference between the gross and real total return indexes is wider. Even so, adjusting gross returns for taxes would likely yield a minimal RRR, if any at all.

Common stock results appear more promising, as shown in Chart 2G, with a real rate of return at an index of 69.33 after adjusting the gross index of 517.50 for inflation.

Small-company stocks, with their total return of $1,277.45 for every $1 invested at the beginning of 1926, were affected less by inflation (see Chart 2H) because they gained so much more than other investments. The inflation-adjusted index for small company stocks was a whopping 171.15.

If fixed-return investments, such as T-bills, T-notes, and T-bonds produce minimal gains, even losses, in after-inflation, after-tax returns, how do they fit into a plan for lifetime investing? I believe secure investments in low-risk, highly liquid, interest-based securities provide a solid foundation from which to build a varied program for wealth accumulation. Having a secure base satisfies many investors' emotional needs for security. During the Great Depression of the 1930s, many investors bought Treasury bills even though they gained no interest. By keeping their money in secure T-bills, they preserved capital when banks were failing. Keeping a part of your portfolio in fixed-income securities need not, however, always yield minimal or negative real rates of return. By accepting a minimally higher level of risk, you can maintain your base without penalizing growth.

INVESTING IN FIXED-INCOME SECURITIES

Despite the discouraging real rates of return from fixed-income securities, you may decide to keep a portion of your investable funds in low-risk, highly liquid securities, such as insured bank savings accounts and CDs; U.S. Treasury bills, notes, and bonds; and money market mutual funds. However, relying too heavily on fixed-income securities could be harmful to your fiscal future. In a recent survey, I found that nearly half of the people answering were losing money on their supposedly risk-free securities on an after-inflation, after-tax basis. Let's examine these low-return instruments that could leave you with guaranteed losses or minimum wealth-building gains before moving on to more likely candidates.

Banks

Savers and investors love the security and convenience of banks—even if the banks cost them a portion of their RRR each year. Currently an estimated $450 billion are resting peacefully in bank savings account drawing 4 1/2 to 5 1/4 percent interest and earning huge profits for bankers. These are not CDs; these savings are what used to be known as passbook savings.

All bank accounts, saving and checking, plus certificates of deposit suffer one overriding fault. They pay as little interest as banks figure they can get away with. When Regulation Q limited how much interest banks could pay on savings accounts, most banks paid the "maximum allowed by law." Most rates have dropped to levels below former Regulation Q limits on savings and money market accounts. I am solidly opposed to turning my money over to people whose express purpose is to pay me as little as they have to in order to get control of my money so they can manage it for their own benefit. Their long-term goals and mine are in conflict. While banks are trying to minimize my returns, I prefer maximizing them.

From 1980 to 1982 when inflation was raging at double-digit rates, banks permitted their patrons to leave their money in low-paying savings accounts. Banks were earning huge profits on those funds by lending them at rates over 20 percent. Only when serious investors begin withdrawing funds to invest in money market mutual funds and T-bills paying 16 to 20 percent, did the bankers cry for help. They still permit patrons to leave their money in low-paying accounts, and then they earn profits from those funds.

Depositors rent their money to banks for less than market interest rates because of fear. They are afraid they will lose their savings unless they are insured by the U.S. government. They feel an emotional need for assurance they can get their money back at any time—even if the bank fails. Banks are also convenient. You can walk in and talk with a living person if you wish. Savers like the peace of mind they gain from knowing their savings are "safe."

Safety is a relative term. First, you must ask, "Safe from what?" Knowledgeable investors look at three levels of safety:

1. Safe return of original capital. If you deposit $100, you feel secure and safe if you know you can get $100 back on demand. The Federal Deposit Insurance Corporation (FDIC) assures your deposits will be returned to you, as long as they do not exceed $100,000.

2. Safety of earnings. Interest earned on bank deposits is also insured by the FDIC as long as capital plus earnings do not exceed $100,000. If your account is approaching $100,000, continued interest accruals could push it over the limit. Be aware that the FDIC does not always insure accounts over $100,000, and it is less likely that accounts over $100,000 will be insured in the future.

3. Safety or retention of purchasing power. Even if your bank savings are insured for capital and earnings, they are not safe from inflation. Insurance against inflation losses is not available.

Money Market Funds

You have an alternative to bank savings accounts and CDs. Invented in 1972 by the Reserve Fund, money market mutual funds revolutionized the banking system in the United States. During the days when Regulation Q restricted how much interest banks and savings and loan associations could pay depositors, small investors had few options. They could invest in the stock market or mutual funds, which had two major faults— high costs and volatile values. Or they could invest in T-bills. Until about 20 years ago, T-bills could be purchased in minimum amounts of $1,000. Because of the building traffic that threatened to swamp the facilities of the Federal Reserve Banks, the minimum was raised to $10,000 with additional increments of $5,000. In the face of these obstacles, many small savers simply accepted the minimal interest rates on bank and S&L saving plans.

The Reserve Fund changed that. Using the mutual fund system, it accepted initial deposits of $1,000 and minimal amounts as additions. Using the collected savings from many small investors, the fund bought jumbo CDs and other short-term money market instruments. The fund paid savers much

higher rates than they could get in the banks and S&Ls, and
the money flowed in.

When savers recognized they could get up to 50 percent
higher returns on their savings in money market mutual funds,
a process of disintermediation began. That jawbreaker term
simply means depositors were changing the location of their
savings from banks and S&Ls to money market funds. Dollar
outflows were huge, and the banks and S&Ls complained to
federal regulatory authorities. Regulation Q was gradually dis-
mantled, and rates paid to depositors were set free to allow
banks and S&Ls to compete for deposits. Banks and S&Ls continue to hold more deposits, not because they offer higher yields,
but because those deposits are insured. The difference in yields
between bank money market accounts (MMA) and money market mutual funds (MMFs) typically runs about 1/2 to 2 percentage points with MMFs paying the higher yield.

Money market mutual funds, as noted earlier, are not insured. More than 600 MMFs now operate; some are limited to
institutional investors. Their total assets rose above $500 bil-
lion in late 1990 and are still climbing. The security for MMF
depositors remains unblemished—no MMF depositor has lost
even one cent.

Money market mutual funds offer a viable alternative to
bank savings accounts, CDs, and T-bills. Note these six advantages:

1. MMFs accept minimal amounts regularly. Although most
MMFs require $1,000 as initial deposits, there are no limits on
additional investments by some and minimal amounts by others. Twentieth Century Cash Reserve Fund will accept any
amount as an initial deposit.

2. No costs are charged to get into a MMF, as they operate
as no-load mutual funds. The MMFs incur operating expenses
and pay management fees, but the yields reported to shareholders are net after expenses and fees.

3. MMFs maintain a constant net asset value (NAV) of $1
per share to preserve capital. They are able to do this by keeping maturities short to minimize interest rate risk and by investing only in secure instruments. MMFs are the only mutual
funds whose NAV does not change.

4. Accounts in MMFs are maintained in computers, and you receive a printout of activity monthly. Earnings are typically paid and reinvested daily and credited monthly.

5. Access to funds in MMFs may be as simple as writing a check. Or you may ask the MMF to wire transfer money to your bank checking account. Most MMFs require checks to be for amounts over some minimum, such as $100 or $500. United Services U.S. Treasury Securities Fund (1-800-873-8637) permits check writing for any amount and for any number of checks.

6. Although they are not insured, MMFs are strictly regulated by the Securities and Exchange Commission and have proved to be a secure repository of cash. The least risky among MMFs are those funds that invest only in U.S. Treasury bills, bonds or notes. A slightly greater risk may be assigned those MMFs that invest in government agency securities other than U.S. Treasury securities. General MMFs may invest in commercial paper, bankers acceptances, CDs, and short-term notes—all with average maturities of 90 days or less. MMFs are proud of their record of no investor losing any part of their investment. During 1989, two sizable companies defaulted on commercial paper being held in the portfolios of several MMFs. The managers absorbed those losses rather than pass them on to investors.

Money market funds have earned a place among investment opportunities for keeping cash secure and liquid. Many investors keep a portion of their portfolios in cash or cash equivalents, meaning some part of the 20 percent may be in T-bills, CDs, or money market funds. All are secure and highly liquid. No long-term investment record of gross and inflation-adjusted returns are available for MMFs because of the limited time they have been around.

Money market mutual funds (uninsured) yield 1 1/2 to 2 percentage points more than bank money market accounts (insured). You can look at this difference in terms of safety and insurance. A 2 percent difference in yield (assumed) might be viewed as the premium you pay for insurance on your money market account (MMA) at the bank. On your $1,000 account, you give up $20 per year (difference between $55 and $75 returns on MMA and MMF, respectively) for the security of FDIC insurance coverage. That $20 is your insurance premium—equal to 36 percent of the bank MMA yield. What are the risks of investing in an MMF? As noted earlier, no investor has lost as much as a penny. That makes the $20 per thousand very expensive insurance.

Money market funds can also have an important impact on your real rate of return (RRR). Under the same conditions noted above and shown in Table 2B, a MMF may earn $7.50 on the $100 principal and you pay a tax at the 28 percent rate of $2.10, leaving $5.40 of after-tax return. Inflation at 5 percent takes away $5 leaving 40 cents for a positive RRR—equal to a 0.4 percent return. Compare that RRR with a bank account's yield of 5 1/2 percent—a loss of over 1 percent. Few investors, probably one in 100, look at their investments on a real rate of return basis. I find that discouraging, because it is an important concept in understanding how their money is working—or not working—for them.

Even though banks are handy and offer security for your money, they operate at the bottom of the ladder of fixed-income securities. Bank savings accounts, money market accounts, and checking accounts fail to offer satisfactory investment opportunities for the fixed-income portion of your lifetime investing program for one simple reason; they are guaranteed losers.

Banks' best offerings are certificates of deposit (CDs) that pay higher interest rates in exchange for allowing them to hang on to your money for some stated period—three months, six months, 1, 2, 3, 5, or possibly 10 years. If you leave the money alone, the bank pays interest at the end of the period or annually or more often on long-term CDs. But if you need the money early, possibly for some emergency, the bank exacts a penalty that might run as high as six months' interest.

Risk-averse investors stick with bank savings accounts and CDs because they forget about inflation. They may know it is there, but inflation is difficult to quantify. No bells ring or bugles blare if your earnings from savings accounts fail to buy as many goods and services at some time in the future as your original investment would have at the time. You must make this decision subjectively.

If you plan to use CDs for part of your portfolio, recognize how important minor differences in yield can be. A term you need to be familiar with is *basis point*. A basis point is 1/100th of 1 percent. That is, 100 basis points make up 1 percent; 50 basis points are equal to 1/2 percent.

If you invest in a CD paying 7 1/2 percent, you can calculate your real rate of return using the same numbers as the example above with a money market fund that pays 7 1/2 percent. Your RRR is a paltry 0.4 percent. A 50-basis point increase in yield (0.5 percent) to 8 percent boosts after-tax, after-inflation return or RRR to 0.76 percent—nearly double the RRR from the 7 1/2 percent yield. These figures ignore state income taxes, as they vary widely.

To earn the higher 7 1/2 or 8 percent interest rate, you agree to keep your money in a bank's CD for some period. Usually, the longer the period, the higher the interest rate.

If you decide to keep a portion of your portfolio in CDs, investigate various options for getting the highest insured yields available. Plan to shop around a bit; after all, every extra basis point counts. Alternatives include:

1. Instead of banks, check the CD offerings from S&Ls. Despite the shoddy reputation of the industry, many soundly managed S&Ls continue operating. Typically, they offer 30 to 60 basis points more interest than CDs with comparable maturities available from banks. Just be sure the S&L is insured by the FDIC, and keep your CDs under $100,000.

2. Credit unions also offer CDs to members. If you belong to a credit union, ask about its CDs. Credit unions may be insured by the National Credit Union Administration (NCUA), a quasi-governmental organization similar to the FDIC. Only federally chartered credit unions are eligible for insurance coverage up to $100,000 per person. Avoid credit unions that are not insured by the NCUA.

3. Ask your stockbroker to search nationally for the best available CD. Brokered CDs offer three advantages: (a) interest rates may be higher than you can find locally; (b) you pay no fee for the brokered service, as the bank or S&L offering the CDs pays a finders fee to the broker; (c) if you have to withdraw your funds from the CD early, the broker may find another buyer and save you a part of the early withdrawal penalty. The broker will charge for reselling your early withdrawal CD, but the cost would likely be less than the penalty from the bank or S&L. As a check on how good your broker is and whether he or she is doing his or her job, look for the Banxquote[R] quotes each Friday in *The Wall Street Journal*. (Banxquote is a registered trademark and service mark of Masterfund, Inc.) The highest yields offered for money market accounts at banks and savings and loans and for CDs at one, two, three and six months and one, two, and five years maturity are reported for amounts of under $100,000 and for jumbos ($100,000). Banxquote also reports each week on the average of broker quotations for three and six months and for one, two, and five years plus changes from the previous week.

   4. Avoid bump-up, variable-rate, and stock market CDs. While some of these offshoots may offer some advantages, chances for disappointment are even higher. Stick with the simple CDs you know about, but shop around for the highest, insured yields.

   If CDs are to be a part of your short-term investment strategy and up to a quarter of your investable dollars might stay with CDs or an alternative fixed-income instrument, consider these additional tactics for managing this portion of your portfolio:

   1. Avoid long-term CDs. Instead, stick with 36-month or less maturities. While long-term CDs offer higher rates, the differences are minimal and fail to compensate you for the risks of committing your money for the long term. One alternative might be laddered or staggered CDs, as noted below.

   2. Investigate the possibility of tiered rates; that is, higher rates for higher amounts. A bank or S&L may offer one rate for CDs of $10,000 and a higher rate for CDs of $50,000. Unless interest is siphoned off regularly, interest accruals over the $100,000 principal amount would be at risk if the bank or S&L should fail.

   3. Automatic rollovers are simple to set up and keep your short-term capital working every day. If you sign up for automatic rollovers, be sure the bank or S&L rolls the maturing CD over into one with the same maturity. A few days before the rollover, call at least three other banks or S&Ls to check on their rates. You are the loser if you don't select the institution offering the highest, insured rate of return.

4. If you expect to keep CDs as a continuing short-term investment, set up laddered maturities. Set up CDs for 6, 12, and 18 months. As each matures, roll it over for another 18 months. This simple system of staggering maturities captures a variety of rising rates and locks them in for 18 months without going out too far into the future.

U.S. Treasury Securities

Treasury bills, more familiarly known as T-bills, are similar in many ways to CDs—the T-bills are direct obligations of the U.S. Treasury, so they are secure. They are short term; the longest maturity for a T-bill is 12 months. Other maturities are three and six months. They are simple to buy and can be bought at original issue with no sales charge directly from the Federal Reserve Bank or branch that serves your area. A secondary market where issued T-bills trade regularly is available if you need money before your T-bills mature.

T-bills differ from CDs is several important ways:

1. The minimum amount you can invest in a T-bill is $10,000 (face amount, not actual cash; see below). Additional amounts are available in $5,000 increments.

2. T-bills are discount instruments and pay no interest. Instead, you buy T-bills at a discount from their face value. At maturity, the U.S. Treasury credits your account with the full face value. The difference between your cash investment and face value is your gain. The Internal Revenue Service (IRS) considers that difference as interest. Because of the discount system, calculating your rate of return can be confusing. The simplest answer comes from calculating your return on the amount of cash actually invested. If you buy a 12-month, $10,000 (face value) T-bill for $9,250, your gain is $750. The discount rate is 7.5 percent. Divide the $750 by the $9,250 cash invested to calculate a return of 8.11 percent on the money actually invested.

3. T-bills are no longer issued as certificates. T-bills are accounted for as data entries, and you receive a computer-generated confirmation. Face amounts are credited to your bank account electronically at maturity unless you elect to roll them over into a new T-bill.

Buying T-bills direct from the Federal Reserve Banks (the Fed) affords you an opportunity to increase your yield from T-bills. Your bank or broker will be happy to buy T-bills at original issue for you—for a fee that may range from $25 to $100 depending on the face amount. The Fed makes it easy for you to buy T-bills direct at no cost.

If you live in a city with a Federal Reserve Bank or branch, stop by during business hours and ask for instructions and a tender—jargon for an application to buy T-bills. If you live elsewhere, write to the nearest Federal Reserve Bank or branch for instructions on how to buy T-bills by mail. Then follow instructions exactly. Typically, the drill calls for you to complete the tender (application form) and send it to the Fed along with a bank cashier's check for the face amount of the T-bill you wish to buy. Your tender and cashier's check must arrive at the Fed before 1 P.M. eastern time on any Monday if you are buying three- or six-month T-bills. Twelve-month T-bills are sold every four weeks.

T-bills are sold to the highest bidders in an auction. The Fed in New York City collects all of the bids from big buyers and tenders from individual investors. Small buyers (those buying up to $200,000 of face value T-bills) agree to accept an average price. Enough T-bills to fill all small orders are set aside. T-bills needed to fill the Treasury's needs are picked from bids arrayed according to price. The highest bids (lowest interest rates) are filled first and on down the array until the Fed fills its needs. All auction bids accepted are averaged, and that is the price small buyers pay.

On Thursday after the Monday auction, the Fed credits your bank account with the difference between the average price and $10,000—or whatever face value of T-bills you ordered. After the stated time, 91 or 182 days, the Treasury credits your bank account with the face amount of your order electronically. A few weeks before your T-bills mature, the Treasury sends a form letter asking if you wish to roll over your T-bill. If you elect to roll your T-bills over, the Treasury sends you a check for the discount on the Thursday following a Monday auction.

For more information, the U.S. Treasury has issued Form PD 800 D, "Information About Treasury Bills Sold at Original Issue," available from Federal Reserve banks and branches or by mail from the Bureau of the Public Debt, Washington, D.C. 20239-1200.

U.S. Government Bonds and Notes

The U.S. Treasury issues notes and bonds, and the only difference is the maturity. Notes may extend from 2 years to 10 years. Bonds may extend from 10 years to 30 years. All are registered to individual or institutional owners, and interest is paid at the agreed rate twice a year—formerly by check but now mostly by electronic entry to investors' bank accounts.

Treasury notes (T-notes) and bonds (T-bonds) have several important characteristics that interest investors:

1. Since T-notes and T-bonds are direct obligations of the U.S. Treasury, they are as secure as our government as far as timely payment of interest and payment of the face value at maturity.

2. Both T-notes and T-bonds are negotiable, and they trade freely on secondary markets. As a result, they are highly liquid. Both T-notes and T-bonds are subject to interest rate risk; that is, their principal value moves up and down in response to interest rates. As interest rates rise, bond prices fall and vice versa. Thus, investors earn regular interest and may realize a capital gain if they paid less than the face value when bonds mature or if they sell at a higher price than they paid before maturity.

3. As with T-bills, investors may buy T-notes and T-bonds at original issue from the Fed without paying a commission using the same general procedure as the one explained above for buying T-bills directly.

You will need to understand the relationship between bond prices and yields. When interest rates rise, bond prices fall, and when interest rates fall, bond prices rise. The two phenomena move together. Here's why:

Suppose you buy a T-bond with a face value of $1,000 with a coupon rate of interest at 10 percent. This means that every six months the U.S. Treasury sends you a check for $50 (or deposits it electronically in your bank account). You buy the T-bond at par, meaning you pay the full $1,000. If the general level of interest should rise to 12 1/2 percent, no investor will pay $1,000 for a bond that pays only $100 in annual interest. So the bond is worth what a willing buyer will pay. For a buyer to earn 12 1/2 percent on your T-bond, he would pay only $800, as $100 in interest equals 12 1/2 percent of $800. Thus, as interest rates rise, the prices of bonds decline. If interest rates decline, the reverse happens.

How have T-bonds fared as an investment? Ibbotson Associates calculated the gross and inflation-adjusted returns for intermediate-term and long-term government bonds.

During most of the 65 years of the Ibbotson studies, interest rates in general rose. An investor in long-term government bonds during the 1980s, a period when rates trended downward, would have gained an average annual return of 12.6 percent. If the investor paid an average 28 percent in taxes, the after-tax return would drop by 3.53 percentage points to 9.07 percent. During the same decade of the 1980s, inflation averaged 5.1 percent. Thus, the after-inflation, after-tax return (RRR) was a positive 3.97 percent. These 10-year average returns are not achieved without some interest rate risk, as prices of bonds cycle up and down with interest rates.

CONCLUSION

Inflation affects the yields of every investment, but none so dramatically as fixed-income instruments that are insured or guaranteed by the U.S. government. Investors trade off safety of principal against total return. When inflation and taxes are taken out, these "safe" returns are minimal—even negative at times. You can't really afford to invest solely in savings accounts at your bank, CDs, T-bills, or money market funds. These cash equivalents afford liquidity and should be a part of every portfolio, but they should be a small part of your investment plans.

Investors with an interest in keeping more of their portfolio in fixed-income instruments appear likely to benefit from keeping funds in intermediate-term U.S. Treasury notes—now known as T-notes and intermediate-term and long-term corporate bonds. While Treasury notes and corporate bonds offer relative stability and safety, they suffer from inflation effects like other fixed-income securities.

Options for wealth building after taxes and after inflation are extremely limited using fixed-income, minimum-risk investments. To gain more leverage over taxes and inflation, you need to consider equities—stocks in a variety of companies. Gains come with risks, so let's learn about the trade-offs between the risks of investing in equities and the wealth-building gains from their higher returns.

CHAPTER 3

MANAGING STOCK RISK

Risks come in different sizes and flood in from many directions to confront and confuse investors. The unrelenting hazards of inflation and taxes emerge as major obstacles along your road to financial security. As the after-inflation, after-taxes margin remaining from total returns of savings accounts, certificates of deposit, U.S. Treasury bills and bonds shrinks, astute investors, and I count you among that group, look for better ways to achieve their objectives. From the data in Chapter 2, it becomes obvious that equities, the shares of both major corporations and small capitalization companies, have provided greater RRR than fixed-income securities. Along with higher returns, however, stocks expose you to new and different risks.

Selecting the right stocks has always been a challenge to investors, but recent structural changes in the stock market make stock picking by individuals even more hazardous. For example:

• Institutions dominate the markets. An estimated 80 to 90 percent of the shares traded on the New York Stock Exchange are between the big hitters—pension funds, mutual funds, and other professional money managers. Huge trades, many in the block-trade category of 10,000 shares or more, can intimidate small players in the market. It's almost like the mice in the elephant savannah. As a small investor, you could get trampled by an elephant-size institutional trader.

• Program traders exploit arbitrage differentials between stock exchange futures markets and a corresponding bag of individual stocks. Using computers and millions of short-term dollars, program traders add volatility and uncertainty to markets. Both can be costly and scary for small investors.

• Real time links with foreign stock markets and plans for 24-hour trading move markets onto a global stage. As a small investor, you may experience difficulty watching markets at home. Adding foreign exchanges and the effects on stock movements abroad complicate your task.

• Insider trading adds a further hazard with unknown dimensions. As much as the exchanges and government investigators are doing, suspicions still lurk that undetected insider trading adds yet another level of uncertainty and risk for investors.

Moving from the relatively limited-risk environment of CDs, T-bills, and T-bonds, thus, introduces new and different risks.

STOCK RISK

Simply stated, stock risk is the risk of picking a bum stock. Whether you select a stock or a broker recommends it, a stock pick seldom performs as you expect. Nobody buys a weak stock deliberately unless they are selling short. Neither do I know of any investor who deliberately buys overvalued stocks. Most investors actively seek undervalued stocks and buy them from investors who believe just as strongly that those same stocks are overvalued. Most of us select stocks that appear to have glowing prospects, that have performed magnificently during recent weeks or months, and that are expected to continue doing well. Other prospects may have hit bottom and are in a turnaround scenario. But projections and expectations can be deceiving. Even the best information and analysis can lead you to a stock that turns out to be a loser. Thus, you need to understand stock risk and how to keep it from wrecking your investment plans.

I ask first-time investors, "How would you invest $1,000?"

They could buy 100 shares, a round lot, of a $10 stock. But if they had $10 million to invest, they would probably not put it all into a single stock. They would probably select 20 to 40 different stocks, recognizing intuitively that putting all their investment in one place makes little sense. Yet, buying only one stock with their first $1,000 pins all their hopes on a single selection—and it could be a bummer.

So how do you avoid picking a bum stock? First, let's define a bum stock. Simply stated, a bum stock is one that declines after you buy it. How much it must decline before it becomes a real loser is subject to personal reaction, but most investors try to avoid issues that fall by more than 10 to 15 percent. According to some frustrated investors, all stocks go down immediately after they buy and go up immediately after they sell. Unfortunately, some truth underlies such wry observations. The market appears to have a mind of its own. It seldom performs as we expect it to and certainly does not respond to wishful thinking.

Diversification is the time-honored solution to stock risk. If you own many stocks, perhaps across a broad range of industries and individual companies within those industries, one bum stock in the collection will do little damage to your total portfolio. Diversification is a means of damage control. If you own 20 different stocks and one declines by 20 percent while the others remain stable, your portfolio's loss is a mere 1 percent overall. Sustaining a small loss on one's portfolio can be acceptable, where a 20 percent loss on a single stock could shake your confidence.

Achieving diversification with individual stocks calls for lots of cash. If you were to buy one round lot (a 100-share block of stock) in 20 different companies with an average price per share of $30, your investment would total $60,000. Because few investors can invest $60,000 in the market at one time, many try to buy low-priced issues in the range of $3 to $8 per share. Or they may buy small numbers of shares of higher priced companies. Three problems immediately emerge from this approach to diversification:

1. Stocks selling under $10 tend to be far riskier than stocks that have been bid up to higher prices. Savvy investors recognize companies that turn in consistently good performances over time. These companies' stock prices advance out of the small-stock price range for good reason; they promise growth with acceptable risk. Attempting to reduce the risk of buying a bum stock by buying several low-price stocks merely substitutes several risks for one risk. In my experience, investors fail to achieve more than minimally effective diversification with individual issues and increase other risks with low-priced stocks.

2. Buying low-price stocks costs more. Since most low-price stocks trade over the counter, the spread between bid and asked prices tends to be greater than exchange-listed stocks even when multiple market makers trade the stock. Adding another one-quarter or one-half point to the buy cost and the sell cost increases the risk because the stock must move further to overcome the burden of the higher costs.

3. Attempting to diversify a portfolio by buying small batches of individual stocks can be even more costly. The investor with too little cash to buy round lots buys in odd lots of less than 100 shares. When you buy stock in odd lots, you pay an additional penalty, possibly two. First, you pay one-eighth to one-quarter points more when buying and get one-eighth to one-fourth less when selling due to the odd-lot penalty. Second, if your stock buy is small, you may pay the minimum commission brokers set to cover their costs for handling small transactions. Minimum commissions may run from $35 to $50 and could exceed the usual 1 to 3 percent of the dollars in a higher priced round lot transaction. If you buy 50 shares of a stock priced at $10, the dollar amount is only $500 and a minimum commission of $40 amounts to an 8 percent bite out of your cash. Another 8 percent commission when selling plus a small spread could mean a round-trip cost of 18 to 20 percent of your investment. Taking out 20 percent of any total return imposes a severe handicap on portfolio performance.

MUTUAL FUNDS—YOUR KEY TO DIVERSIFICATION

Buying shares of mutual funds achieves three objectives at once:

1. You gain wide diversification instantly. Diversified mutual funds typically invest in at least 20 different issues to meet rules set down by the SEC. One fund, Janus 20, invests in the minimum number of individual stocks to meet its objectives. Fidelity's Magellan Fund invests in about 850 stocks to disperse its $15 billion of assets across a broad spectrum of stocks in practically every industry in the United States. When you buy shares of a mutual fund, you own a slice of each stock in the fund's portfolio. If a stock owned by a broadly diversified mutual fund falters, its decline in value has a minimal effect on your shares' value. Volatility and your exposure to risk vary among different mutual funds, as managers embark on different roads to meet a variety of objectives. Even so, diversification protects you and minimizes the effect of picking a bum stock on your portfolio.

2. The diversification you gain from buying mutual fund shares comes with a surprisingly low price tag. You need not invest $100,000 to $500,000 to gain proper diversification. Minimum initial investments in mutual funds typically run $1,000 to $3,000. A few funds, such as the 20th Century family of funds, will open an account with no minimum. The 20th Century funds do charge a flat fee of $10 per year if an account falls below or fails to reach $1,000. Load funds—those funds that levy a front-end or back-end sales commission—cost more than no-load funds, but both cost less than multiple purchases and sales of small numbers of individual stocks.

3. Selecting a mutual fund removes much of the emotion from stock picking. You can become enamored with a stock following a glowing account in your local newspaper or one of the popular financial magazines. You may identify with the product a company produces and neglect to ask the tough questions about its financial performance. For whatever reason, mutual funds come with a diversified, almost faceless image that generates less emotion—and that's good. One of my goals is to help you eliminate emotion from your investment decision making. Buying diversified mutual funds adds a measure of discipline because decisions tend to be made on the basis of financial data rather than image.

The mutual funds industry is huge. In 1990, the amount invested in about 3,000 mutual funds topped $1 trillion. Almost half of that total, or nearly $500 billion, was invested in money market funds. Mutual fund investments grew from $100 billion at the beginning of the 1980s to more than $1 trillion by the end of 1990, a 10-fold advance. Roughly 25 percent of the money invested went into stock funds. Along with the increase of assets, the number of investors holding shares in mutual funds grew from 17.5 million in 1981 to 54.7 million in 1989. Although you may already be familiar with many of the characteristics of mutual funds, the following will help you understand their unique advantages for helping you achieve your financial goals.

ORGANIZATION

Mutual funds operate as corporations; a few are organized as limited partnerships. As a shareholder in either type of mutual fund, you will probably not know the difference. Like other corporations, mutual funds sell shares. However, instead of using the collected capital to make things or provide services, mutual funds invest capital collected from shareholders in stocks, bonds, or other securities according to the fund's objectives.

Some funds invest in the stocks of small, emerging corporations. Other funds limit investments to the shares of mature, dividend-paying corporations. Another group of funds invests only in bonds, some only in U.S. Treasury bonds. Each of the thousands of mutual funds attempts to exploit some specific market niche by following a unique policy. Because of this wide variety, you can surely find a fund that satisfies your needs.

How many shares your investment buys varies by fund, but the price of shares is meaningless. Mutual funds with low share prices, for example, are not riskier than shares at high prices.

Typically, mutual funds do not issue certificates but keep investor records as computer data entries. Computer systems enable funds to record and track fractional shares, usually to three decimal points, for added flexibility and convenience. Mutual funds send confirmations of their activity monthly, quarterly, or anytime you invest new cash or redeem existing shares. After closing the books for the year, mutual funds send Form 1099 to each investor and to the Internal Revenue Service to aid in the computation of income taxes.

TAXATION

Taxes on mutual funds are figured differently from individual shares of stock. Income derived from a fund's investments and appreciation of the shares or other securities owned by the mutual fund flow to shareholders. Regulations require mutual funds to distribute at least 98 percent of realized capital gains and income to shareholders to avoid paying income taxes as corporations. Unrealized gains are not taxed. Most funds distribute income and realized capital gains yearly to avoid double taxation, once at the fund level and again by individuals. A few mutual funds hold onto gains and income and pay taxes on them as a matter of policy. Copley Fund is one that does this. Such plans avoid the yearly taxes paid by shareholders but could increase overall taxes, as rates paid by corporations exceed the rates paid by individuals.

While mutual funds pass realized gains through to shareholders, they do not pass along realized capital losses. Gains are realized when a fund sells stocks from its portfolio at prices higher than the stock's cost basis. Losses result when selling prices are lower than cost. Realized losses are deferred and used by the fund to offset later gains. Both realized and unrealized losses show up in the net asset value of shares.

As a year-end tax tip, you may wish to sell shares showing a loss to offset other gains. Immediately rebuying shares in the same fund would violate the "wash sale" rule and defer the loss until the next sale. A wash sale results when an investor, attempting to establish a loss, sells and rebuys substantially the same security in 30 days or less. However, buying a different but similar fund is OK.

SHARE PRICES

Share values are calculated once a day after the close of markets. A few sector (one-industry) funds price shares hourly. Share prices represent the net asset value (NAV) of shares. To calculate the NAV at the end of each day, a manager "marks to market" the value of each stock or bond holding. That is, the manager multiplies the number of shares by the closing price to obtain their capital value. The total of the shares' value is added to any cash being held, interest accrued, and assets in the process of collection. Liabilities are then subtracted. Liabilities include the day's operating costs, such as a day's portion of the annual management, legal fees, and transfer agent and custodian bank fees. Marketing costs, such as mailing prospectuses to potential shareholders, advertising, toll-free telephone costs for selling and similar costs are part of the management fee. If the mutual fund deducts a 12b-1 fee from the assets, it reduces the asset total. More about 12b-1 fees later.

The resulting total of assets less liabilities is divided by the number of shares outstanding to reach the net asset value, one of the most important facts you need to know and remember about mutual funds. Why? First, the NAV is the number reported in newspaper tables daily. You can track a fund's performance by the daily changes reported for the NAV. Second, the NAV accounts for all assets including realized and unrealized capital gains or losses when you buy or sell.

If the fund is a bond fund, the current value of each bond in the fund's portfolio is similarly marked to market (priced daily based on sales of identical or similar bonds or estimates if trade prices are not available) to obtain a true valuation of the fund's holdings. The fund computes the NAV for a bond fund in the same way as for a stock fund.

Computing a daily NAV is a problem for a fund that holds real estate and is the major reason for the lack of a true real estate fund, that is, one that buys real estate directly. Obtaining a daily appraisal of properties' value for computing an NAV at each day's close of business is not practical. The funds proclaiming themselves as real estate funds actually invest mainly in REITs (real estate investment trusts) whose shares trade on one of the markets and close with a known value each day. Besides investing in REITs, so-called real estate mutual funds may also invest in other indirect investments related to real estate, such as the shares of real estate sales corporations and development companies.

EXPENSES

Expenses affect the NAV directly; dollars spent for management fees or other costs reduce income to shareholders on a dollar-for-dollar basis. One way to compare the cost of mutual funds is to compare their expense ratios. The expense ratio is the relation of all expenses to the assets of the fund. If a fund's assets totaled $100 and expenses were $1, the expense ratio would be 1 percent. A table near the front of a fund's prospectus spells out these costs in a format dictated by the SEC. Expense ratios may range from 0.25 to more than 3.0 for a variety of reasons, including size, type, and management policy decisions.

Size of a fund affects the expense ratio because a fund with many shareholders and millions, perhaps billions, of dollars of assets can spread expenses over a broader base. The management company of new funds with a limited number of shareholders may waive some or all of the management fee and a portion of the operating expenses to reduce expense charges that could degrade the performance while a fund is getting started. Many of the managers of money market funds absorb portions of the management fee, and these benefits drop directly to the bottom line.

Type of fund may also affect expenses. An index fund with few management decisions can reduce the management fee. Vanguard's 500 Index Trust, a large fund that follows the investments of the Standard & Poor's 500 index, reports the lowest expense ratio in the industry, near 0.25. That is 25 cents for every $100 of assets. International funds, on the other hand, spend more money on research, including travel to foreign countries, to gain information on which to base investment decisions and may have another level of taxes and fees imposed by the country. International funds may hedge their positions by trading futures and options to minimize the effect of currency exchange variations. So-called junk bond funds may not rely only on rating organizations for information but spend analysts' time digging into company records to assess risks. If the fund invests in high-yield municipal bonds to produce tax-free income, analysts may probe into the various government agencies' taxing authority and credit problems on their own. These added efforts to avoid losses also boost costs.

Deliberate fund management decisions may increase or decrease expense ratios. The infamous 12b-1 fees charged against assets increase expenses and reduce bottom-line results for investors. I can see no useful result for shareholders in buying shares of a mutual fund that charges 12b-1 fees. SEC regulations, paragraph 12b-1, allow mutual funds to spend up to 2 percent of the fund's assets for promotion if the managers so choose. The fund's manager will benefit, but not you. A study commissioned by the SEC found that 12b-1 fees added a bigger burden than a front-end load over 20 years and failed to advance the size or profitability of the funds charging the fees. However, if a fund manager agrees to absorb all or a portion of the management fee to be more competitive or attract new shareholders, you can benefit, as expenses are lower.

Note particularly the level of management fees. These expenses are set by the manager. For no apparent reason some managers charge higher fees than others. The Vanguard family of funds is one of the most efficiently administered group of funds in the industry and charges minimal management fees.

MUTUAL FUND CATEGORIES

The most important categories are grouped generally according to their objectives. The largest number of mutual funds with the simplest concept is the group of money market funds.

Money Market Funds

Money market funds offer an alternative to bank and S&L saving accounts, CDs, and T-bills and are explained in detail in Chapter 2. Money market funds offer convenient places to park savings with high liquidity. They function as combination checking and savings accounts, as they pay market interest and you can write checks on the account. MMFs may require checks to be above some minimum amount, such as $100, $250, or $500. But United Services U.S. Treasury Securities Cash Fund processes checks written for any amount and in any number. The fund requires an initial minimum investment of $1,000, but no fees are charged as long as your account balance does not fall below $500. The fund will not automatically return canceled checks to you, but it retains a microfilm record and will supply copies of specific checks when requested at no charge.

MMFs increase the liquidity of diversified stock or bond funds within a family by telephone switching. If you wish to access Stock Fund A, for example, you could telephone Stock Fund A and switch some part of your account to Money Fund A within the same family of funds. Then you could write a check on Money Fund A immediately.

If you market-time stock or bond mutual funds, as detailed in Chapter 5, MMFs provide a safe haven for your cash during those times when technical indicators indicate the market is in a declining trend. Your funds continue to earn interest and capital remains constant, as MMFs maintain their $1 per share value. Neuberger & Berman's Money Market Plus was an exception, as it included securities with long maturities in its portfolio. Since its maturities exceeded the new SEC limit, it changed its name to the Neuberger & Berman Ultra Short Bond Fund.

Diversified Stock Funds

Diversified stock mutual funds invest in stocks of corporations. They are grouped into four broad categories.

Aggressive Growth Funds

Aggressive growth funds seek opportunities to profit from many new and emerging companies as well as turnaround situations that appear to offer rapid growth. Another term for this group may be *capital appreciation funds*, as managers concentrate on stock value growth. They consider income from dividends as secondary to their major objective of rapid growth. Aggressive growth funds tend to invest mainly in over-the-counter securities, hoping to get in on the ground floor or at the point where growth is fastest. Significant risks accompany these tactics, and aggressive growth funds report volatile results—sharply

TABLE 3A
Aggressive Growth Funds

Fund	Assets as of 12/31/90 ($Million)	5-Year Annual Compound Rate of Growth
AIM Weingarten Equity	803.1	17.8%
Babson Enterprise Small Companies	80.0	7.4%
Columbia Special	121.6	14.9%
Fidelity Growth	601.7	15.2%
Fidelity Magellan	12,325.7	15.1%
T. Rowe Price New Horizons	855.7	5.9%
Scudder Development	310.4	9.9%
Stein Roe Stock	225.8	12.2%
Strong Opportunity	131.9	16.2%
20th Century Growth	1,908.0	15.8%
20th Century Ultra	455.9	17.6%
Value Line Leveraged Growth	236.1	12.8%

up in bull markets and just as sharply down in bear markets. Over several market cycles, you can expect a compound rate of return of 12 percent or more with this fund group. The trade-off is the risk of losing 30 to 40 percent of your investment one or two times during a 10-year period.

Aggressive growth funds typically rate betas greater than 1. Beta is an index of risk and volatility that uses the Standard & Poor's 500 index (S&P 500) as an index base equal to 1.0. A mutual fund with a beta of 1.2 would be expected to grow 20 percent faster than the S&P 500 during bull markets and to fall 20 faster during bear markets. Managers of aggressive growth funds typically either roll over their portfolio more often than most other managers in their search for fast-growing stocks or take long-term positions with little turnover. Representative aggressive growth funds are listed in Table 3A with a five-year summary of their performance and size.

Growth Funds
Growth funds tend to be less aggressive than their riskier counterparts. Volatility is less—betas range from 0.8 to 1.0—indi-

TABLE 3B
Growth Funds

Fund	Assets as of 12/31/90 ($Million)	5-Year Annual Compound Rate of Growth
Acorn	769.5	10.1%
AMA Classic Growth	22.8	5.0
Babson Growth	221.3	10.3
Berger 100	15.0	15.4
Bull & Bear Capital Growth	46.7	2.5
Columbia Growth	270.7	12.7
Dreyfus Growth Opportunity	428.7	9.8
Gintel Capital Appreciation	29.0	10.8
Growth Industry Shares	62.9	12.0
Janus Venture	276.9	16.3
Neuberger & Berman Manhattan	368.6	11.2
T. Rowe Price Growth Stock	1,396.5	11.1
T. Rowe Price New America	95.7	9.5
T. Rowe Price New Era	707.5	11.1
Safeco Growth	65.4	8.2
Stein Roe Special	388.3	14.1
20th Century Select	3,191.4	12.9
USAA Growth	243.3	10.0
Vanguard Morgan	697.1	11.7

cating that growth funds tend to follow the overall market closely. Although growth funds also focus on capital appreciation, many of the companies whose stocks these funds hold pay dividends. Income is still not their main objective, but dividend-paying stocks, particularly those that increase dividends regularly, also tend to grow consistently. Over several market cycles, you can expect returns to compound at 10 to 12 percent annually with a risk of losing 20 to 30 percent of your investment once during 10 years.

Growth funds tend to hold the stocks of major corporations known to spend heavily on research and development, believing this is one route to future growth. The 3M Company, for example, rolls out new products regularly, and its sales reflect an increasing proportion from new products introduced within the past five years. Other companies that spend heavily on research, such as the biotechnology companies, computer makers, and software producers, have not reached a sound financial plateau with a record of consistent sales to warrant inclusion in portfolios of growth mutual funds and are usually found in aggressive growth funds. Representative growth funds are listed in Table 3B.

No rigid rules segregate specific funds within these broad groupings. Some analysts may consider a fund as aggressive while another will rate the fund a growth fund. But few analysts have difficulty separating aggressive growth funds from conservative growth funds.

Conservative Growth Funds

Conservative growth funds carry the mix of capital appreciation and income one step further with a greater emphasis on consistent asset value growth and dividend distributions. You can expect growth of 9 to 10 percent compounded yearly with the prospect of a 15 to 20 percent loss during 1 year in 10. Volatility drops even lower than the growth category; betas range from 0.5 to 0.7.

Conservative growth funds tend to hold shares in even bigger corporations than those held in growth funds. Growth patterns and dividend distributions will have shown consistency over longer periods. Some analysts might say conservative growth funds show little bounce or they are stodgy. During the 1980s, conservative growth funds delivered better total returns than either aggressive growth or growth funds. However, over the 66 years studied by Ibbotson Associates, small stocks, those carried in most aggressive growth fund portfolios, outperformed blue-chip stocks by about 20 percent but with greater risks. Investors could expect a loss of 10 to 20 percent at least 1 out of 10 years. Representative mutual funds in the conservative growth category are listed in Table 3C.

Balanced Mutual Funds

Balanced mutual funds tend to be even more conservative than those in the conservative growth category and carry even less risk. Betas for balanced funds may run from 0.3 to 0.5. Other

TABLE 3C
Conservative Growth Funds

Fund	Assets as of 12/31/90 ($Million)	5-Year Annual Compound Rate of Growth
Babson Value	22.0	10.6%
Dreyfus Third Century	199.3	11.3
Evergreen	580.0	7.2
Financial Industrrial	340.3	9.4
Founders Growth	87.8	12.0
Gradison Established Growth	131.4	11.7
Ivy Growth	185.3	10.7
Janus	1,156.1	15.0
Legg Mason Value Trust	636.2	5.5
Lindner	651.0	10.6
Mathers	299.7	15.1
Neuberger & Berman Partners	730.2	10.7
Nicholas	1,379.7	10.1
Penn Mutual	1,030.8	18.6
T. Rowe Price International Stock	548.4	8.5
Safeco Equity	53.8	11.8
Vanguard World—U.S.	354.8	11.5

names for this category are all-season, growth income, or equity income. The names tend to be self-explanatory. All-season, for example, implies these mutual funds balance their portfolios in attempts to do well in good and bad times. Growth income and equity income in the names of some funds indicate their balance between holding stocks for some growth plus bonds or high-dividend stocks for income. Total returns will average 8 to 9 percent over several market cycles with the chance for a loss of 5 to 15 percent in 1 of 10 years. Balance is the key—a balance between growth and income. Persons in retirement need this kind of balance—some growth to keep pace with inflation plus dividends to supplement income from Social Security and a pension. Distinctions between a few of these mutual funds and those categorized as conservative growth can be blurred. Not all analysts agree on which funds should be in each category. Representative no-load mutual funds meeting the balanced or all-season guidelines are noted in Table 3D.

TABLE 3D
Balanced Funds

Fund	Assets as of 12/31/90 ($Million)	5-Year Annual Compound Rate of Growth
AARP Growth & Income	265.2	10.6 %
Analytic Option	107.3	10.3
Copley	27.5	7.9
Evergreen Total Return	1,100.0	6.6
Fidelity Fund	1,065.9	12.3
T. Rowe Price Growth-Income	475.0	7.1
Bull & Bear Equity	9.4	7.2
Dodge & Cox Balanced	82.5	12.8
Financial Industrial Inc.	549.7	13.5
Founders Equity Inc.	13.7	9.4
Lindner Dividend	149.6	8.5
Permanent Portfolio	80.8	5.8
Safeco Income	174.6	8.1
USAA Cornerstone	551.7	12.2
Value Line Convertible	34.8	6.5
Value Line Income	141.0	10.1
Vanguard Wellesley	1,019.7	10.6
Vanguard Wellington	2,432.0	11.1

Bond and Fixed-Return Funds

Bond and fixed-return funds form another broad category. This group may be divided into a couple of types.

Taxable Bond Mutual Funds
Taxable bond mutual funds aim primarily for income, and they come in two varieties. Corporate bond funds invest in the debt instruments of corporations. Many different types of corporate bond funds exist based on maturities and quality. A bond fund may call itself a short-term, intermediate-term, or long-term bond fund.

Knowledgeable investors recognize that risks are lower the shorter the term of the bonds in a fund's portfolio. Short-term bonds carry less risk because of the shorter period during which interest rates may change and a lower risk of default. But returns tend to differ only slightly from the returns of money market funds where there is no risk of capital. Intermediate-term bond funds have produced the most consistent real and risk-adjusted returns, as they minimize interest risks and maximize returns. Long-term bond funds offer the potential for capital gains if you buy shares when interest rates are high. When interest rates are high, prices of long-term bonds may be discounted by as much as 40 to 50 percent. As interest rates drop, prices of bonds climb and permit traders or investors to claim capital gains.

Other bond funds may specialize by holding high-yield bonds, a well-known euphemism for junk bonds. Risks may be high but so are current returns. As the value of junk bonds changes, sometimes radically, due to the fears of default or actual defaults, capital values of junk bonds vary greatly. Junk bond funds' total return (yields plus distributed capital gains and changes in NAV) can be negative even with high payouts.

Investment-grade and insured bonds are other niches staked out by bond fund managers to reduce risks. Investment-grade bonds are rated AAA or AA or the similar top four grades by bond rating organizations, such as Standard & Poor's. Risks are minimal because the corporations selling the bonds have established impeccable credit ratings. Investment-grade bonds take their name from the suitability of these bonds for trust portfolios and investments adhering to the "prudent man" philosophy.

Insured bonds offer a second layer of risk protection by being insured by a company that takes on the liability of making good the principal and interest if the underlying company fails. Insured bonds actually offer two layers of security, as the insurance company will insure only bonds from the most creditworthy corporations. The catch 22 situation for investors is that insurers are least likely to insure those bonds that need insurance coverage.

A second major category of taxable bond funds limits holdings to government issues. Some bond funds hold only notes and bonds issued by the U.S. Treasury to keep credit risks to an absolute minimum. But don't be lulled to sleep by the government guarantee, as interest rates still affect the NAVs, and in turn, the total return from Treasury-only bond funds. Other government bond funds include issues from government agencies other than the U.S. Treasury, such as the Federal Housing Authority. GNMA (Government National Mortgage Association) certificates, while not bonds, are instruments backed by the full faith and credit of the U.S. government. Special funds hold only these GNMA certificates and aim mainly for low-risk income. The GNMA funds, however, do not offer the capital gain potential available with U.S. Treasury bond funds because, when interest rates drop, mortgage holders refinance their loans, thus removing the mortgage from the GNMA pool.

Tax-Free Bond Mutual Funds

Tax-free bond funds buy only municipal bonds and pass through the income free from federal taxes to shareholders. Keeping state tax implications aside for the moment, the benefit from holding tax-free bond fund shares depends on your marginal tax bracket, defined earlier. The formula is simple: Divide the tax-free return available from a tax-free bond fund by 1 minus your marginal tax bracket to find the equivalent taxable return. For example, a 7 percent tax-free rate at the federal level is equivalent to a 9.72 percent taxable rate for persons in a 28 percent marginal tax bracket (7 divided by .72 [1 − .28] = 9.72). You may figure the advantage in the other direction by deducting the federal tax from a taxable return to see how it compares with a tax-free return.

State income taxes affect your decisions two ways:

U.S. Treasury bills, notes, and bonds deliver interest that is taxable at the federal level but escapes all state taxes. Most states exempt that interest even though it passes through a mutual fund. Originally, states were taxing U.S. Treasury securities' interest but lost in numerous court cases when mutual funds sued the states. Thus, if you hold shares in a money market fund that limits its investments to T-bills, the interest income escapes state income taxes. Less clear is the interest from government agency issues, but the funds are attacking and appear likely to prevail.

State and local municipal bond interest is not subject to federal income taxes, but it may be subject to state income taxes. Muni-bonds issued within a state will usually carry an exemption from that state's income tax if the buyer lives within the state. State-specific tax-free bond funds buy bonds issued only within a single state to preserve the state tax exemption. An in-state investor pays neither state nor federal income tax and receives what is known as "double tax-free" income. Populous states, such as New York, California, Massachusetts, and others, support specific funds that provide the double tax-free income. An individual outside of New York could buy shares in a mutual fund holding only New York muni-bonds, but that investor would be liable for his or her own state's taxes on the interest. State tax exemption extends only to residents of the state issuing the muni-bonds. If you should live in a state without an income tax, consider the returns from a single-state tax-free fund in competition with a widely diversified tax-free fund. At times, the state-specific muni-funds pay higher rates, due possibly to the poor credit risk of the state.

Some cities or local taxing districts impose yet another layer of taxes. In these jurisdictions, muni-bonds may carry an exemption from local, state, and federal income taxes. These bonds are known as "triple tax-frees," but whether a muni-bond fund can pass through interest totally tax free remains questionable. To assure totally tax-free interest, a muni-bond fund would need to invest only in tax-free bonds issued by the local taxing authority.

Alternative minimum tax (AMT) laws throw another wrench into the works. When Congress changed the income tax laws in the massive overhaul of 1986, it took aim at the substantial tax-free bond interest that was not dumping income into federal coffers. The law now requires high-income taxpayers to consider an alternative tax based on preference income. One source of preference income is muni-bond interest paid on bonds that do not meet the definition of "essential services." Muni-bonds issued to finance roads, schools, port facilities, sewers, water-treatment plants, and others escape any AMT. Muni-bonds issued to finance low-cost housing, incentives for a company to locate in a community, and other so-called nonessential services produce preference income. Muni-bonds subject to the alternative minimum tax are known as AMT bonds. A heavy investor in AMT bonds could end up paying more taxes on income that was supposedly tax free. The investor could end up making less than buying a taxable bond fund and paying taxes on the interest.

Tax-free mutual fund managers experience trouble in dealing with AMT muni-bonds. Mutual fund managers are attracted to the AMT muni-bonds because they tend to pay as much as 50 to 60 basis points more interest. Higher rates are due to the possibility the interest may be subject to AMT, and thus, reduce net after-tax income to the investor. Presumably, only the interest from AMT muni-bonds would be added as preference income and that could be some percentage of the total income distributed. The problem could present a monumental accounting headache. One solution is a tax-free bond fund composed entirely of AMT bonds would yield more income to an investor who is unlikely to fall within the AMT limits. So far as is known, no mutual fund group is offering such a fund.

Unit Investment Trusts

Unit investment trusts (UIT) are similar to mutual funds holding taxable or tax-free bonds but with significant differences. A unit trust may hold a collection of bonds totaling $100 million. If you buy a share of a unit trust for $1,000, you buy a piece of the total trust assets. A brokerage firm may collect the bonds and sell shares to clients, charging a 4 to 5 percent commission. Contrary to a mutual fund, the trustee does not manage the trust assets, that is, the trustee doesn't buy more bonds or exchange bonds. The trustee collects interest payments and passes them along to shareholders. When an issue is paid off, the trustee returns a shareholder's portion of the capital. Eventually, all of the bonds are paid off and the trust goes out of existence.

About $100 billion is currently invested in unit investment trusts, so they are a viable alternative to mutual funds holding bonds. Typically, more tax-free bond unit trust exist than those holding taxable bonds. Two advantages accrue to unit trust shareholders:

1. Ongoing expenses are far lower than annual expenses for mutual funds. Since the trustee simply holds the bonds and passes income and capital to shareholders without any active management, costs are minimal. Since expenses detract dollar for dollar from shareholders' income, the low expense ratios of UITs are advantageous.

2. Unit investment trusts offer widespread diversification to minimize risk.

Unit investment trusts also can be disadvantageous:

1. Liquidity of UIT shares is limited. The brokerage that sold shares originally may make a secondary market for shares, but sales tend to be costly. If interest rates rise, the value of UIT shares will decline, and there is little shareholders can do to preserve their capital. They will likely receive full value for shares when bonds in the trust mature, but waiting could involve years. On the other hand, when bonds are selling at large discounts due to higher interest rates, shares of UITs sold earlier may be available at attractive discounts.

2. Since UITs are not actively managed, shareholders receive their portion of principal payments as bonds in the trust are paid off. These small returns of capital can be a nuisance to reinvest. Bond mutual funds routinely reinvest the capital from paid-off bonds into new issues.

Sector Funds

Another large group of mutual funds disdains the single main benefit of the mutual fund concept, broad diversification, to invest in narrow niches. Known as sector funds, they invest in defined industry segments. One sector, for example, is the health-care industry, where funds invest in the shares of hospital management corporations, drug manufacturers, manufacturers of medical and hospital equipment, and other medically related companies. Fidelity, Financial Programs, and Vanguard fund families offer a number of sector funds.

Because sector funds lack broad diversification, they exhibit more volatile and erratic net asset value patterns than those of most diversified equity funds. A mutual fund performance scoreboard usually lists sector funds among the top performing funds and also among the lowest performing funds.

Although the wide selection of sector funds has been popularized by Fidelity Funds, the concept is not new. Major mutual funds concentrating in gold or precious metals, energy sectors, utilities, and chemicals have been around for decades. Generally, diversification tends to be greater in these older specialized funds than in the new sector funds.

MUTUAL FUND TYPES

Mutual funds may be organized as open-end funds or closed-end funds. Although both offer diversification to minimize stock risk, you need to understand the basic differences between them to make sure you aren't taken advantage of by a fast-talking security salesperson.

Open-End Funds

Open-end mutual funds are the ones you are most likely to think about when you hear the term mutual fund. They far outnumber closed-end funds. Open-end simply means the fund can sell as many shares as it finds buyers. Fidelity Magellan, for example, sells more shares as investors put more money into the fund. If investors redeem more shares than they buy, the fund reduces the number of shares it manages. Net asset value is not affected by the number of shares bought or sold; it is determined by the value of the portfolio holdings. Market action and the investment savvy of Fidelity Magellan's portfolio manager are mainly responsible for changes in the NAV. Following are major characteristics of open-end mutual funds:

• You purchase shares in an open-end fund only from the fund itself. If you buy shares in an open-end, no-load fund, you contact the fund directly by telephone or mail. If you buy shares through your broker, he or she deals with the open-end fund and charges a commission. Only the mutual fund manager can issue new shares or redeem existing shares. One exception to this procedure appeared recently when the Jack White Co. set up a mini-exchange to buy and sell shares of a limited number of mutual funds without going to the fund manager.

• Shares in open-end funds are tracked by computer entries.

Certificates documenting share ownership can be issued, but they complicate trading and record keeping. Share totals are reported in fractions to three decimal places as data entries, and certificates cannot be issued for fractional shares. Consider a computer-issued confirmation as your proof of ownership and retain it for as long as you own shares plus an additional six years. Confirmations provide the data you need to figure income taxes and offer proof if you should be challenged up to six years later by the IRS.

• Net asset values of shares in open-end funds are computed at the end of each business day. The NAV is the bid price for load fund shares and the only price for no-load fund shares. Don't consider this point inconsequential; it means there is no spread between the buy and sell prices for shares of no-load, open-end funds. In all other round-trip transactions, the spread between the bid and asked price is another element of cost. A commission (load) is added to the NAV to reach the asked price for load funds. Calculating the NAV is detailed earlier in this chapter. When you buy shares, you receive the NAV figured at the end of the day your order arrives. Deadlines vary; some funds require checks or wire transfers to arrive before 2 P.M. eastern time. Other funds accept orders up to the 4 P.M. market closing time. If you send a check, the money will be invested at the closing NAV for that day, but normally you may not withdraw any of your shares or transfer them to a money market fund until your check clears. Holding periods vary among funds.

• Redeeming shares in an open-end mutual fund calls for different procedures than selling shares of stock. Normal redemption requires a letter indicating the account number, number of shares to be redeemed (all or a portion), the name and address where funds are to be sent, and a signature guaranteed by an authorized officer of a national commercial bank or a broker whose firm is a member of the New York Stock Exchange. See the sample letter in Chart 3A. A few mutual funds permit a limited redemption of shares without a guaranteed signature; ask first. Otherwise, if your redemption letter arrives without a signature guarantee and one is required, your money will be delayed. Ordinarily, when a redemption request is received in

CHART 3A
Sample Redemption Letter

Date

0000 Mutual Fund
Address
City, State, Zip

Gentlemen:

     Please redeem _____ shares of 0000 Mutual Fund. My account number is _____. Please send proceeds to the following address (state your full address) as soon as possible.

                              Sincerely,

                              Your Name

Signature Guarantee _____
                      Authorized Signature

If you wish to redeem all shares in your account, write: Please redeem all shares of 0000 Mutual Fund.

Some funds may accept a redemption request under some dollar limit without a signature guarantee. To avoid possible problems, it is safer to get a guarantee. Authorized officers of commercial banks and member firms of the New York Stock Exchange can guarantee signatures. Notarized signatures are not acceptable.

---

good order, the fund will send you the money the next day or in no case later than seven days.

    A quicker way to redeem shares is to open a money market fund in the same family of funds as your equity or bond fund. To redeem shares, simply telephone the fund and ask them to transfer cash to the MMF. If you have check-writing privileges, you simply write a check for the cash you need.

    • Open-end funds enjoy complete latitude in selecting objectives. You will find open-end funds owning stocks, bonds, both taxable and tax-free, money market instruments, shares of U.S. and international companies, and precious metals. The open-end fund organization has few limitations on innovation.

Closed-End Funds

Closed-end mutual funds may be widely diversified or limited to a specific objective, such as investing in the securities of a single country. Otherwise, they differ markedly from open-end funds. Major characteristics of closed-end funds are:

• The number of shares in a closed-end fund remains constant, in contrast to the constantly varying number of shares in open-end funds. A closed-end fund begins as an initial public offering (IPO) underwritten by a brokerage firm or a group of firms. An IPO for a closed-end mutual fund may include 10 million shares or some other number fixed by the fund manager.

• After issuance, shares in a closed-end fund trade on one of the exchanges or over the counter. Share prices depend on supply and demand and trade like the shares of other corporations. You buy and/or sell shares through a broker and pay a commission on each transaction. There is no equivalent of a no-load, open-end fund among closed-end funds. Although the NAV may be computed daily, it does not determine the price of closed-end fund shares.

• Actual prices of closed-end fund shares vary during the day as trades are effected. If shares trade at a price lower than the NAV, they are said to be discounted. If shares trade at a price higher than the NAV, they trade at a premium. Most closed-end funds trade at a discount from their shares' NAV. Both the price movement and the discount or premium affect profit and loss potentials when trading closed-end funds.

• Closed-end mutual funds are poor candidates for market timing (see Chapter 4). Commissions and spreads on trades exact such a heavy toll on timing transactions, that market timing with closed-end funds is impractical.

Financial newspapers, such as *The Wall Street Journal* or *Investor's Business Daily*, and metropolitan newspapers report the NAVs of open-end funds daily if those funds have sold shares to at least 1,000 shareholders. However, reports on the discount or premium of shares in equity closed-end funds appear only once a week in *The Wall Street Journal* on Mondays with prices at the close of the previous Friday's markets. If closed-end funds are listed, the actual share prices may be available daily but without the discount or premium position.

Investors should avoid buying shares of a closed-end fund at the time it is offered. You may be enticed by a broker who says the shares are available without commission. But brokers do not work without an incentive, and the fund underwriters pay brokers a concession, equal to about 7 percent of the shares' value. If the shares you buy "without commission" earn a 7 percent concession for the broker, you are buying 93 cents of assets for every $1 invested. Instead of buying at the offering, wait for several weeks or months. For a short period after the offering, underwriters will support the price. When all shares are sold, they allow the price to find its own level of value. Shares in closed-end stock funds often drop to a discount of 5 to 10 percent from their NAV within a few months. Occasionally, shares in a closed-end, single-country fund will soar to a premium, as investors perceive the country to be a source of growing values. But don't count on it. Wait for a better buying opportunity.

You may profit from investing in closed-end funds three different ways:

1. If you buy closed-end Fund A at a 20 percent discount when its NAV is 10, you pay $8 per share, not including commissions. If the NAV remains the same but the discount declines to only 10 percent, you can sell at $9 and turn a profit of $1 for each share, again without considering commissions. Note that the value of the shares (NAV) has not changed.

2. You could buy closed-end Fund A at $8 when the NAV is $10 at a 20 percent discount. If the NAV advances to $11 and the discount remains at 20 percent, actual share prices advance to $8.80 and you again turn a profit, 80 cents for each share.

3. If you were to buy closed-end Fund A at $8 when the NAV is $10 (20 percent discount) and sell when the price advances to $9.50 and the NAV moves to $11, you gain two ways. The NAV advances by $1 and the discount drops to 14 percent for an overall gain of $1.50 per share or a percentage profit of 18.75 percent.

You may also lose in any of the three ways if conditions

reverse. Plus, unlike open-end mutual funds, commissions apply to both purchases and sales of closed-end fund shares and you lose on the spread.

PROSPECTUS

Much maligned and seldom read, the mutual fund prospectus remains your key source of information. If you buy shares from a broker, he or she must send you a copy of the fund's prospectus. Failing to do so violates the law. Although the SEC can require a mutual fund to send you a prospectus before you invest, the SEC can't force you to read it.

A prospectus is light years from an entertaining read, but it can supply critical information. It can also be a dandy soporific if you are an insomniac. Even so, studying the prospectus is your responsibility. If you choose not to read the full document, at least read the two important sections: the summary of fees and expenses and the summary of important information.

Summary of Fees and Expenses

You find the all-important data on loads (commissions), redemption fees (contingent and otherwise), exchange fees, if any, and other transaction fees plus annual operating expenses and the management fee in the summary of fees and expenses (see Charts 3B and 3C). Projections of these costs and expenses over 1, 3, 5, and 10 years based on a 5 percent annual return and a redemption at the end of each period will help you compare total fees between funds. You will also see the amount of a 12b-1 fee spelled out, if the fund charges distribution costs to assets. Also look for the expense ratio.

Summary of Important Information

The summary of important information usually begins on the cover or the first page. There are several important segments to look for.

CHART 3B
Examples of Expenses and Fee Schedules for a No-Load Fund

Generic Income Fund

The following table illustrates all expenses and fees that shareholders of the fund will incur. The expenses and fees set forth below are for the 1991 fiscal year.

Shareholder Transaction Expenses

Sales charge on purchases	None
Sales charge on reinvested dividends	None
Redemption fees	None
Exchange fees	None

Annual Fund Operating Expenses

Management expenses	0.13%
Investment advisory fees	0.15
Shareholder accounting costs	0.15
12b-1 Fees	None
Distribution costs	0.04
Other expenses	0.04
Total operating expenses	0.51%

The purpose of this table is to help you understand the various costs and expenses that you would bear directly or indirectly as an investor in the fund.

The following example illustrates the expenses you would incur on a $1,000 investment over various periods, assuming (1) a 5% annual rate of return and (2) redemption at the end of each period. The fund charges no redemption fees of any kind.

1 Year	3 Years	5 Years	10 Years
$5	$16	$29	$64

CHART 3C
Examples of Expenses and Fees Suitable for a Fund with a Contingent Redemption Fee

Precious Metals Fund

The purpose of the fee table is to assist the investors in understanding the costs and expenses that you would bear directly or indirectly as an investor in the fund. For more complete descriptions of the various costs and expenses, see following sections of this prospectus.

Shareholder Transaction Expenses

Contingent deferred sales charge (as a percentage of the lesser of total cost or net asset value of shares redeemed)	4.00%
Exchange fee (per exchange)	$5.00

Annual Fund Operating Expenses
(as a percentage of average net assets)

Management fee	0.58%
12b-1 Fee	0.53
Other expenses	0.67
	1.78%

For example: You would pay the following expenses on a $1,000 investment, assuming (1) 5% annual return and (2) redemption at the end of each period:

1 Year	3 Years	5 Years	10 Years
$57	$73	$91	$199

Objectives

The manager will state the fund's objectives and the plans for achieving them. If a fund's objective is growth, look for a statement similar to, "The fund's primary objective is long-term growth of capital with secondary objectives of regular income and preservation of capital. The fund invests primarily in common stocks."

If the fund's objective is income, look for a statement similar to, "The fund's objective is to maximize current income and the prospect of increasing dividends with a secondary objective of capital appreciation. The fund invests primarily in dividend-paying common stocks of large, mature companies."

An aggressive growth fund may include a policy statement similar to, "The fund may borrow from banks to buy stocks and to hold them or buy stocks on margin using broker funds. This use of leverage is considered to be speculative." Aggressive growth funds may state in their policy their intention to buy or sell options and/or futures to hedge stock positions or to gain more income. These speculative activities mark aggressive growth funds as risky but potentially more profitable in bull markets.

Initial Purchase and Repurchase Minimums
A fund that requires an initial investment of $1,000 may permit following deposits of $10 to $100 or more. Twentieth Century Funds will open accounts with any minimum investment and accepts any amount as additions. A fee of $10 will be charged for every year the balance drops below $1,000, however.

How to Redeem Shares
The prospectus will also detail whether you must send a letter requesting redemption of shares with a signature guarantee for any amount or only for an amount over some minimum. Can you redeem shares by telephone? Are wire transfers to your checking account permitted? How about check writing?

Switching Requirements
Can you switch money from one fund to another by telephone? By overnight letter or fax? Look for any fees or restrictions on the number of switches permitted, particularly if you plan to market-time your funds.

In their search for a compromise between full disclosure and readability, a number of fund managers, mainly among the no-load groups, provide short versions without such details as a listing of securities in their portfolios. If you want or need this information or other details, write or call for an SAI, Statement of Additional Information, that is replete with technical and detailed data. Another source of portfolio information is the quarterly or annual report of a fund.

If you fail to study the information in a prospectus, you invest in mutual funds at a disadvantage.

DISTRIBUTION METHODS

Open-end mutual funds market their shares to buyers by one of three methods: loads, low loads, and no loads.

Load Funds

Load funds distribute shares through stockbrokers or financial planners who earn a commission on sales. The commission in the jargon of Wall Street becomes a load. According to Webster's, a load is a heavy burden—how much of a burden you will see later. The SEC limits commissions to a maximum of 8 1/2 percent of the money invested, equivalent to 9.3 percent of the money that actually buys shares. Many brokers prefer to sell shares in funds that offer the higher commissions. However, funds distributing shares with an 8 1/2 percent load appear to be dwindling as the number and variety of high-performing no-load funds compete aggressively.

An 8 1/2 percent load prevents you from earning a return from $850 of a $10,000 investment. Not only does the broker keep the $850, but you also lose future earnings from the $850—the equivalent of $8,199 after 20 years at an average rate of 12 percent compounded yearly. The 8 1/2 percent commission is the full charge for a round trip; you can redeem shares at no cost. Loads provide the incentive for brokers to sell shares and more than half of the mutual fund shares sold today are sold by brokers. That percentage is slipping as investors discover no-load funds.

Commissions vary by fund and the size of investments. Numerous funds now levy loads of 4 to 4 1/2 percent for bond funds and 5 to 8 1/2 percent for domestic and international stock and specialty funds. The more you invest, the lower the load. If you were to invest $1 million, for example, the front-end commission may drop to 1 percent. While 12b-1 charges are often misunderstood, they constitute one of the biggest ripoffs in the mutual fund business.

The broker has no responsibility for managing the portfolio of any mutual funds he may sell to you; he is strictly a salesperson. Recognize that the broker and his firm keep the commission; none of it goes to the fund. Thus, all mutual funds operate as no-load funds, except those that collect a low load of their own.

Low-Load Funds

A number of mutual fund families charge a commission to invest directly in some or all of their funds. Fidelity, for example, charges a commission of 3 percent to invest in Magellan Fund, one of the family's most popular funds. If you should decide to invest $10,000 in Magellan, Fidelity would invest $9,700 for you and keep $300 for itself. This is a low load (commission) that flows into the mutual fund's coffers and is not paid out to a broker for acquiring your account. The 3 percent load pays for some of Fidelity's distribution expenses.

Low loads are typically under 4 percent, with many funds charging 1 or 2 percent. Fidelity and other fund families omit commissions on bond and money market funds. Except for the low load, mutual fund families typically function like no-load families and deal directly with investors by mail or telephone.

No-Load Funds

No-load funds skip brokers and sell shares directly to individual investors. All marketing and sales costs are paid out of the manager's pocket. Using their own money, not yours, no-load funds advertise in newspapers, in financial magazines, and by mass mailings to existing shareholders and lists of known mutual fund investors. The important difference is that with no-load funds, all of your money goes to work for you. There is no siphoning off of commissions. The $850 from a $10,000 investment that goes to a broker earns income for you instead. Look at load and no-load funds as a 100-yard dash. If you buy shares in a load fund, you give your no-load competitor an 8 1/2-yard head start, Your load fund must run faster to catch up. Few do.

Paying an 8 1/2 percent load to buy mutual fund shares is like investing in the market just before it drops 8 1/2 percent for a huge one-day loss. That is the equivalent of a drop of 255 points on the Dow Jones Industrial Average from a value of 3,000. No-load families of funds, such as Vanguard, Value Line, T. Rowe Price, Dreyfus, Fidelity, and other fund families offer an exciting array of more than 700 funds. New funds are being added regularly. Service to individuals is a key part of the no-loads' sales strategy because their growth—even their continued existence—depends on treating investors courteously and quickly by telephone or by mail. Because they deal directly with individuals, no-load funds have reduced the process of investing to three steps.

1. Call or write the fund of your choice for an application. Sources of information on picking the right fund abound, and performance statistics are available in newsletters and in financial magazines, such as *Money, Forbes,* and *Business Week.* If you plan to start an IRA or Keogh plan, ask the fund's representative for a special application.

2. Study the prospectus that will accompany the application and sales information. Fill out the six to eight blanks on the application. Note whether it is to be a single or joint ownership account. If it is a joint account, both owners must sign the application. Check the boxes for telephone switching and check writing if they are offered. Note also if you want dividends and capital gain distributions reinvested in more shares. Unless you specify another alternative, dividends and capital gains will be automatically reinvested.

3. Return the application along with your check in the envelope provided. Check for a minimum initial deposit in the prospectus and on the application. A few days later you will receive a computer confirmation of your account and the beginning balance.

A few of the major no-load fund families, such as Fidelity and Dreyfus, maintain sales offices in large markets for personal service. A salesperson will answer questions and open your account immediately.

TABLE 3E
35 Fund Families in the "Uppercrust"

Fund Family Name	Perfor-mance Rating	Risk-to Reward Rating	Customer Service Rating	Fees Rating	Com-posite Rating
Columbia	A-	A-	A	A+	A
Merriman	A-	B	A+	A+	A
Scudder	B+	B+	A	A+	A-
Fidelity	B+	B+	A+	A	A-
Twentieth Century	B	B+	A+	A+	A-
T. Rowe Price	B	B+	A+	A+	A-
Vanguard	B	B+	A+	A+	A-
Neuberger & Berman	B+	B+	A-	A+	A-
AARP	B	A-	A-	A+	A-
SIT "New Beginning"	A-	A	B-	A+	A-
Dreyfus	B+	B+	A-	A	A-
Financial Programs	B	B	A+	A+	A-
Janus	B+	B	A-	A+	A-
USAA	B	B+	A-	A+	A-
Harbor	B	B	A-	A+	A-
Value Line	A-	B+	B	A+	A-
Nicholas	B-	B	A	A+	A-
Founders	C+	B	A+	A	B+
Stein Roe	B+	B+	B	A+	B+
Strong	B	B	A-	A	B+
Plymouth	B+	B+	A+	B-	B+
Safeco	B-	B+	B+	A+	B+
Babson	B-	B	B+	A+	B+
Boston Co.	C+	B+	A-	A	B+
Lexington	B-	B-	B+	A+	B+
Rushmore	C	B	A	A+	B+
Sentinel	A-	B	B+	B+	B+
Equitec Siebel	B+	B	A+	B-	B+
IAI	B	B+	C+	A+	B+
Westcore	A-	B+	B-	B+	B+
Vista	B+	B	B-	A	B+
Evergreen	B	B-	B+	A+	B+
Winthrop	A-	B+	B-	B+	B+
Mimlic	B+	B+	B-	B+	B+
GIT	C	B	B+	A+	B+

Source: *Jay Schabacker's Mutual Fund Yearbook 1991*

THE "UPPERCRUST" FUND FAMILIES

Each year Jay Schabacker compiles the *Mutual Fund Yearbook* (Phillips Publishing Co., 7811 Montrose Road, Potomac, MD 20854). In the 1991 edition, Jay surveys 108 medium and large mutual fund families. The purpose of the survey is to determine which funds have good performance, high reward-to-risk ratios, quality customer service, and low fees. Of the 108 families, 35 earned a composite quality rating of B+ or better. The list of the 35 "uppercrust" fund families appears in Table 3E.

CONCLUSION

Picking and investing in a mutual fund that meets your current objectives is only the first step. Monitoring performance and diversifying among different funds or money managers is critical to optimum long-term performance, a problem I call "stock-picker" risk. How you can reduce stock-picker risks is the subject of Chapter 4.

CHAPTER 4

MANAGING STOCK-PICKER RISK

Just as stock risk is the possibility of picking a bum stock, stock-picker risk is the possibility you may lose by following a less-than-successful stock picker. Managers of mutual funds are stock pickers, or bond pickers if the fund is a bond fund. They have been known to own the wrong stocks or bonds occasionally—even frequently. As a result, your mutual fund could be out of sync with the market. If you rely on one market analyst, broker, newsletter writer, mutual fund manager, or friend too closely to select stocks, you increase your risk. Relying on just one advisor for guidance poses additional risks if the market they specialize in turns against you. Surprisingly few market gurus are right most of the time for a variety of reasons, but mainly because markets change.

A particularly trying period for mutual fund investors extended from 1965 through late 1974. The average for all equity mutual funds came in at a dismal annual increase of 1.55 percent compounded for 10 years. During this period, one standout mutual fund appeared—International Investors, managed by John C. van Eck. International Investors was up 360 percent. John van Eck was not a genius, but he had invested primarily in gold-mining stocks that boomed as the price of gold rose to $850 an ounce. Most gold-mining stocks and all gold funds that invested in them would have posted banner performance records during those years.

Experts or money managers may shine in the spotlight of public acclaim following a spectacularly prescient call on the market direction or a stock pick that zooms into the public's attention. But top-performing stock pickers seldom follow through with a continuing series of outstanding picks. If this is the reality, how can you reduce your chances of following a high-flying stock picker into the dumper? Market watchers recognize that markets often make managers rather than the reverse.

Few investors find a manager for their money with whom they can feel complete confidence. Always in the back of their mind is the nagging doubt, "I wonder if I could be doing better." As a result, they seldom leave their money with a manager long enough to prove out the manager's strategy. As I survey seminar attendees, I find that less than 1 percent of those answering have ever owned a fund for five years that has lived up to the investor's expectations at the time of the original investment. Investors may try and try again to find just the right combination of funds, only to fail. Finally, between disappointing fund manager results and bear markets, they throw in the towel and go back to the bank. Returns may be slim at the bank, but they know exactly what they will be getting—no room for disappointment fed by promises that failed. Retreats to the safety of a bank spell defeat for the reasons I detailed in Chapter 2. Inflation and taxes make it very unlikely that CDs will leave a positive return.

You can improve returns from your investments by using money managers with whom you are comfortable. A huge part of that feeling of confidence comes from knowing what to expect. Let's look at several strategies for avoiding losses from stock pickers who fail to live up to your expectations. One of the easiest strategies to implement is the one that eliminates the stock picker by investing in index funds. Diversification is another strategy; use several money managers just as you diversify among stocks by buying shares in mutual funds.

SETTLING FOR AVERAGE

Attempting to compare your stock picker's performance to some norm or another picker can be an unsettling exercise. Should you compare your fund's performance or your portfolio's performance with the total return from certificates of deposit at your bank? Probably not. Should you compare your fund's performance with the Dow Jones Industrial Average (DJIA)? Your fund might stack up favorably if it had invested in many of the same stocks that comprise the DJIA. How about comparing your fund's performance to the Standard & Poor's 500 index? Because of its wide diversity, the S&P 500 is a frequent benchmark. Two problems emerge from such comparisons:

1. The S&P 500 and other averages charge no expenses. Because every mutual fund incurs expenses in its operations, trying to keep up with the unmanaged S&P 500 index is much like a boxer competing in a match with one hand tied behind his back. A fund manager has to be better than S&P 500's average just to break even.

2. The S&P 500 index is weighted according to the size of the company. Weighting gives the price changes for large companies more influence on the index than price changes for smaller companies' stocks. While the S&P 500 enjoys widespread respect for its role of summarizing market activity, it may not represent your funds' objectives or your personal objectives for growth.

COMPARING FUND PERFORMANCE

How does no-load mutual funds' performance compare to the DJIA and the S&P 500? Load funds are not included in the following reports because of the difficulty of adjusting total returns for front-end load charges. For example, if you held a fund that charged an 8 1/2 percent front-end load for two years, its total performance would be degraded by 4.25 percent per year. Few overcome a handicap of that size consistently. Comparing load funds with no-load funds without considering the effect of the front-end sales commission is not only unfair, but also presents a scenario in which investors cannot play a role. If you cannot buy shares in a load fund without paying a commission, how can you compare results without factoring in the load? Numerous reporting publications ignore the cost of getting into load funds.

One useful tool for examining mutual fund performance is to compare specific funds or groups of funds with the S&P 500 or the DJIA. You might consider either or both of these widely followed indicators of market activity as a benchmark. If your fund does better than the S&P 500 or DJIA, you could reasonably conclude your fund performed better than the market. How likely is this to happen? That is, how often or for what period might you expect your mutual fund to perform better than the market as represented by the S&P 500 or the DJIA? Let's examine what happened to no-load mutual fund performance during one period for clues.

In January 1991, 66 out of 263 equity no-load mutual funds turned in better composite performances than the S&P 500. The composite performance rating was an average of 1-, 3-, 6-, and 12-month total returns. That is, 25.1 percent or one quarter of the mutual funds outperformed the S&P 500, according to **NoLoad Fund*X*, a newsletter that reports on the performance of more than 600 no-load mutual funds monthly. Over the same period, only 61 funds or 23.2 percent of the same group of no-load funds outperformed the DJIA. Performance ratings ranged from a positive 33.1 score for Financial Strategic Portfolios-Health to −53.5 for Bull & Bear Special Equity Fund. The comparable rating for the DJIA was 2.3 and for the S&P 500 was 1.4—both positive, but barely. Numerous low-load funds showed up in the ratings array in addition to the 263 pure no-loads. Fidelity Select Biotechnology topped all funds with a rating of 40.5. Even allowing for the 3 percent low load, the rating far exceeded the S&P 500. Numerous low-load funds appeared on the negative performance list too, with Fidelity Pacific Basin Fund turning in a rating of −25.5.

A similar analysis of different periods discloses that some percentage of funds is always doing better than the S&P 500 and the DJIA. However, this group of top-performing funds rotates, and no group consistently performs better than the averages. You can expect some percentage of funds to outperform either the S&P 500 or the DJIA because those indicators of market activity are averages. In any average compilation, some entries will always be higher and some lower than the average.

INDEX FUND INVESTING

Investing in one of the index funds avoids stock-picker risk because there is no stock picker. An index fund, such as the Vanguard S&P 500 Index Trust, includes stocks in its portfolio that match the makeup of the S&P 500. Since the S&P 500 is a weighted index, the fund holds roughly the same proportion of specific stocks as their weight in the index. When Standard & Poor's replaces a stock in its index, Vanguard 500 Index Trust sells the outgoing stock and buys shares of the replacement stock. This happens often enough that, as soon as a new stock is announced for the S&P 500, the price for the new stock rises because of the demand from index fund buying.

Two other index funds aim to match the performance of the S&P 500—the Dreyfus People's Index Fund and the Fidelity Spartan Market Fund. Both are relatively new, but because they are index funds, the lack of a long-term track record doesn't matter.

Other index funds' objectives are to match the performance of different indexes constructed for their own purposes.

• Vanguard's Index Trust-Extended Market Portfolio aims to match the performance of the Wilshire 5000 index, less the 500 stocks included in the S&P 500 index. The Wilshire 5000 is a huge index of more than 6,000 small- and medium-size companies traded on the New York Stock Exchange, American Stock Exchange, and over the counter. The Extended Market Portfolio does not attempt to hold shares in all of the companies in the index. The fund's managers pick and choose groups of stocks that appear to match the overall Wilshire Index.

• Vanguard's International Equity Index Trust-European Portfolio aims to match the performance of the Morgan Stanley Capital International Europe Index by owning shares in the securities in the index. The Morgan Stanley index includes companies in 13 European countries.

• Vanguard's International Equity Index Trust-Pacific Portfolio aims to the match the performance of the Morgan Stanley Capital International Pacific Index of companies located in Japan, Hong Kong, New Zealand, Australia, and Singapore.

• Rushmore Stock Market Index Plus Fund aims to match the performance of the S&P 100 index, but also attempts to improve income performance through option transactions. The S&P 100 index is the base for the popular OEX stock index option contract and represents stocks on which options are available on the Chicago Board Options Exchange.

• Other index funds include Benham Gold Equities Index Fund that is not broadly diversified. It is an index fund only if you make allowances for its industry focus; it limits holdings to the stocks of 30 North American gold-mining and fabricating companies. Gateway Index Plus Fund invests in index options and is not a true index fund; don't be misled by the word *index* in its title.

The Vanguard 500 Index Trust has been around since 1976, and it closely mirrors the market's performance as measured by the S&P 500 index. Investors consider it a proxy or stand-in for the market. If you want to "buy the market," the simplest tactic is to buy shares in the Vanguard 500 Index Trust. Settling for average, if you consider the S&P 500 index as average, isn't all bad. Since only a quarter of the no-load mutual funds equal or better the performance of the S&P 500 index, you can expect to do better than three-quarters of the investors in no-load mutual funds.

An index fund, such as the Vanguard 500 Index Trust, can be a useful fund for dollar-cost averaging and market timing—both strategies explained in detail in later chapters. Since there is no stock picker, your results from investing in systems will equal what happens in the market rather than what might happen to a single stock or mutual fund.

DIVERSIFYING AMONG STOCK PICKERS

Just as diversification can be the answer to stock risk, so can diversification relieve your anxiety about following the wrong stock picker. Instead of relying on a single money manager, stock picker, or mutual fund manager, spread your investments among several.

Fund of funds

A simple strategy for diversification of stock pickers is to invest in a fund that invests only in the shares of other mutual funds.

T. Rowe Price started two Spectrum funds in 1990 to invest in the shares of other Price funds. Spectrum Growth Fund invests in the shares of the Price Growth Stock Fund, New Horizons Fund, New Era Fund, International Stock Fund, Growth & Income Fund, Equity Income Fund, and Prime Reserve Fund, a money market fund. Spectrum Income Fund invests in the shares of Price Income Fund, Prime Reserve Fund, High Yield Fund, Equity Income Fund, International Bond Fund, GNMA Fund, and Short Term Bond Fund. The two Price Spectrum funds offer two approaches to diversification, one aimed at growth and one aimed at income. Within each broad category, individual funds offer another layer of diversification because each fund manager is a different stock picker.

Vanguard offers its STAR Fund that invests in the shares of other Vanguard mutual funds. The mix is about 50 percent in a combination of Windsor and Windsor II with lesser allocations of Explorer, Morgan, GNMA, Investment Grade Portfolios, and Money Market Fund, Prime Reserve.

FundTrust is a family of funds that invest in other mutual funds with varied objectives. Five funds range from the Aggressive Growth Fund, Growth Fund, Growth & Income Fund, Income Fund, and Managed Total Return Fund to Money Trust, a money market fund with a constant NAV of $1 per share. FundTrust levies a 1 1/2 percent front-end load charge, but charges no redemption or exchange fees. All FundTrust funds, except Money Trust, charge 12b-1 fees that range from 0.31 percent for the Growth and Income funds to 0.07 for the Managed Total Return Fund.

Flex-Fund–Muirfield Fund is one of the family of Flex funds but is the only one that invests in the shares of other mutual funds. None of the assets in the Muirfield Fund is in other Flex funds. The Muirfield Fund aims at long-term capital appreciation by investing in funds with those objectives. Flex-Fund—Muirfield Fund charges no front-end load or redemption fees but does levy a modest 12b-1 fee.

Two Merriman funds offer fund-of-funds diversification. Timed Capital Appreciation Fund invests in the shares of aggressive growth and growth funds during bull markets and shelters capital in money market funds during bear markets. Timed Asset Allocation Fund invests in the shares of other funds, allocating 50 percent in aggressive growth funds, 20 percent in fixed-income funds, 20 percent in international funds, and 10 percent in precious metals funds. Investments in each of the four categories are timed separately, according to timing models designed to monitor each of the four markets. More on market timing in Chapter 5.

T. Rowe Price and Vanguard funds of funds charge only one set of fund expenses because they invest only in other family member funds. With only one layer of expenses, the Price and Vanguard funds of funds compete with other mutual funds under the same ground rules.

The two Merriman funds of funds impose two layers of expenses, one for their own operation and one for the funds in which they buy shares. The two layers of expenses are justified by the funds' broad diversification and the internal market timing discipline that attempts to avoid major losses. With their defensive strategy of market timing in place, the two Merriman funds can pick boldly from a mix of international, small-capitalization, and aggressive domestic growth funds with minimum risk of major losses. These trades of other no-load funds avoid the commissions and spreads common when trading individual stocks and bonds.

FundTrust also imposes two layers of expenses, including a 1 1/2 percent load. While it stays fully invested at all times, it justifies the compensation by continuously switching funds according to the managers' perception of which funds or fund groups are likely to perform best. Wide diversification and a range of investment objectives are expected to overcome the low load, two layers of expenses, and 12b-1 charges to the FundTrust shares. Flex-Fund–Muirfield Fund, an internally timed fund, also imposes two layers of fund expenses.

A number of years ago, the fund of funds concept foundered on the reefs of two layers of management costs, but conditions were far different from those in the market today.

First, today's funds of funds invest only or mainly in no-load funds and thus avoid the high front-end commissions, although some of the funds of funds impose front-end loads (commissions).

Second, diversification available under the fund of funds concept is widespread. Merriman, Muirfield, and the two T. Rowe Price funds have been available for only a short time, too short for meaningful results. But Vanguard STAR fund has been around since 1985. During that period, it has turned in a 10.1 annual compound return, placing it in the middle decile of performance ratings according to *The No-Load Fund Investor*. Vanguard STAR is classified as a balanced or total return fund, indicating it's conservative approach.

PICKING YOUR OWN FUNDS

Mutual fund managers are highly visible stock pickers. In contrast to private money managers who seldom publicize their results, the performance reports of mutual funds and their managers appear regularly in newsletters and financial magazines. One of the most comprehensive annual presentations of comparative results appears in *Forbes'* annual mutual fund issue in early September each year. Another source of detailed information on 1,100 mutual funds is the *Business Week Annual Guide to Mutual Funds*, a book available from McGraw-Hill. If you use a computer, a quarterly updated disk from Investability (520 N. Michigan Ave., Chicago, IL 60611) reviews the performance of 2,600 mutual funds on an after-load basis for 1-, 3-, 5-, and 10-year periods plus each fund's beta and other indicators of risk. Quarterly reviews of mutual funds appear in *Money* and *Kiplinger's Personal Finance Magazine*.

So much information appears about mutual funds that you and many other investors may be totally confused. Or you could use this wealth of detailed information to pick a diversified group of fund managers on your own. But there are pitfalls in this approach, too. For example, how do you sort out track records as a guide to picking funds?

Advisors may tell you to pick certain funds according to their long-term performance record, 5 years certainly and 10 years preferably if a fund has been around that long. Advisors look to the past because mutual funds are prohibited from forecasting their performance. A study by Darryll Hendricks, Jayendu Patel, and Richard Zeckhauser published in National Bureau of Economic Research, Inc., Working Paper No. 3389, titled, "Hot Hands in Mutual Funds; The Persistence of Performance, 1974–87," found that top-performing funds in one year continued as top-performing funds the following year. The authors equated the persistence of performance by leading mutual funds to the managers' "hot hands." The fund managers were apparently on a roll and were doing something right. While the paper is scholarly and highly technical, the message coming through points to short-term results as an effective guide for picking funds. However, markets change and the "hot hands" label may shift to other managers quickly. How long the "hot hands" approach continued was not determined, unfortunately.

Over five-year periods, significantly different results came to light from a study of 25 funds by **NoLoad Fund*X** founder and editor Burt Berry. He examined the performance of the 25 load and no-load mutual funds that had topped performance evaluations over successive five-year periods. How did the top-performing 25 funds perform during the following year and the following five years? The record was both enlightening and disappointing. For the five years from December 1980 through December 1985, Vanguard High Yield Stock Fund turned in the top performance with a five-year gain of 258.8 percent. During the next year, it dropped from 1 to 138 in the rankings with a one-year performance gain of 22.0 percent. Over the next five years, from December 1985 through December 1990, the fund dropped to a ranking of 813 out of 905 funds and its five-year gain was a minimal 6.2 percent.

The fund that was second over the five years from 1980

through 1985 was Oppenheimer Target with a five-year gain of 258.6 percent, only 0.2 percentage points behind Vanguard High Yield Stock Fund. One year later, it ranked 779th out of 905 funds and gained a minimal 8.3 percent. Over five years, it dropped to a rank of 670 out of 905 funds and reported a total five-year gain of 36.2 percent. Fidelity Magellan ranked third in the rankings out of 506 funds for the 1980–85 period with a five-year gain of 248.9 percent. The next year it ranked 107th out of 905 funds and reported a gain of 23.7 percent. As of December 1990, Fidelity Magellan ranked 59th out of 905 funds and reported a 97.2 percent gain for the five years from December 1985 through December 1990, the highest gain for any of the funds ranked in the top 25 for the 1980–85 period.

From 1980 through 1985 the Vanguard 500 Index Trust ranked 244th out of 506 funds. The next year it ranked 251st out of 905 funds and gained 18.1 percent. Five years later it ranked 118th out of 905 funds and had gained 82.5 percent over the five years. As noted earlier, the Vanguard 500 Index Trust mimics the S&P 500 index closely and is considered as a proxy for what happened in the broad market. You could expect it to be above the middle but less than the top.

Berry studied what happened to the 25 top-performing funds over one- and five-year periods in successive groups beginning with 1976. Results were generally similar; different funds assumed top positions during one period to be replaced by others the next periods. Thus, picking funds based on a fund manager's five-year record could be counterproductive. While 10-year records have not been studied in the same way, a fund's performance over a longer period, certainly over a period embracing many market cycles, could be more predictive. Because fund performance appears to be highly changeable, as managers move in or out of sync with the market, picking funds for investment can benefit from either of three disciplines:

1. Diversifying among a variety of funds. Despite the reputations of money managers for their role in hiking performance, markets are known to have made managers rather than managers making markets.

2. Following the leaders could keep your assets in those funds directed by the manager with the current "hot hands." Tracking the "hot hands" funds yourself to find the point when one manager's hot hands begin to cool and another takes over calls for massive number crunching. Fortunately, numerous sources supply the information needed to keep invested in the funds that shift positions as the top producers. Sounds simple, but the practicability of changing funds often can be time-consuming and produces monumental problems at tax time, as the capital gain or loss on each sale must be reported separately. Combine frequent switching with investments in a variety of funds to gain diversification and you could encounter horrendous record-keeping problems. And unless you tracked these varied investments closely, you may not know whether you are winning or losing. Frequent switching with its consequent numerous tax liabilities is more practical if it occurs within an IRA. There, the tax consequences of multiple switching do not apply. But switching between fund families inside or outside of an IRA involves a passel of paperwork.

3. Market timing, the strategy of moving into and out of funds according to market conditions and how your specific funds may be responding to those changing market conditions, is detailed in the following Chapter 5.

If you decide on your own plan to minimize stock-picker risk, begin by first defining your investment objectives. If you decide to invest in growth, pick at least five different growth funds. Spread your investable cash among the five growth funds you select and expect to keep it there for three to five years. The key is to own enough good funds to get you out of the guru chasing business.

If you decide to invest in conservative or balanced funds, pick at least five different funds and spread your money among them. You could decide on a diversified approach with some money in aggressive growth, some in conservative growth and some in bonds. Your portfolio should represent a level of risk and diversification according to your age and objectives. If you elect to spread money around in different risk categories, combine that with diversification to minimize stock-picker risk by investing in three to five funds within each category. Diversification, the key to managing stock risk, is also the key to minimizing stock-picker risk.

CHAPTER 5

MARKET RISK AND MARKET TIMING

Stocks and the mutual funds that invest in them tend to move together. One day a market may be up, pulling prices higher, usually for reasons that are explained only later. The next day, with little change in the financial news, the market may be down, with more stocks declining in price than rising. On a short-term basis, the market appears to have a mind of its own, behaving randomly and with little rhyme or reason. This constant, rhythmic motion creates little discipline and much emotion for most investors. Without some way of summarizing these actions—of getting rid of the noise and spikey movements—trying to make sense of the market would be even more difficult than it is. Indexes or averages in great variety summarize market movements. These include the venerable Dow Jones Industrial Average, which reaches back over 100 years when its 11 stocks included nine railroads because they were the most important corporations in the late 1800s, and the mammoth Wilshire 5000, which actually includes more than 6,000 stocks. And not all indexes or averages relate to the prices of stocks.

One of the most helpful indicators of market activity is the advance/decline (A/D) line, the ratio of stocks advancing in price to those declining in price. The A/D line measures the breadth of market activity and usually goes along with the general direction of broad market moves. If the A/D line fails to follow some of the averages that include only the prices of a few stocks, then technicians may rightfully suspect a forthcoming change in market direction. The study of averages, indexes, charts, and graphics is the realm of technical analysis, which will be discussed later.

The market has a maxim for this tendency of stocks to move together—"A rising tide lifts all boats." The metaphor is apt, as one pictures water and boats, even the float itself, rising with an incoming tide. We know this isn't true in the stock market, of course. At no time do all stocks rise or fall together. During even the most active up day, some stocks decline in price. During a down day, a surprising number of stocks may rise in price. A stock may rise or decline without any known reason except that most other stocks are rising or falling. Thus, the price of a stock or a mutual fund may rise or fall from market forces alone. You can't afford to ignore the force of market movements or trends.

How much of the movement in a stock's price is market related? A generally accepted range for the market's effect on the direction of a stock's price is about 60 to 70 percent. That is, if a stock should rise 10 points, about 7 of those points on average will be due solely to the overall market's action, leaving 3 points to reflect the fundamentals of the stock.

When I was a stockbroker from December 1966 to January 1969, I would telephone prospects about a company, about its sales, earnings, management, balance sheet, and—they loved this one—takeover possibilities. People liked to hear most about those subjects that were the most difficult to quantify, and takeover possibilities was high on the list. But after you buy a stock based on its own story, it turns out that only 30 percent of the money you make comes from the story; 70 percent of the money you make comes from the market. Higher correlations, up to 95 percent, apply to market effects on mutual funds because a large, broadly diversified fund tends to move with the market and becomes a microcosm of the market. Thus, we come to the risk of market action on a stock's price.

MARKET RISK

Surveys indicate first-time mutual fund investors believe they will receive three primary benefits from their new investment; (1) professional managers who will pick a diversified group of "good" (undervalued) stocks; (2) a chance for better than bank returns; and (3) when those professional managers perceive there is an appreciable downside risk, they will liquidate the portfolio of stocks and put the money somewhere safe. Certainly, a mutual fund reduces the risk of picking a bum stock through diversification. But mutual funds offer little or no defense against market risk, and, at times, that unmanaged risk can produce huge losses.

When a broadly diversified mutual fund is fully invested, its ratio of winners and losers will likely mirror the ratio of advancers to decliners in the market. A sector or specialized fund reacts to its own market forces that may or may not be in concert with the overall market. Individual stocks often move counter to the market but will generally move with the market about 60 to 70 percent of the time. Thus, you gain no defense against broad market declines by sticking with individual stocks. And since mutual funds' diversification offers little defense against market action, what can you do to minimize market risk? The answer is: market timing.

MARKET TIMING

Since the direction of the market determines about 70 to 100 (for Vanguard's S&P 500 Index Trust) percent of the direction of a mutual fund's price, ideally you would like to be fully invested when the market is moving up and to be out of the market when it is moving down. Simple as it appears, that is market timing. You remain in your diversified mutual fund as the market is rising, but you sell your shares when the market begins to decline to protect your capital. The cash you received from the sale of the shares doesn't sit idle. While you relax on the sidelines as the market declines, your cash earns interest in a money market fund, T-bills, or other cash equivalents.

When the market bottoms out and begins moving up again, your retained capital buys more shares than you sold because prices are lower and you have the extra money from money market fund interest.

Stepping in and out of the equity market according to overall trends can ratchet the value of your investments higher and higher without the distressing losses many investors suffer during major bear markets. Market timing is often oversold as a panacea that solves all investor problems. It isn't, but it helps to solve the problem of market volatility better than any other system I know—even with its foibles and imperfections I detail later.

Effective market timing systems work because losses hurt worse than gains help. For example, if your investment of $10,000 in stock mutual funds should decline by 25 percent during a market dip, pullback, or retracement—pick whichever term you're most comfortable with—it drops in value to $7,500. To gain back the $2,500 lost during the dip, your mutual fund must advance by a third, 33 1/3 percent, to break even again at $10,000. Sometimes the break-even waiting period is a long time in coming. You may remember when the Dow Jones Industrial Average reached a new high of 1,052 in 1972 and then dropped, it was more than 10 years before the market as measured by the DJIA surpassed 1,052.

Many advisors look across the valley (declining market and later recovery) to an upswing later. I prefer to sit on the sidelines with my money earning safe interest in money market funds during a decline and invest again as the market begins moving up. The strategy for reducing losses is to market-time mutual funds, combining mutual funds' diversification as a defense against stock risk with market timing as a defense against declining markets.

I have made the process of market timing sound better than it really is. For example, no system for timing the market will improve performance over being fully invested during an uptrend. A handful of individual stocks and high-performing mutual funds will outpace the broader market, of course. Exemplary performance of certain funds falls within the 30 to 40 percent of price movement not directly affected by market forces.

CHART 5A
Ideal Market Timing

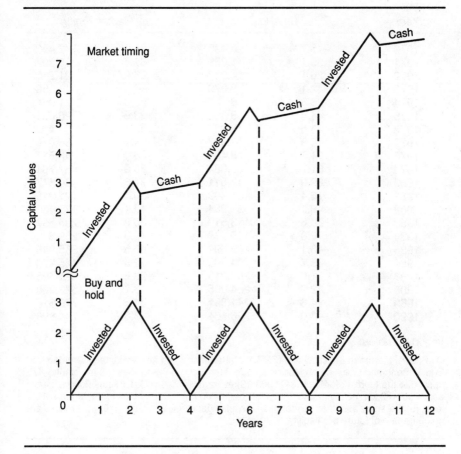

An ideal market timing system aims to keep you fully invested during markets trending up. But its most important function is to keep you out of markets trending down. A graphic representation of the ratcheting up appears in Chart 5A. This isn't the way it really happens. How often have you bought a stock at 10 with the expectation that it would move up to 15 and then it actually does move to 15? As you may have experienced, it often moves down rather than up. When market timers show the scenario of racheting up by successive moves out of and back into the market, they don't show getting out at the

TABLE 5A
Buy and Hold versus Market Timing for Fidelity Magellan

Year	Buy/Hold		Market Timing	
1970	−15.7%	$8,430	24.5%	$12,450
1971	35.1	11.389	31.7	16,397
1972	30.1	14,817	28.9	21,215
1973	−42.1	8,579	−7.5	19,550
1974	−28.3	6,151	7.9	21,094
1975	44.4	8,882	23.5	26,051
1976	35.5	12,035	32.4	34,492
1977	16.3	13,997	4.4	36,010
1978	31.7	18,434	26.4	45,517
1979	51.7	27,964	26.9	57,761
1980	69.9	47,511	74.3	100,677
1981	16.4	55,303	20.4	121,215
1982	48.1	81,904	43.1	173,459
1983	38.6	113,519	35.8	235,557
1984	2.0	115,789	10.3	259,819
1985	43.1	165,694	40.5	365,046
1986	23.7	204,963	16.5	425,279
1987	1.0	207,013	23.8	526,495
1988	22.7	254,005	8.7	572,300
1989	34.6	341,891	34.6	770,316
1990	−4.6	326,164	−3.3	744,896

Important notes:

(1) Paul A. Merriman & Associates (PM&A) started managing funds with the Merriman Equity, Bond and Gold Switch Models on July 31, 1983; (2) the models are hypothetically applied to the funds before July 31, 1983; (3) average 90-day U.S. Treasury Bill rates are assumed while in money market funds; (4) results do not include taxes or management fees; (5) the study assumes dividends and capital gains are reinvested; (6) past results are no guarantee of future profitability.

top or getting in at the bottom for one overriding reason—you wouldn't believe it. You will believe you can get in slightly above the bottom and out soon after the top. But market timing doesn't have to be that good to leave you with a great return— better than almost any other investment you can find in the market today.

Let's look at two distinctly different mutual funds and their performance with and without market timing to back up that assertion. Most salespersons ask you to look at a buy-and-hold program for a fund, such as Fidelity Magellan, that grew from $10,000 in 1970 to $326,160 by the end of 1990. Using a simple

TABLE 5B
Buy-and-Hold vs. Market Timing for Value Line Special Situations

Year	Buy/Hold		Market Timing	
1970	−34.4%	$6,560	10.5%	$11,050
1971	17.6	7.715	35.9	15,017
1972	−11.0	6,866	−4.5	14,341
1973	−45.5	3.742	−1.6	14,112
1974	−29.5	2.638	7.9	15,227
1975	47.0	3,878	34.0	20,404
1976	52.8	5,922	57.8	32,197
1977	12.3	6,650	3.5	33,324
1978	21.2	8,060	17.0	38,990
1979	43.6	11,575	26.0	49,127
1980	54.4	17,871	78.4	87,642
1981	−2.2	17,478	8.5	95,092
1982	23.1	21,515	30.7	124,285
1983	19.4	25,689	21.4	150,882
1984	−25.5	19,138	−5.7	142,282
1985	−21.1	23,176	19.3	169,742
1986	5.1	24,358	−7.5	157,011
1987	−9.1	22,141	19.4	187,471
1988	3.3	22,872	−7.6	173,223
1989	21.7	27,835	21.7	210,812
1990	−4.5	26,582	−0.9	208,915

See Table 5A for important notes.

trend-following market timing program over the same period more than doubles the final value of the investment to $744,896. Table 5A reveals the year-to-year variations.

But Fidelity Magellan is a standout fund. What happens if you apply market timing to a less productive fund? Value Line Special Situations on a buy-and-hold basis for the same 21 years from 1970 through 1990 grew from an initial investment of $10,000 to $26,582, not exactly stellar performance. However, under the same market timing discipline, the original $10,000 grew to $208,915—not as good as Fidelity Magellan with market timing but almost eight times better than buy-and-hold results, as shown in Table 5B. The market timing discipline used is proprietary, but it is reported in the Fund Exchange. It also happens to be the least productive of the four systems used in managing the Merriman timed funds. The footnotes in Table 5A explain other important conditions.

CONFESSIONS OF A MARKET TIMER

If you try to manage market risk, and there is no question that you can, you may feel uncomfortable at times because you are going to look sufficiently different from your neighbor or fellow investor that you may feel as if you are out in left field.

One sure way to manage market risk is—never go into the market. If you are one of the 44 percent of investors who never leaves the safety of the bank, you have perfect protection from market risk. October 1987 happens and you and the others with their assets in the bank didn't lose a penny.

If you plan to manage market risk, you want to be out of the market when it is declining. And you want to be in the market when it is rising. You understand the theory, but how do market timing systems actually perform in the real world?

Lower Risk-Adjusted Return

During the 21 years represented in Table 5A, the market timing discipline called for the investment to be out of both Fidelity Magellan and Value Line Special Situations about 40 percent of the time and in U.S. Treasury bills until money market funds became available. While the money was in a money market fund, practically no risk was involved. During the buy-and-hold program, the funds were exposed to market risk 100 percent of the time. Thus, you can see that on a risk-adjusted return basis, you are far better off in a market timing program. Unfortunately the higher returns at lower risks are the end of the good news. At this point, I want to confess to the following:

Confession No. 1. One out of every three trades was a losing trade. As an investor, would you be willing to accept an approach that you knew would cause you to lose money on one third of your trades? A losing trade results from selling shares at a price lower than they were bought. In fact, there are times when these systems produce as many as three losing trades in a row. Are you willing to take or can you withstand the emotional stress and strain of three losing trades in a row? You might conclude that market timing doesn't work.

Confession No. 2.   More bad news. On 40 percent of the trades, when the system went back into the market, we got back into the stock or bond fund at a price higher than we last sold. One of the Merriman market timers, Charlie Hooper, actually gets back into the market 60 percent of the time at a price higher than he got out. Even so, the impact of his system yields results that exceed those posted in Table 5A for Fidelity Magellan and Table 5B for Value Line Special Situations. Those "losing" moves are difficult for most investors. Imagine you buy a stock at 10, get out at 9, and buy back in at 11. Such tactics are difficult emotionally for investors, but if you are going to use market timing strategies, you must accept such reversals as part of the strategy.

Confession No. 3.   Market timing strategies do not beat buy-and-hold all of the time. Fidelity Magellan on a buy-and-hold basis beat market timing 12 out of the 21 years studied from 1970 through 1990 (see Table 5A). Market timing is not financial nirvana; it attempts to give investors what they want most—something between bank safety and the stock market. I call it "a piece of the action with peace of mind."

If you examine Fidelity Magellan's record carefully, you will discover a 42 percent loss in 1973 followed by a 28 percent loss in 1974. Losses like this forced most investors back to the bank, promising, "I'll never invest in the stock market again." Further, if you had owned Fidelity Magellan in October 1987, you lost about 22 percent in only one day. The goal of market timing is to minimize such losses, but defensive strategies exact a price. During bull markets, market timing strategies tend to cut out little pieces of that advance. This is what happens. The market is rising but then begins to decline. Our system says, "Get out!" So we get out only to see the market resume its upward climb. We must follow the discipline, so we get back in. During these snippets of the bull market action, we are out of the market. The overall result is that market timing underperforms buy-and-hold in a bull market. For example, in 1986 Fidelity Magellan was up 23.7 percent, but my trend-following market timing produced a profit of only 16.5 percent. And 1989 produced the same disappointing comparative results for timing—a 22.7 gain for buy-and-hold versus a gain of 8.7 percent for market timing.

Market timing works long term. It tries to be an insurance policy against catastrophic events. It can't guarantee that; nobody can, but it tries. As we look ahead, we would like to know whether the next one, two, three or more years will be good years. If you knew the markets would be up, you could dispense with market timing. But do you expect to buy fire insurance just before the fire? Or collision coverage just before a truck rear-ends your car? Most of us keep insurance on the books continuously, hoping we won't need it.

IMPACT OF MARKET TIMING

Newsletter writers claim wild, sometimes outlandish, gains from market timing. Their services are often grossly overstated. But if you use market timing strategies in combination with fairly aggressive mutual funds, the 15, 18, and maybe even 20 percent returns can be legitimate long term. What do we need to get that? A study that goes back to 1926 shows that $10,000 invested in a growth index grew to be worth more than $12.7 million for a compound rate of return of 11.3 percent. During that period, 1 out of every 3.2 years was a losing year.

The systems we use and publish in the *Fund Exchange* have historically picked up about 89 percent of the gains during the average profitable year and about 1 to 5 percent in losing years. That doesn't mean we don't have losing years—we do. But the average result during the buy-and-hold losing years is a small profit for market timing. If we captured 85 percent of the gains during profitable years and broke even, rather than gaining 1 to 5 percent, in losing years, the $10,000 original investment would have grown to more than $400 million for a compound rate of return of 18.3 percent.

It is not how you do in the good times that matters; it is how you do in the bad times that separates the great returns from the mediocre returns. It is not how much money you earn that counts, it is how much money you keep. Market timing is no different from your personal or business life. It is how you deal with adversity that determines whether you will be a winner or loser.

If we choose as a goal to capture at least 75 percent of the average profitable year and lose 25 percent of whatever a buy-and-hold program lost, continuing the example of the study that began in 1926, we would still have almost $50 million after 65 years. That is an average 14.3 compound rate of return over the period and almost four times the result of a buy-and-hold strategy.

Despite what you may read in the popular press about how market timing doesn't work, it does and it can. Why are these writers so negative about market timing? Why will they declare that market timing is more risky than buy and hold? A major reason these individuals are negative stems from their personal experience. They may have tried it based on how they "felt" about the market. Or they based timing decisions on a computer model that was not productive during the period they used it. Either way, they got in or out at the wrong times. If your money rests in a money market fund out of risk's way 40 percent of the time and only at risk in the market 60 percent of the time, how can anyone conclude market timing is more risky than being in the market 100 percent of the time? Obviously, being in the market every day exposes an investment to greater volatility. The proof of the lower volatility is displayed in the betas of timed funds that range from 0.22 to 0.39.

Nay-sayers rebut by saying that if you are out of the market as much as 40 percent of time, you might miss part of the bull market. What if you were in cash and the market takes off like a rocket? You will miss an early part of the rise. This will happen. But the results shown in Tables 5A and 5B were created by getting in late after the early rise had started and getting out late after the decline had begun. When a writer warns that you might miss part of a bull market, why is he or she silent on the prospect of missing part of a bear market? The reason financial advisors, brokers, and planners don't tell the whole story is that the financial community has made its living based on selling stories of optimism. Reality is hard on people. Market timing works, but it is tough emotionally on the average investor.

To help you work through the emotional mine fields of market timing, I recommend using more than one market timing system. Diversification among market timers or market timing systems reduces market timer risk, as detailed in Chapter 6. Using several market timers is analogous to using several stock pickers to minimize stock picker risk, as we found in Chapter 4.

The name, buy and hold, tells it all. You buy shares in a mutual fund and hold them while the market cycles up and down. Few investors duplicate these results because they may buy shares in one or several funds, but they don't hold them long enough to experience true buy-and-hold results. In this context, comparing performance of a market timing strategy with buy and hold is a myth. The myth assumes an investor buys and holds shares in a mutual fund long enough to participate in one or more market cycles. Over the same period, the market timer moves in or out of the market according to his or her indicators. Few investors are able to keep either discipline, unfortunately. But disciplined investors using market timing can expect superior results over most long periods.

A professional market timer moves into or out of the market according to a disciplined system. A "feel for the market," hunch, or emotional reactions to news or pronouncements of market gurus do not influence the successful market timer. The only systems I will use or recommend rely strictly on technical indicators and ignore what others may think or believe. Several of the trends that may indicate the direction of the market are the prices of market indexes or individual funds, a market's advance/decline line, the ratios of new highs to new lows, or the relationship of up volume to down volume. Because of most market timers' unwavering reliance on indicators, you need to understand how technical analysts use them. I'm not trying to turn you into a technician, but understanding how we arrive at various indicators will give you more confidence in using them. Developing your own indicators could take far more time than we have allocated to managing your personal finances.

VARIETY IN MARKET TIMING

Two broad categories of market timing systems are currently being used by successful market timers with varied results.

Trend Following

Many of the popular market timers follow a trend-following strategy. These trend-following systems are the ones I have the greatest confidence in and use in managing the Merriman timed mutual funds. As market timers, we invest in stocks or mutual funds during bull markets and in money market funds during bear markets by following one or more indicators. Following in this chapter is a full description of trend-following systems.

Forecasting

Technicians or fundamentalists with a bent toward trend forecasting rather than trend following attempt to forecast the market's direction on a long-term basis. Forecasters aim to get out of stock mutual funds before the market heads south and to get back into stock mutual funds at or near the bottom of a market cycle before the market begins rising. Although their goal is the same as the trend followers, these analysts use different tools to assist in forecasting direction, including price-earnings ratio for the Dow Jones Industrial Average, Standard & Poor's 500 index, or other major indexes. For example, when the P-E ratio moves to historically high levels, analysts figure the market is too high and forecast a drop. Similar up and down limits on other fundamentals applied to averages and indexes may signal a change in market direction.

Interest rates are strong precursors of market direction and figure strongly in many forecasting systems. Strategies built around interest rate movements depend on a second-order correlation. That is, forecast indicators depend on how interest rates can be expected to affect the stock market. Stock prices tend to follow interest rate patterns inversely. That is, as interest rates decline, stock prices move up—generally. One of the most powerful market direction initiators is the Federal Reserve Board's action to raise or lower the discount rate, the interest the Fed charges member banks for loans. When the Fed cuts the discount rate, stocks almost invariably rise. Further, as the Fed eases interest rates through changes in monetary policy, stock prices tend to rise. But when the Fed raises interest rates to rein in an overheated economy, stock prices usually tumble. Market timers using interest rates as indicators look for telltale signs of the Fed's intentions to get a jump on what may happen and when.

TREND FOLLOWING BASICS

Trend reversal is another term for *trend following*. Action of the market itself indicates whether you should be in or out. Being "out of the market" means to have parked your money in a money market fund or other cash equivalent. I recommend money market funds because of their convenience, competitive interest rates, and safety.

Trend following is just that; you follow the trend. When prices head south (trend lower), the market is telling you to get out of stock mutual funds, thus the term *price reversal*—prices are reversing to head down after an upswing or are topping out. So it's time to bail out. At the bottom of the cycle when your money is safely parked in a MMF, prices reverse and begin climbing. This is your clue to move back into stock mutual funds. Indicators pinpoint when you should get out of a bear market and when you should get into a bull market. However, no trend-following system will pinpoint exact tops or bottoms of market cycles. At a minimum, we aim to capture more than 75 percent of the up move and avoid more than 75 percent of the down move.

Finding reliable indicators that tell you when to move into or out of your mutual funds is the key to successful market timing. And the primary tool for analyzing market activity and developing indicators is the moving average. A moving average may also be used as a tool for smoothing data; that is, to remove the spikey daily or weekly ups and downs to disclose the underlying cyclic or trend direction.

TABLE 5C
Computations for Two Moving Averages

Week Number	NYSE Comp.	10-Day Total	10-Day Average	Weight Factor	Weighted Index	10-Day Total	Weighted Average
1	120.74			1	120.74		
2	121.50			2	243.00		
3	121.38			3	364.14		
4	123.14			4	492.56		
5	120.20			5	601.00		
6	118.87			6	713.22		
7	118.82			7	831.74		
8	119.19			8	953.52		
9	120.12			9	1,081.08		
10	120.62	1,204.58	120.46	10	1,206.20	6,607.2	120.13
11	120.34	1,204.18	120.42	55			
12	119.86	1,202.54	120.25				
13	118.95	1,200.11	120.01				
14	117.75	1,194.72	119.47				
15	118.14	1,192.66	119.27				

A moving average is, first of all, an average. And averages come in a variety of sizes and shapes. Also, the average, however constructed, moves with time. Most moving averages used for market timing are computed daily or weekly.

The simple average, known more precisely as a *mean*, is the most familiar. Calculate a mean by totaling all the numbers in an array and dividing the total by the number of entries. The first series in Table 5C computes a mean by totaling 10 weekly closes for the New York Stock Exchange Composite index and dividing the total, 1,204.58 by 10 for an average of 120.46. To convert the weekly series of NYSE index closes to a moving average, drop the closing figure for week No. 1 and add the closing figure for week No. 11 for a total of 1,204.18 and a new average of 120.42. Continuing with each new week's closing figure produces a series of 10-week averages that "move" forward one week at a time; hence the term *moving average*.

A weighted average adds another factor. Columns on the right in Table 5C show a weighting by week number with most recent weeks given greater value than earlier weeks. For the first 10 weeks in this example, each of the closing figures for the NYSE index is multiplied successively by a weighting factor from 1 through 10. The weekly figures are progressively heavier to total 6,607.20. A mean of these numbers is 120.13 (6,607.2 divided by the total weight of 55), slightly different from the unweighted mean. Successive weekly averages are calculated by dropping the earliest week and weighting the latest 10 weeks using the same 1 through 10 weights. Some strategists believe the weighted average produces more reliable data. Various weightings provide different results, as well.

Exponential averages also attribute more weight to recent numbers. Although calculating an exponential average may appear complex, developing an array of exponential averages as a first step in constructing a moving average is actually simple, particularly if you have access to a personal computer. Computing an exponential average avoids the need for adding a long string of numbers as the first step in calculating the mean or weighted mean. The formula for calculating the exponential average is

$$EA = [(A - B) \times SC] + B$$

where EA is the exponential average, A is the newest data entry, B is the previous exponential average and SC is a smoothing constant. An example will help you follow the calculations. First, the smoothing constant. The formula is

$$\text{Smoothing constant} = \frac{2}{(N + 1)}$$

where N is equal to the number of days or weeks to be averaged. Sticking with the 10-week average for this example, N is equal to 10. The calculation

$$\text{Smoothing constant} = \frac{2}{(10 + 1)} = \frac{2}{11} = 0.18$$

Calculating the first exponential average

$$EA = [(120.74 - 120.74) \times .18] + 120.74 = 120.74$$

Since there is no previous exponential average to substitute for B in the formula, the calculation assumes the previous EA (B) equals the current week's number. The second data point is calculated as follows:

Second EA = [(121.50 - 120.74) x .18] + 120.74

= [.76 x .18] + 120.74

= .1368 + 120.74 = 120.88

To begin a new series, you must calculate exponential averages for at least the number of periods averaged before the exponential average stabilizes. In the example in Table 5D, EAs beginning with week No. 11 are stable and statistically reliable. All you need to compute the EA for week No. 11 is the NYSE Composite index close for the week (120.34) and the previous week's EA (120.26). Using these numbers and the formula developed above computes the new EA of 120.26 for week No. 11. You would not need to know any of the closing index figures for prior weeks. Setting up the formulas on a computer spreadsheet program permits computing new EAs in minutes. Note that the EA for week No. 11, 120.25, is close to the simple mean from Table 5C of 120.42.

The period selected for a moving average depends on your objective. If you are looking for long-term trends, a 52-week

TABLE 5D
Calculating Exponential Moving Average

Week Number	Daily NYSE Comp.	Exponential Average	+1.5%	-1.5%
1	120.74	120.74	122.55	118.93
2	121.50	120.88	122.69	119.06
3	121.38	120.97	122.78	119.15
4	123.14	121.36	123.18	119.54
5	120.20	121.15	122.97	119.33
6	118.87	120.74	122.55	118.93
7	118.82	120.39	122.20	118.59
8	119.19	120.18	121.98	118.37
9	120.12	120.17	121.97	118.36
10	120.62	120.25	122.05	118.44
11	120.34	120.26	122.07	118.46
12	119.86	120.19	121.99	118.39
13	118.95	119.97	121.77	118.17
14	117.75	119.57	121.36	117.78
15	118.14	119.31	121.10	117.52

moving average smooths the weekly data points to permit a look at broad movements. A 25-day moving average of interest rates enables an analyst to look at short-term rate cycles. No hard and fast rules define the period for a moving average used in market timing. A 39-week period is common. We used a 33-week moving average for a previous timing system built on the three Dow Jones averages. Mark Hulbert, editor of the *Hulbert Financial Digest*, a newsletter that rates the performance of stock pickers and mutual fund market timers, has studied the effect of period length on timing results and found that almost any period—short, intermediate, or long—will produce satisfactory results. Different periods appear to work better in some markets than others. Which period will likely work best during the next cycle is not known, another reason for using multiple timing systems if you are going to do your own timing. The period length of the system you choose will depend on how often you want to trade, the size of losses you can accept before getting out, and the switching limitations of the funds you choose to time.

USING MOVING AVERAGES

Moving averages function in combination with a plot of actual mutual fund prices. If the mutual fund price line, plotted to the same time interval as the moving average, is above the moving average, as in Chart 5B, you should be invested in the market. When the moving line of mutual fund prices moves down and penetrates the moving average; that's the signal to switch out of your stock mutual fund and park your cash in your money market fund. The downward trend of closing mutual fund prices signals a bear market trend that is likely to continue. You should be out of your stock fund taking refuge in your MMF during the bear market.

As long as the fund price line remains above the moving average, remain in your stock fund. Your signal to move out of the stock fund and into the MMF occurs when the fund price line penetrates the moving average to the lower side. As long as the fund price line remains below the moving average, you

CHART 5B
Moving Average

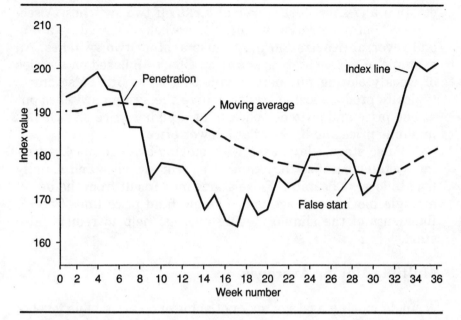

keep your money in the MMF where it retains its capital value of $1 per share.

Ideally, a series of these in and out switches produces a ratcheting up of the value of your investments, as diagramed in Chart 5A. Note that the line representing the value of your total investment retreats slightly from a high figure before a switch from your stock fund to the MMF. Also, the market moves up a bit before a switch from your MMF into your stock fund. Trend following means the combination of fund price line and moving average follow the trend before signaling a move into or out of the stock fund.

REFINEMENTS TO MARKET TIMING

False starts, also known as *whipsaws*, can toss a monkey wrench into the works of an ideal moving-average market timing system. A false start occurs when the fund price line penetrates the moving average, continues the move for a short period, and then reverses to penetrate the moving average again. The penetration and short-term reversal kicks off two switches. A second cycle of penetration within a few weeks followed by a second reversal penetration may cause another two switches. An example of a false start is shown in Chart 5B based on a series of weekly closing numbers detailed in Table 5E. False starts typically produce losing trades, where the system switches out at one price and switches back in at a higher price or switches in at one price and back out at a lower price.

False starts play havoc with moving-average market timing systems because they cause frequent switches and usually lead to losses of capital. False starts may result from the use of a single moving average and a single fund price line. Two refinements of the simple moving average help to reduce false starts:

Multiple Moving Averages

A single moving average may not achieve an acceptable level of reliability. A second moving average or a different index may be used to confirm a switch signal before an actual switch from an MMF to a stock fund or vice versa occurs. For example, the fund price line moves up and penetrates the moving average in Chart 5B. Before switching from your MMF to your stock fund in accordance with the signal in Chart 5B, your market timing system might call for a confirming signal. Such a signal might come from a moving average based on the S&P 500. If the S&P 500 line penetrated the S&P 500 moving average constructed over the same period, the switch signal would be confirmed and you would switch out of the MMF into the stock fund. A similar confirmation, that is, downward penetrations of the mutual fund moving average and the S&P 500 moving average, would be needed before switching from the stock fund back into the MMF. The theory here is that a broad market signal from the S&P 500 confirms the emerging bull market trend noted when the stock fund price line penetrates its moving average.

Another form of double-moving-average confirmation is a moving average constructed to a different time line. For ex-

TABLE 5E
Closing Prices and Moving Average Data

Date	Index Close	Moving Average
June 27	193.87	190.01
July 5	194.45	190.35
July 11	197.11	190.86
July 18	198.83	191.48
July 25	195.10	191.83
Aug. 1	194.38	192.14
Aug. 8	186.54	191.94
Aug. 15	186.54	191.76
Aug. 22	174.22	190.79
Aug. 29	177.78	190.06
Sept. 5	177.93	189.35
Sept. 12	177.09	188.59
Sept. 19	173.91	187.64
Sept. 26	167.52	186.30
Oct. 3	170.80	185.20
Oct. 10	164.97	183.75
Oct. 17	163.59	182.26
Oct. 25	170.60	181.28
Oct. 31	166.17	180.04
Nov. 7	167.47	178.93
Nov. 14	174.68	178.34
Nov. 21	172.73	177.64
Nov. 28	173.91	177.04
Dec. 5	180.11	176.86
Dec. 12	180.25	176.70
Dec. 19	180.35	176.58
Dec. 26	180.60	176.51
Jan. 2	178.63	176.34
Jan. 9	170.97	175.73
Jan. 16	173.00	175.30
Jan. 23	180.16	175.39
Jan. 30	186.02	175.89
Feb. 6	195.38	177.00
Feb. 13	201.18	178.50
Feb. 20	199.26	179.86
Feb. 27	200.74	181.32

Computations for Chart 6B.

ample, you may be relying on a moving average keyed to 39 weeks. A second moving average built on a 25-week schedule picks up a different cycle of the market. A switch signal from either system will not initiate a movement of capital from the MMF or stock fund in either direction. Only when both systems signal a switch, when one confirms the other, would you move capital in either direction.

Double-moving-average systems can reduce false starts. But computing two moving averages and watching the interplay of two systems can be frustrating. Typically, waiting for one moving average system to confirm a switch signal delays the move. While waiting for the confirming signal, you may lose more of a bull market's move while you are sitting in the MMF or lose more of your capital before moving out of a stock fund into the safety of the MMF. These small potential losses are the price you pay to avoid false starts.

Filter Zones

Instead of switching from a stock fund to an MMF or vice versa on a signal from a moving-average system, you could wait until the price line extends some specified distance beyond the moving average. This refinement to the moving-average system is known as a channel, filter, or buffer zone. The theory is that if the fund price line penetrates beyond the moving average without retracing its movement, the move is for real. Or if the fund price line extends beyond the moving average but not past the edge of the filter zone, it could retrace a portion of its movement, even penetrate the moving-average line again, without causing a false start. A typical filter zone may extend 1 1/2 percent above and below the moving average. Thus, a fund price line that has been below its moving average would need to penetrate the filter zone extending 1 1/2 percent higher than the moving average before signaling a switch from MMF to stock fund. A similar filter zone along the underside of the moving average would delay a switch out of the stock fund into the MMF.

Width or depth of a filter zone results from experience or a computer simulation of results. For example, a computer programmed to define a filter zone that would eliminate all false starts over a history of 10 or 15 years could come up with a filter zone so wide as to make the moving-average market timing system unworkable. Running the program again and again permits optimization—a filter zone wide enough to eliminate most false starts but not so wide that you could miss a substantial portion of the bull market or take an equally substantial loss at the beginning of a bear market. Such a program would still allow false starts to occur.

MARKET TIMING SIGNALS

Some trend-following market timing systems tend to be complex, as detailed above. You can also develop your own with the aid of a computer. Downloading market index or averages data from a source, such as the Dow Jones Retrieval Service or CompuServe, via modem avoids the time-consuming task of entering data manually. Once the raw data are available, manipulating the information to try various schemes or plans can be a fascinating, creative exercise. You may try a variety of different indexes of market activity as a base for a moving average. For example:

• The Dow Jones Industrial and Transportation averages tend to move through wide swings to reflect the price actions of the large capitalization companies, those known as the blue chips. A trend-following system based on either or both could be effective if you invest in a stock fund that includes many of the same stocks as those in the index.

• The S&P 500 takes a much broader view of the market that includes many over-the-counter stocks in high-technology arenas that tend to move faster in both bull and bear markets. Vanguard's 500 Index Trust mimics the S&P 500 closely. Timing signals generated from a system built on the S&P 500 index could be applied against the Vanguard Index Trust. Vanguard discourages active switching, so you will have to use a long-term system. Applying a blue-chip market timing system against the Rushmore Fund—Stock Market Index Plus Portfolio could be equally viable, and Rushmore encourages market timers.

• Some combination of four or five stock funds could be indexed together as a proxy for some group of funds, such as small-capitalization funds, international funds, precious metals funds, and other groups. As noted earlier, these funds may march to a different drummer from those broadly diversified, big-capitalization funds.

• Confirming signals may be taken from a different index, a moving average of interest rates, commodities price index as a proxy for inflation, or any of a number of other possibilities. Only your creativity would appear to limit the possibilities.

Testing

After you develop your own market timing system, the question is—how effective would the system have been over some reasonable number of years that should include at least two complete market cycles? We compare simulated results from using a market timing system with a buy-and-hold program using the same funds or market indexes. You could, for example, apply your market timing system to the weekly closing figures of the NYSE Composite index. A buy-and-hold comparison would disclose how much better or worse your timing system would have performed over the period. Bottom-line or end-result figures tell only part of the story. If a market timing system earned a 1 to 5 percent annual compounding advantage over a buy-and-hold system, for example, that would be a significant advantage. Even if your system produced results similar to a buy-and-hold program, you would be ahead because your timing system would have produced the same results with less risk, as your program kept you in no-risk money market funds for part of the time. You should also examine the simulation for other results:

• How often did the market timing system call for a switch? Typically, a practical system may switch an average two to four times a year. A bond fund system might switch more often, up to 8 or 10 times a year on average. Frequent switches may cause some mutual funds to refuse your requests to transfer assets from a stock fund to a money market fund or vice versa. Switching incurs transaction expenses for a fund. Too many switches increase a fund's expense ratio, and managers are extremely sensitive to costs. An excessive number of switches also increases your tax accounting problems.

• How often did false starts occur? False starts are troublesome for the reasons detailed earlier and because they can be emotionally unsettling.

• What were the percentages of profitable and losing trades? You must expect some losing trades along with the profitable trades when using market timing. Typically, an active trend-following market timing system might involve losing trades 30 to 40 percent of the time. If you are market-timing a particularly volatile fund, such as a gold fund, you might run into losing trades as often as 60 percent of the time. Note the example in Table 5F for United Services Gold Shares. Even so, market timing results exceed buy-and-hold programs because losses are controlled.

TABLE 5F
Buy and Hold versus Market Timing for United Services Gold Shares

Year	Buy/Hold		Market Timing	
1975	−38.9	$6,110	−5.3	$9,470
1976	−41.1	3,599	5.0	9,944
1977	39.9	5,035	11.8	11,117
1978	9.0	5,488	−8.4	10,183
1979	187.2	15,762	142.6	24,704
1980	78.9	28,198	78.4	44,072
1981	−28.0	20,303	1.1	44,557
1982	72.4	35,002	107.6	92,500
1983	1.0	35,352	6.3	98,328
1984	−29.6	24,888	1.0	99,311
1985	−26.8	18,218	−21.7	77,760
1986	37.9	25,123	28.7	100,077
1987	31.4	33,011	22.2	122,294
1988	−35.7	21,226	−8.9	111,410
1989	64.7	34,959	35.6	151,072
1990	−34.2	23,003	−16.8	125,692

See Table 5A for important notes.

USING OTHERS' SIGNALS

Unless you enjoy the challenge of developing, testing, and using your own trend-following market timing system, you will probably prefer to follow one or more market timers. Using a market timer's signals simplifies your program. After deciding which mutual fund or funds you wish to invest in with the help of a market timer, you invest and follow the timer's switch signals by moving into or out of the fund on cue. More on the strategies in later chapters. Your source of signals may be:

Newsletter. Most market timers supply their clients with progress reports through a monthly newsletter. If the market timer's system generates a switch signal, it appears in the newsletter that could arrive several days or weeks after a signal's effective date. If the timer works with a number of different investment opportunities, such as domestic bond, domestic stock, international bond, international stock, and precious metal funds, he or she will use a different timing system for each type of asset.

Hot Lines. Most effective market timers supply up-to-the-minute information by telephone. A phone-answering setup plays a tape of updated information to newsletter subscribers who dial a special number. Hot-line tape recordings may be updated daily but at least weekly to shorten the time between recognizing a switch signal and communicating the signal to subscribers. Calls are to regular numbers, not toll-free numbers, so subscribers pay for the call. If the hot-line number is a 900 number, expect to pay a fee for each call. If a switch signal should occur between regular hot-line update schedules, a special bulletin will often appear on the tape. Thus, anyone relying on hot-line information must call frequently. Only active subscribers will have access to the hot-line number, as it is changed frequently to eliminate freeloaders who might be tempted to use switching information without subscribing to the newsletter.

Overnight Notices. For an extra fee, subscribers to newsletters receive notices of switch signals the morning after a switch signal appears from closing market prices. Or notices may be dispatched by fax to subscribers with facsimile machines.

Normal Mail Notices. For a lesser but still extra fee, subscribers to a few newsletters may receive switch signals via a postcard that could arrive one to five days later.

Switching promptly on cue is critical to the user's success. *Telephone Switch Newsletter*, for example, closes its week after the market closes on Thursdays. Before the debacle in October 1987, it issued a switch signal on its hot line after Thursday's market close and sent overnight notices to subscribers to exit the market Friday. Subscribers who switched out at prices posted at the close of the market on that Friday escaped the 508-point fall in the DJIA the following Monday. Unfortunately, many subscribers did not call the hot line and did not receive the switch signal. The four Merriman market timing systems had switched out of the market earlier and sat out the huge decline. But for many, it didn't help because they didn't follow the discipline. If you subscribe to a newsletter or hot-line source of switch signals and you don't follow through, you're wasting your subscription money.

If you subscribe to more than one newsletter, each following a different system, avoid mixing switch signals. Don't, for example, start a market timing program with Newsletter A and switch after a signal from Newsletter B. If you wish to use both systems, start two programs, one that follows the signals from Newsletter A and one that follows Newsletter B. Following a market timing system with the help of a newsletter with or without hot-line support should keep your time commitment within the one hour per month that we promised.

CONCLUSION

Market timing may be controversial for some advisors and market watchers. A look at the facts, however, shows clearly that market timing works over the same periods usually noted for buy-and-hold investors. But successful market timing depends on controlling costs with no-load mutual funds and paying attention to the instructions from market timers. Internal timing of mutual funds, where managers structure their portfolios in response to market indicators to minimize losses and protect gains, offers investors a simple way to avoid difficult tax reporting problems.

You will note frequent references to more than one market timing system. Using multiple market timers is one system for coping with market-timer risk (the risk of following a single nonproductive market timer), as you will see in the following chapter.

CHAPTER 6

MANAGING
MARKET-TIMER RISK

Market timers are technicians who analyze market conditions as they search for indicators that will tell them when to enter and when to exit the market. If controlling market risk is important to you, then understanding and controlling market timer risk is just as important. Market timers as a group may be as diverse as stock pickers. Different market timers produce timing signals as different as night and day. Some timers may recommend being in the market while other timers are recommending getting out or staying out of the market. Timers are not unlike stock pickers; one professional stock picker is buying an "undervalued" security from another professional who is selling because the same stock is "overvalued." With so much disparity between market timers, you should not depend on a single source of timing signals. If a diversity of stock pickers is a defense against stock-picker risk, then look for several market timers or market timing systems as a defense against market-timer risk.

Market action may determine 60 to 70 percent of the direction of a stock's price and up to 90 percent of the direction of a broadly diversified stock mutual fund's NAV (price), as noted in Chapter 5. Thus, market trends can be far more important to your investment's growth than the fundamental study of a company and its stock or of a mutual fund's portfolio.

MARKET TIMING BASICS

The concept of market timing is controversial. Many market watchers pooh-pooh the idea that anybody can consistently forecast what the market may do. But most market timing systems do not depend on forecasting market direction. Most timing systems are trend following and depend on cues from the market's present direction rather than a long-term forecast.

Timing systems are not faulty, in most cases. It is their implementation that is bad, mainly due to a lack of discipline or a lack of belief in the effectiveness of the system. Following a market timing system is not unlike those stock pickers who attempt to emulate such giants as Warren Buffet, Michael Price, Peter Lynch, and others. Successful stock pickers are patient and follow their strategies with unwavering discipline. Attempts to imitate often fail because fledgling stock pickers lack patience and diligence, not because their analyses or strategies are faulty.

The objective of market timing is to minimize market risk while generating reasonable returns. Technicians attempting to take advantage of the effects of market movements on investor portfolios are generically known as *market timers*. Within this generic class are technicians who practice varied forms of wizardry and with varied success, again not unlike successful, mediocre, and unsuccessful stock pickers.

Market timers attempt to be in the market during a rising trend of prices (bull market) and out of the market during a declining trend of prices (bear market).

Being "out of the market" means to have your assets invested in a money market fund, T-bills, or other cash equivalent, as noted in Chapter 5. Money market funds are ideal parking places for funds when you are out of the market because capital values remain constant at $1 per share. And your capital continues to earn money market interest.

Being "in the market" means to have your assets invested in an equity or bond mutual fund. While invested in equity or bond funds, your assets are at risk. Equity funds may be broadly diversified funds holding shares of major corporations. Other diversified mutual funds may hold shares of small, emerging-growth companies. Or an equity fund may invest in stocks outside the United States, in gold-mining shares, or in the shares of companies within a narrow segment of the market, such as utility companies.

Switch signals are the stock in trade of market timers' efforts; they are intended to tell you precisely when to move from money market funds into equity funds and when to move from equity funds into money market funds. If the market begins to decline and you are invested in equity funds, a late sell signal means your capital declines in value before you move it to the safety of a money market fund. After bottoming out, the market may move up sharply before a late buy signal indicates you should move out of the money market fund and back into your equity fund. If your investment program calls for minimizing stock-picker risk through diversification, you may repeat the process with several funds.

Most switching systems make 100 percent moves; that is, when signals call for being in an equity fund, all of your investable cash is committed to one or more equity funds. When signals call for being out of the market, 100 percent of your investable cash is safely at rest in one or more money market funds. Moving all of your investable funds into or out of equity or bond funds can be emotionally unsettling. Yet, prompt moves in either direction are critical to market timing success. The impact on your emotions can be particularly difficult if a move in or out produces a loss. Losing trades and getting back into an equity fund at a higher price than you exited are hazards of market timing. Losing trades may occur as often as one out of three times, but the long-term benefits of protecting against large losses far outweigh the short-term reverses. Count on it!

MARKET TIMERS

Some market timers disclose their systems. That is, they freely explain exactly which data they are using and how they manipulate it to produce the signals for entering or exiting the market. You may study their track record and discover how well or poorly their signals have worked during past markets.

The usual performance study compares a market timer's record of results with one or more mutual funds' records on a buy-and-hold program. Recognize that performance studies between a market timer's results and a buy-and-hold program over the same period only simulates reality on both sides, as both are hypothetical. Few investors buy and hold shares in a fund for 3, 5, or 10 years. Thus, even though comparisons of a market timer's results over a 10-year period offer solid and convincing data, an investor won't live through the same experience for two reasons: (1) Impatience will likely cause the investor to change direction and not hold shares for the full period. (2) A large, successful $1 billion fund will never be a flexible, aggressive $100 million fund again. Events will not repeat; Nixon will never be president again; you can never buy the past.

A market timer's signals may be published for actual dates, rather than simulated data, but few investors supposedly following the signals actually switch from equity funds to money market funds or from money market funds to equity funds immediately after receiving a switch signal. Don't misunderstand me; performance results are important building blocks for developing confidence, but few investors follow through.

At one large seminar, I asked over 100 attendees how many subscribed to five or more newsletters. A few hands went up. When I asked how many subscribed to three or more newsletters, more hands were raised. Most of the attendees raised their hands when I asked how many subscribed to at least one newsletter. Then I asked, "How many of you who subscribe to at least one newsletter follow the directions of your newsletter advisor explicitly? That is, how many of you switch one way or the other as soon as you receive a switch signal?" Not a single hand was raised. Market timing works, but only if you make it work for you.

If you wish to crunch the numbers, you can duplicate the trend-following system used by Tele*phone Switch Newsletter* or Donoghue's Timing Signal system on your own. Both market timers depend on moving average systems, similar to those detailed in Chapter 5.

Other market timers use proprietary systems; that is, the tools and analytical methods used to produce timing signals are not disclosed. You won't know how these market timers manipulate data to direct movements into or out of the market. If you elect to follow directions from a market timer, whether he or she discloses the system or holds it proprietary is of little concern. You are mainly concerned with the effectiveness of the signals.

MULTIPLE MARKET TIMERS

Because no system or strategy is perfect, I believe strongly in using multiple market timers for diversification, and I use four different equity systems in the management of our equity funds and in our newsletter. The biggest challenge for investors is to accept the 100 percent move—totally in equities one day, for example, and totally in a money market fund the next following a timing signal to sell. The resistance I sense among clients to the 100 percent move is almost totally emotional.

Each of the market timing programs, including my own, is proprietary. There is nothing sneaky or underhanded in not fully disclosing one's system. Years of effort, fine-tuning, and testing have gone into developing each timing system. No copyright protection is available for market timing systems. Disclosing how a system was developed and constructed allows other technicians to develop similar, even identical, systems without going through the agony of evolving and testing their own system. While the end product of a market timing system is simple—a signal to enter or exit the market—little about the systems themselves is simple. I am not suggesting that you become a technician, only that you understand that signals rely on data and historically proved patterns of activity. You can use them with confidence to improve your investment results.

Table 6A compares the results of the four market timing systems I use in my management programs and covers the 11 years from the beginning of 1980 through the end of 1990. Market timing results are also compared to a buy-and-hold program of the Standard & Poor's 500 index for the same 11-year period. Individual market-timer results are compared to an average of the four timers' results.

TABLE 6A
Equity Timing Signals, 1980-1990 Comparative Results (12/31/79-12/31/90)

	S&P 500 Index with Dividends	Hooper*	Lipstadt†	Merriman‡	Wright§	Average
1980	32.9%	43.0%	47.7%	37.2%	27.4%	38.8%
1981	-4.0%	8.5%	8.7%	5.0%	13.4%	8.9%
1982	20.7%	33.4%	25.9%	28.8%	15.6%	25.9%
1983	22.5%	20.8%	22.4%	18.8%	22.5%	21.1%
1984	6.5%	2.6%	4.9%	10.5%	4.6%	5.7%
1985	31.4%	28.5%	29.8%	29.0%	32.2%	29.9%
1986	18.7%	19.7%	20.0%	2.9%	13.1%	13.9%
1987	5.8%	24.0%	28.4%	21.5%	27.2%	25.3%
1988	16.5%	9.5%	3.6%	6.5%	16.9%	9.1%
1989	31.5%	30.3%	7.8%	31.5%	31.5%	25.3%
1990	-3.3%	1.8%	10.9%	-3.3%	-4.8%	1.2%
	391.1%	610.7%	542.9%	432.0%	495.6%	524.8%
Compound Rate of Return	15.6%	19.5%	18.4%	16.4%	17.6%	18.1%

* Charlie Hooper, Progressive Investing, P.O. Box 446, Burlington, VT 05402.
† Stan Lipstadt, PSM Investors, Inc.,, 121 Judy Farm Road, Carlisle, MA 01741.
‡ Paul A. Merriman, PM&A, Inc.,, 1200 Westlake Ave. N., Suite 700, Seattle, WA 98109.
§ David Wright & Kenneth Sleeper, U.S. Fund Timing, 2114 Hill St., Santa Monica, CA 90405.

138

Table 6A contains a wealth of data for the analysis of performance of multiple systems on a diversified portfolio. Note the variability of performance between the different timers and the S&P index. The variability among the four different timing programs proves the need for multiple market timers. For example, although Merriman and Wright had the best records of the four in 1989, their systems were out of sync with the market in 1990. On the other hand, Lipstadt, who was the worst of the bunch in 1989, had a great year in 1990. I find most investors can't accept being too different from the market. Multiple systems tend to smooth the curve and make timing less radical, as each of the systems will experience periods of exceptional and mediocre performance.

HOW TO USE MULTIPLE TIMERS

I use all four market timing systems in managing both the three Merriman timed equity mutual funds and in the private management of clients' funds outside our family of mutual funds. Clients who prefer doing it themselves and switching their own funds may follow the signals published in the *Fund Exchange*. Or you may subscribe to other timing newsletters and follow their signals with portions of your investable funds. Names and addresses of other timing newsletters are noted in Resources at the end of the book.

Based on the positions of four distinctly different timing systems, the *Fund Exchange* recommends a quarter, half, three quarters, or all of a client's funds be committed to stock funds. If one market timer is in the market and three are out of the market, *Fund Exchange* recommends to subscribers that one fourth of their invested funds be committed to the equity fund or funds of their choice and three fourths of their funds remain in their money market fund. If all four market timers are in the market, then investors should commit all of their funds to stock funds. Under adverse market conditions, 100 percent of investor cash may be safely parked in money market funds or T-bills. Using multiple market timers spreads both the financial and emotional risks. I use the four timers, and I recommend you diversify among market timers to reduce market-timer risk.

Which stock fund or funds you select for market timing can affect bottom-line results. You add another element of risk when you pick a specific fund, whether it be an aggressive growth fund or a more conservative growth-income fund. Obviously, different funds will hold different stocks or bonds in their portfolios. One way to avoid stock-picker risk is to market-time one or more of the index funds. The most popular index fund is the Vanguard 500 Index Trust that mimics the S&P 500 index. The Vanguard 500 Index Trust is also the largest index fund with $2.7 billion of assets and the one with more than 14 years of actual experience.

Instead of picking four different funds and committing each to a different market timer, you could select the Vanguard 500 Index Trust and three other index funds and market-time each by following signals from four market timers. Each timer and fund should be kept separate. If market timer A calls for a switch from equities to money market funds, switch only the capital in one fund, with that fund representing 25 percent of the portfolio of funds. Let each timing system stand on its own merits using an index fund as the vehicle. You gain stock diversification and, by using four market timers, you gain market-timer diversification to reduce market-timer risk. The index funds you use could represent the blue-chip sector through the Vanguard 500 Index Trust or the small-capitalization sector through the Vanguard Extended Index Trust. Even with index funds you can build a portfolio that represents distinctly different segments of the market. See Chapter 11 for the names of other index funds.

PAPERWORK AND TAXES

Suppose you elect to invest in four different aggressive growth funds. Further, you elect to market-time each one with a separate market timing discipline. You must keep four separate tax tracks to gain this minimum level of diversification.

Tracking results from as many as four different mutual funds and following four different market timers can be a paperwork nightmare. Every time you switch from a stock or bond fund into a money market fund is a sale. If you buy in at one NAV (net asset value) and switch out (sell) at a higher NAV, you benefit from a capital gain. And the IRS wants its piece of the action. To make sure you pay taxes on only your capital gains, you must keep track of the cost basis of each mutual fund's shares. Rules are not difficult, but you must follow them precisely.

The cost basis of your capital invested in a stock fund is the initial cost plus the dollar amount of any dividends or capital gains reinvested in more shares. This updated cost basis is the figure you use to calculate capital gains or losses at the time you switch 100 percent of the capital in the stock fund into the money market fund.

No similar problems result from switching capital from your money market fund into the stock fund because the NAV for money market funds always remains at $1 per share. You will likely switch more money out of the money market fund than you started with, but the difference represents income from interest, not capital gains. You can see that switching from stock fund to money market fund and back, a round trip, two to four times within one year complicates reporting gains and/or losses to the IRS at tax time. Fund managers committed to market timing were not unaware of the problems switching caused for investors. Their answer is the internally timed fund.

TAXES AND INTERNALLY TIMED FUNDS

When a fund manager switches from stocks or bonds to cash equivalents, investors are unaware of the move until months later. Even then, few investors keep track. Internal trading may yield capital gains or losses for the fund, but shareholders are not affected except at year end. Then the fund sends Form 1099 to shareholders apprising them of dividends paid and realized capital gains distributed during the year. About 84 percent of mutual fund shareholders automatically reinvest dividends and gains distributions in more shares. Normally, mutual fund investors pay income taxes on the dividends and capital gain distributions from other sources to avoid cluttering their records.

Realized capital gains are those resulting from the sales of stocks or bonds by the fund manager in his or her attempts to maximize total return. Unrealized capital gains show up in higher net asset values, as the higher prices for shares owned by the fund raise the value of the fund's net assets. Realized capital losses offset realized gains at year end, and distributed gains, if any, are net after losses. If the fund's actions should result in net capital losses—that is, realized losses exceed realized gains—the net losses are not distributed to shareholders. The losses are retained, however, to offset gains in later years, if any; they are not lost. Thus, shareholders in mutual funds that practice internal timing deal with only one Form 1099 Information Return and tax reporting is greatly simplified.

Internally timed funds do much more than simplify your tax reporting chores. Managers of internally timed funds erect defenses against losses, as they understand the difficulty of making up for losses once incurred. Managers of internally timed funds assume the responsibility for getting out of markets trending down to preserve capital. Internally timed funds are not simple; as there are two basic types.

Top-Down Funds

Internally timed funds that practice top-down timing rely on one or more market timers to signal switches. The managers of top-down internally timed funds are not stock pickers primarily; they are market technicians and market pickers. As noted earlier, the three Merriman timed stock funds are top-down funds. The managers switch out of stocks and park the cash in T-bills or money market funds when market timers flash a switch signal to exit the market. Since I use four market timers, from 25 to 100 percent of the funds' capital may be either in stocks or money market funds. Because two of the Merriman funds, the Capital Appreciation and Asset Allocation funds, are funds of funds, the switches are into or out of other mutual funds rather than stocks. Being invested in several funds provides another layer of diversification and eliminates trading costs, as all funds used in the two Merriman funds are no-loads. When our market timing systems indicate the funds should be out of the market, they move to T-bills or money market funds.

In addition to the three Merriman funds, the other no-load, top-down internally timed funds are noted in Table 11D. All of the other internally timed funds switch according to one market timing system. They tend to be either fully committed to stocks or bonds or totally out of the market with capital parked in cash equivalents.

Bottom-Up Funds

Another group of defensively managed funds practices value investing. Managers of these funds emphasize stock selection and are constantly looking for good values. They may end up mostly in cash, but only if they cannot find undervalued stocks. When stock values rise to unsustainable heights, these managers sell shares to take a profit. At times, these bottom-up managed funds may be mainly or wholly in cash. Janus Fund is an example of an internally time fund that moves between stocks and cash on an individual basis. Shortly before the market crashed October 19, 1987, Janus Fund was almost totally in cash, believing, rightfully as it turned out, that the market was poised for a downturn. The managers moved in immediately after the crash and acquired stocks at depressed prices.

Mathers Fund is another bottom-up fund that practices value investing. When the managers cannot find stocks at what they consider to be good values, they leave portions of the fund's assets in cash. This philosophy differs strongly from the managers of 20th Century, Fidelity, and most Vanguard funds that remain fully invested at all times. The manager of Mathers Fund, who considers himself to be a "value timer," uses 12 criteria for evaluating individual stocks before adding them to the fund's portfolio. At times, Mathers Fund may be as much as 90 percent in cash, waiting for the right time and price to buy. In January 1991, Mathers Fund's assets were about 90 percent invested in Treasury notes. This combination of retaining assets in cash when stocks become pricey has paid off handsomely;

compound rate of return over the five years ending with 1990 was 15.4 percent. Total return for 1990 for Mathers Fund was 10.4 percent. Other bottom-up funds are listed in Table 11C.

If you keep your eye on the bottom line, you don't need to worry about what kinds of securities the manager is buying, only whether his or her defensive mechanisms are in sync with the market and producing profits for shareholders or protecting their capital against losses.

CONCLUSION

Diversification of mutual fund's investments helps to protect you from picking bum stocks. But mutual funds' instant diversification can be ineffective in minimizing the effects of market risks. You need some system of market timing to keep you out of markets trending down. You also need more than one market timing system to protect your investments against major market risks and the prospect of one market timer or market timing system being out of sync with the market. You need to diversify your investments among several market timers.

CHAPTER 7

MANAGING EVENT AND ASSET RISK

EVENT RISK

The risk of loss following a major and unexpected happening that unsettles the stock market is known as *event risk*. Iraq's invasion of Kuwait was not anticipated and immediately kicked the stock market into a downward slide. Before it reversed direction, the Dow Jones Industrial Average had declined about 20 percent, from tickling the underside of 3,000 to under 2,400. For reasons few pundits are willing to disclose except after the fact, the market turned around and began another upward climb that took it to just over the 3,000 level on the DJIA in one of the shortest times on record for such a major advance. The major event was the beginning of Desert Storm. The assassination of President Kennedy and the heart attack of President Eisenhower keyed similar shocks to securities markets earlier. The 508-point drop in the DJIA on October 19, 1987, was a disastrous and sickening plunge of the stock market not connected with any world-shaking event.

Unfortunately, major unsettling events provide little or no warning. Few defenses exist to counter event risk because of its sudden impact. But ways and means are available for limiting losses due to event risks.

ASSET RISK

Closely associated with event risk is asset risk, the possibility of being invested in the wrong type of asset in a particular market that may decline for months or years. For example, if you were invested in long-term bonds and interest rates began a steady climb, the prices of bonds would decline for as long as interest rates continued to rise. From 1979 to 1982 when inflation ranged from 11 to 14 percent and the prime rate reached 21 1/2 percent, many bonds sold at discounts of 40 to 50 percent. Some municipal bonds were yielding as much as 13 to 14 percent. Those periods were sorry times for holders of long-term bonds—but excellent times for bond buyers.

Being invested in growth stocks from 1969 to 1974 produced significant losses. In 1973, Fidelity Magellan plunged 42.1 percent and in 1974 dropped another 28.3 percent. Gold and silver stocks were the places to be during the early 1980s when gold reached a never-repeated high of $850 per ounce and silver reached a remarkable $50 per ounce. Mutual funds invested in precious metals mining companies proved to be highly profitable, just as growth stocks were laggards. In the middle and late 1980s when leveraged buyouts and takeovers commandeered the investment stage, junk bonds flooded the market to pay for the multibillion-dollar deals that cast headlines on financial pages day after day and drove stock prices higher. But when reality settled in again, the junkers toppled and sank as if there was no bottom. Investors lost heavily, as bonds defaulted or stopped paying interest. It was another case of being in the wrong asset at the wrong time. Such is asset risk.

One defense against both event risk and asset risk is to diversify your holdings among different types of assets. Just as real estate investors claim "location, location, location" as the key to profits, savvy investors, with an eye to protecting themselves from as many risks as possible, call for "diversification, diversification, diversification."

The ultimate diversification is to be invested in an array of alternative assets so that some will show a profit regardless of what happens to different markets around the world. Different investments respond to varied market conditions, worrisome or upbeat economic developments, and a mix of worldwide events. Inflation affects economies and the correction of conditions that start and continue inflation can be painful, as the high interest promulgated by the Federal Reserve Board in 1980–82 proved. Inflation was stifled and brought under moderate control, but the price was a major recession. World events and different economic conditions call for a variety of investment defenses.

One of the major defenses against investment risks is market timing. But market timing is only partially successful in combating event and asset risks. As a defense against asset risk, experts recommend assets be allocated so that at least one asset will be a winner regardless of what happens to the world, the economy, or the market. It is hoped the winning asset will be sufficiently profitable to offset expected losses in the declining asset.

ASSET ALLOCATION

You can diversify your assets by investing in gold, domestic and international stocks and bonds, currencies, real estate, and money market funds. These different investment vehicles prosper or falter in various markets but are extremely unlikely to advance or decline in unison.

Gold

Gold is a time-honored hedge against inflation. If inflation should get out of hand again, as it did in the late 1970s and early 1980s, gold's price could rise sharply, as investors sell stocks and bonds and buy gold in an attempt to protect the purchasing power of their assets. Gold is often called the *ultimate money* and is accepted worldwide. People living in India, the Persian Gulf, France, and other countries often forgo banks; instead they collect and hide gold as their private hoard of wealth. Gold has remained a reliable store of value for 5,000 years and appears likely to continue in that role. When Germany's inflation ran out of hand in 1923, the country finally issued a new currency based on a gold standard and stopped inflation in its tracks. Gold's prime value rests on its scarcity, ready recognition, difficulty of increasing the supply, and resistance to chemical change.

Most asset portfolios do not hold gold bullion or gold coins. Portfolio managers prefer to hold stocks in gold-mining or fabricating companies. Gold in bullion bars or coins earns no income. It only becomes more valuable if its price rises. While some gold is used industrially, mainly in electronics and jewelry, prices primarily reflect investor or monetary interest. As inflation or world tensions increase, so does the price of gold, as investors exchange paper money for solid money.

Governments can and do print currency or expand credits to undermine or debase the value of their paper money, a process as old as the Romans who clipped bits of gold from coins. Witness the wild inflation of South American countries, as they attempt to buy prosperity by printing more money. As a monetary metal, gold has earned and continues to hold a unique position as a hedge against uncertainty in the world of money. Be careful not to equate a hedge with an investment. A hedge aims to protect against a loss, while an investment aims to earn a return.

Growth Stocks

Growth stocks prosper when economic conditions appear strong or a turnaround from a weak economy appears imminent. Growth stocks tend not to prosper in an economy plagued by high inflation because high inflation brings on higher interest rates. Thus, growth stocks will likely be in a decline if gold is strong. In our developing global economy, growth stocks in some countries may be rising while growth stocks in other countries are declining. Total diversification of growth stocks would call for investments in several countries or purchases of shares in international stock mutual funds.

Bonds

Bonds increase in value when interest rates appear to be headed lower. When inflation expectations are declining, the inflation bias built into interest rates will also be declining. Under those conditions, bonds, prosper but you may miss a strong upsurge in stocks. Gold will be in a decline.

Currencies

Some currencies have tended to be a steady-as-she-goes asset because of the strict control those governments exert over monetary and fiscal policies. With only a minimal growth in the money supply in Switzerland, for example, inflation is close to zero and interest rates change direction seldom and move in either direction with glacial speed. Swiss francs retain a quality image of stability, while dollars, pounds, and deutsche marks may be changing value in relation to each other. Swiss francs are accepted only a bit less readily than gold because Swiss francs are based on gold.

Money Market Funds

Money market funds represent ready cash and liquidity. Earnings are related to short-term economic conditions as opposed to the long-term conditions that affect government notes and bonds. Treasury bills would be equally productive as money market funds and more secure, but the costs of acquiring them and possibly turning them over before maturity are higher than cash deposited in money market funds.

Collectibles

Diamonds, art treasures, and other collectibles from stamps and coins to Chinese antiquities appear in some portfolios. Diamonds may be a girl's best friend, but they also constitute high-density wealth. Diamonds may be concealed in incredibly small spaces to avoid confiscation and are prized for this quality in Third World countries. Diamonds are also recognized worldwide for their value and resemble gold in this characteristic. Costs associated with collectibles, particularly the spread between bid and asked prices, can penalize their profitability. Collectible dealers tend to be the primary beneficiaries of investing in collectibles.

Real Estate

Real property—raw land, commercial property, or homes—cycles with inflation and interest rates. Tax policies also affect real estate values, as the tax-shelter mania in the late 1970s and early 1980s proved. Overbuilding was rampant, and poorly planned projects were thrown together more for tax consider- ations than for economic reasons. Even so, real estate, despite its problems with liquidity, commissions, and settlement costs, has been a major wealth builder for patient investors. Real estate has been an effective long-term hedge against inflation. If the real estate produces income as well, investors can gain two ways.

ASSET ALLOCATION FUNDS

A number of mutual funds offer investors shares in a diversi- fied portfolio of assets allocated to reduce event and asset risks. Among the most widely known are:

Permanent Portfolio

Constructing a portfolio of precious metals, U.S. and foreign currencies, stocks, and bonds as a defense against event and asset risk is an alternative investment strategy given wide ex- posure by Harry Browne in his book *Why the Best-Laid Invest- ment Plans Usually Go Wrong & How You Can Find Safety and Profit in an Uncertain World* (William Morrow & Co., 1987, New York). Browne called his asset allocation plan the Perma- nent Portfolio. His concept calls for collecting assets in a fixed combination, hence the name Permanent Portfolio. It would weather catastrophic events and all manner of economic news to prosper in what has become, in his terms, "an uncertain world." Assets are allocated in four equal parts of gold coins, bonds, T-bills, and money market funds, and shares of growth mutual funds. For a portfolio of $100,000, approximately $25,000 would be allocated to each of the four major investment groups.

A mutual fund matching Browne's Permanent Portfolio has been around since 1982 and is managed by Terry Coxon. The Permanent Portfolio Fund allocates its assets slightly different from the quarterly divisions noted in Browne's book. The fund has 20 percent of its assets in gold, 5 percent in silver, 10 percent in Swiss francs, 15 percent in U.S. and foreign real estate and natural resource companies, 15 percent in U.S. stocks, and 35 percent in T-bills and other dollar assets. Although classified as a no-load mutual fund, the Permanent Portfolio charges a flat $35 one-time account initiation fee and $1.50 per month for account maintenance.

Performance has been spotty. During 1990, total return was a loss of 3.9 percent. For the five years ending in 1990, the annualized return averaged 5.9 percent, placing it among the lowest 20 percent of funds for that period. During the bear market of August 25, 1987, through December 4, 1987, which included the market meltdown of October 27, the Permanent Portfolio lost 8.4 percent. That loss was considerably less than the 32.7 percent decline registered by the S&P 500 during the same period. During the bull market period of September 12, 1986, through August 25, 1987, the Permanent Portfolio Fund reported a total return of 20.2 percent, less than half of the 49.4 percent return posted by the S&P 500 for the same period. For the 12 months ending June 30, 1991, Permanent Portfolio reported a total return of 2.0 percent. Thus, performance has been relatively stable with a low overall total return that is below that of many fixed-asset-allocation models.

Managers of the Permanent Portfolio adjust allocations quarterly. Their aim is to maintain the allocations permanently. If the stock segment of the Permanent Portfolio grows to exceed its 25 percent allocation, some of the stocks will be sold and the cash invested in the other segments to retain the desired distribution of assets. An analysis of results since the Permanent Portfolio Fund began indicates the makeup of the fund appears to be overly conservative. It does better in down markets by declining less than the average market index or most other mutual funds. In up markets, its performance lags that of index funds or most traditionally managed stock or balanced funds.

USAA Cornerstone

Another fixed-percentage asset allocation fund similar in concept to the Permanent Portfolio is USAA Cornerstone. Cornerstone includes five asset categories with 20 percent of the fund's value in each. The five categories are gold, foreign equities, real estate, U.S. government bonds, and U.S. equities. Cornerstone rebalances percentages quarterly.

Performance has been uneven, but it was a top-performing fund when both equities and gold shares were doing well. According to *The No-Load Fund Investor*, USAA Cornerstone Fund reported a five-year annual average compound rate of return (CRR) of 13 percent at the end of 1990, one of the highest CRRs in its group. For the 12 months ending June 30, 1991, Cornerstone reported a gain of 1.1 percent in total return.

Blanchard Strategic Growth Fund

Blanchard Strategic Growth Fund is an asset allocation fund similar to the Permanent Portfolio but with one major difference. Instead of adjusting the makeup of the fund's portfolio to maintain the strict percentages in specific types of assets, Blanchard fund managers shift allocation percentages according to their perceptions of the market and their expectations for future movements. Such a posture is similar to that of the market timer who switches out of stocks in a bear market and moves to a money market fund. When forecasts indicate a rising market, money is moved from money market funds into growth stocks to take advantage of rising prices.

By switching percentages of assets, the Blanchard Strategic fund managers attempt to catch cyclical gains of different types of assets from their beginnings and to get out of declining assets as early as possible. The policy is to allow one asset category to run if it is profitable rather than cutting it back to a fixed percentage each quarter, as in the case of the Permanent Portfolio and USAA Cornerstone. A different manager controls the investments for each asset and an overall manager sets asset allocation percentages according to his or her perception of the market. The Blanchard fund is typical of the second general type of asset allocation funds with variable allocations.

In mid-1987, the Blanchard Strategic Growth Fund (BSGF) was diversified as follows: 18 percent in U.S. stocks, 25 percent in foreign stocks, 12 percent in precious metal investments, 15 percent in fixed-income investments divided 4 percent for the U.S. and 11 percent for foreign, and cash reserves of 30 percent. For the 12 months ending January 31, 1988, the Blanchard Strategic Growth Fund reported a total return of 6.7 percent. This period included the major decline of October 1987. For the six months ending on January 31, 1988, the Blanchard fund showed a decline of 14 percent. Even though the fund's assets were diversified to avoid event risk, the shares still suffered a decline similar to a group of 60 conservative growth funds that declined an average of 14.5 percent.

More recently, Blanchard Strategic Growth Fund has lagged the market. For the 12 months ending June 30, 1991, BSGF lost 3.1 percent while the S&P 500 gained 7.1 percent and the Dow Jones Industrial Average gained 4.1 percent.

Bailard, Biehl and Kaiser Diversa Fund

Another of the variable allocation funds is Bailard, Biehl and Kaiser Diversa Fund (BB&K) which holds varied percentages of U.S. stocks (5 to 50 percent), real estate stocks (5 to 50 percent), international stocks and bonds (5 to 50 percent), U.S. bonds (5 to 50 percent), and cash equivalents (0 to 25 percent). Asset allocations are varied among the five categories within wide margins according to how the managers see the market developing. All five categories will be represented in the fund at any time, but allocations can and are changed widely and frequently.

BB&K Diversa Fund reported a loss of 2.8 percent for the 12 months ending June 30, 1991, compared to a total return for the S&P 500 of 7.1 percent. For the period from December 1, 1987, through December 31, 1990, BB&K Diversa Fund reported a total return of 13 percent, placing it in the lowest 20 percent of funds in its category, according to *The No-Load Fund Investor*.

Vanguard Asset Allocation Fund

Started in 1988, Vanguard Asset Allocation Fund offers a simple allocation plan: common stocks, bonds, and money market funds. Some money managers would call this fund a balanced fund rather than an asset allocation fund. Percentages are not fixed, as managers vary the mix according to their perception of the market. Due to its limited life, only short-term performance figures are available. For the 12 months ending June 30, 1991, Vanguard Asset Allocation Fund reported a total return of 8.6 percent.

Fidelity Asset Manager

Fidelity Asset Manager is one of the newest asset allocation funds, organized in 1989. Like Vanguard's Asset Allocation Fund, Fidelity Asset Manager limits investments to three categories— equities, bonds, and money market instruments. Equities can vary from 10 to 50 percent, bonds from 20 to 60 percent, and money market instruments from 0 to 70 percent. Typical allocations run about 30 percent for equities, 40 percent in long- and intermediate-term bonds, and the remaining 30 percent in money market instruments. Only limited performance figures are available. For the 12 months ending June 30, 1991, Fidelity Asset Manager reported a total return of 15.8 percent.

Merriman Timed Asset Allocation Fund

Merriman Timed Asset Allocation Fund (MTAAF) is structured to provide three levels of diversification.

    1. The Merriman TAAF is a fund of funds. It invests fund assets in other no-load mutual funds, each of which is diversified to reduce risk.

    2. Assets are allocated as follows: 50 percent in equity funds, 20 percent in fixed-income funds, 20 percent in international funds, and 10 percent in precious metals funds. The allocation of assets is intended to spread risks among different types of funds to minimize losses.

    3. Each of the asset categories is timed individually. If the equity portion of the MTAAF is in a bear market, that 50 percent of the portfolio is parked in money market funds. While the portion devoted to equities is in money market funds, the other categories could be invested in their special sectors. At any one time, one or more of the asset categories could be out of the market and in money market funds. Rarely will all asset categories to be in or out of the market together. A different timing discipline (proprietary) controls each of the four asset categories, as each reacts to different market conditions. Percentage allocations are adjusted quarterly to retain essentially the same allocations.

Since the Merriman Timed Asset Allocation Fund is relatively new, having started in May 1989, only short-term performance figures are available. For the 12 months ending June 30, 1991, total return for MTAAF was up 5.9 percent compared to the S&P 500 at 7.1 percent and the Dow Jones Industrial Average at 4.1 percent.

The Merriman Timed Asset Allocation Fund was designed following a study of the difference between two approaches to asset allocation over a 13-year period. This study of an asset allocation fund approach in combination with market timing produced significant results, as noted in Tables 7A and 7B. In this program $10,000 was allocated as follows:

• $1,000, or 10 percent, was invested in United Services Gold Fund, one of the industry's most volatile funds. Conversely, it has been one of the most profitable in gold bull markets.

• $2,000, or 20 percent, was invested in international equities. Scudder International was the choice because it is one of the few that have been around since 1978. Other international equity funds have performed better in recent years.

• $2,000 was invested in U.S. corporate bonds. Dreyfus A Bonds Plus was the fund of choice because it represents much less risk than high-yield bonds. A later study indicated a high-yield fund would have produced results about 2 percent higher per year for each scenario.

• $5,000, or 50 percent, was invested in several aggressive growth funds and market-timed using three of the equity timing models we are currently using.

TABLE 7A
Results of Market-Timed Asset Allocation—No Rebalancing

Year	Gold $1,000 % Gain or Loss	Gold $1,000 Return	International $2,000 % Gain or Loss	International $2,000 Return	Bonds $2,000 % Gain or Loss	Bonds $2,000 Return	Growth $5,000 % Gain or Loss	Growth $5,000 Return	Total Return % Gain or Loss	Total Return Return
1978	-8.40	$916	27.30	$2,546	8.20	$2,164	25.70	$6,285	19.10	$11,911
1979	142.60	2,222	20.20	3,060	8.30	2,344	32.10	8,302	33.70	15,928
1980	78.40	3,964	29.10	3,951	25.20	2,934	71.50	14,239	57.50	25,088
1981	1.10	4,008	-6.50	3,694	10.50	3,242	4.30	14,851	2.80	25,795
1982	107.60	8,321	8.50	4,008	18.40	3,839	27.70	18,965	36.20	35,133
1983	6.30	8,845	23.80	4,962	12.60	4,323	21.40	23,023	17.10	41,153
1984	1.00	8,933	8.20	5,369	17.50	5,079	5.10	24,197	5.90	43,578
1985	-21.07	6,995	49.20	8,010	17.00	5,942	26.30	30,561	18.20	51,508
1986	28.70	9,002	41.70	11,351	9.80	6,525	11.20	33,984	18.20	60,862
1987	22.20	11,000	11.70	12,679	10.00	7,177	21.00	41,121	18.30	71,977
1988	-7.20	10,208	19.90	15,202	10.10	7,902	4.30	42,899	5.90	76,201
1989	35.60	13,843	26.80	19,276	8.60	8,582	15.40	49,494	19.70	91,195
1990	-16.80	11,517	-0.10	19,257	7.00	9,182	2.80	50,880	-0.40	90,836

Number of gains: 46
Number of losses: 6
Years with return less than money market rates: 4
Years with return greater than money market rates: 9

TABLE 7B
Results of Market-Timed Asset Allocation—Annual Rebalancing

Year	Gold $1,000 % Gain or Loss	Gold $1,000 Return	International $2,000 % Gain or Loss	International $2,000 Return	Bonds $2,000 % Gain or Loss	Bonds $2,000 Return	Growth $5,000 % Gain or Loss	Growth $5,000 Return	Total Return % Gain or Loss	Total Return
1978	-8.40	$916	27.30	$2,548	8.20	$2,164	25.70	$6,285	19.10	$11,911
1979	142.60	2,890	20.20	2,863	8.30	2,580	32.10	7,667	33.70	16,200
1980	78.40	2,890	29.10	4,183	25.20	4,056	71.50	13,892	57.50	25,020
1981	1.10	2,530	-6.50	4,679	10.50	5,529	4.30	13,048	2.80	25,786
1982	107.60	5,353	8.50	5,596	18.40	6,106	27.70	16,464	36.20	35,519
1983	6.30	3,563	23.80	8,299	12.60	7,548	21.40	20,346	17.10	37,756
1984	1.00	4,015	8.20	8,603	17.50	9,343	5.10	20,892	5.90	42,853
1985	-21.07	3,355	49.20	12,787	17.00	10,028	26.30	27,062	18.20	53,232
1986	28.70	6,651	41.70	15,086	9.80	11,690	11.20	29,597	18.20	63,224
1987	22.20	7,726	11.70	14,124	10.00	13,909	21.00	38,251	18.30	74,010
1988	-7.20	6,868	19.90	17,748	10.10	16,297	4.30	38,596	5.90	79,509
1989	35.60	10,712	26.80	20,163	8.60	17,270	15.40	47,746	19.70	95,891
1990	-16.80	7,978	-0.10	19,159	7.00	20,521	2.80	49,280	-0.40	96,946

Number of gains: 46
Number of losses: 6
Years with return less than money market rates: 4
Years with return greater than money market rates: 9

During the 13 years, gold was extremely volatile. International funds performed better than they had historically because the dollar declined and a few key foreign economies prospered. Bonds provided an extra kick, as interest rates plummeted during the 1980s, after struggling in the late 1970s. Stocks, particularly aggressive growth stocks, outperformed their historic 10-year average returns. All in all, the 13 years studied may not be representative, and the next 13 years could be far different and produce significantly different results. None of the figures includes any allowance for taxes or management fees. And, of course, the past is never a guarantee of future performance.

Table 7A assumes the $10,000 was allocated among the different asset categories only once, at the outset in 1978. Table 7B assumes the portfolios were rebalanced annually to maintain the initial allocation percentages. Note these results from the two studies:

• The unbalanced system (Table 7A) produced 12 profitable years before suffering a less than 1 percent loss, while the balanced system (Table 7B) suffered no losing years, a record few programs can duplicate. With no rebalancing (Table 7A), the average annual compound rate of return was 18.5 percent. With annual rebalancing (Table 7B), the average annual compound rate of return was 19.1 percent.

• Rebalancing produced 5.2 percent more money at the end of the 13-year period and did so with much less risk. Note the differences in the gold and bond columns of both tables. Rebalancing pushed more money into low-risk bonds and less money into high-risk gold.

CONCLUSION

Event and asset risks are troublesome because they are so unexpected. Major market disruptions can occur suddenly and for any reason. Attempts to allay event and asset risks by diversifying assets among a variety of categories have been only moderately successful. Allocation of assets to minimize event and asset risks tends also to limit growth during those periods un-affected by unexpected disruptions.

Later, in my action plan (see Chapter 11), I will lay out specific plans for investors with varied objectives, including a different approach to asset allocation.

CHAPTER 8

BE WARY OF FINANCIAL ADVISORS

(CAVEAT EMPTOR— LET THE BUYER BEWARE)

Another risk you need to be aware of is the risk of doing business with the wrong person. Advice on what to do with your money comes from so many sources, you can easily be confused. Business sections in local newspapers, specialized newspapers such as *The Wall Street Journal* and *Investor's Business Daily*, and magazines such as *Money, Forbes*, and *Kiplinger's Personal Finance Magazine*, plus radio and television stations spew forth a continuing volume of economic data, market reports, opinions, and forecasts. Even the professionals can't hope to keep up with the flow of information that could affect your investments. Typically, individual investors are intimidated by gurus and so-called experts. They lack confidence to proceed on their own, and they look for help. Help may be as handy as a phone call or a newsletter, but the quality and ethics associated with much of the help they seek may be suspect. The purpose of this chapter is to make you aware of possible pitfalls when you seek help in managing your financial affairs.

STOCKBROKERS

One convenient source may be a neighborly stockbroker. If you haven't found a broker, one will find you. Few individuals with means escape. A variety of marketing ploys can put you on their hit list:

• Invitations to attend a free investment seminar attract individuals looking for information. Regardless of the subject—tax-free bonds, options, managed accounts, or whatever—when you attend, you become a prospect for that broker.

• Fliers or brochures explaining some investment opportunity may arrive in your mailbox. Or the investment may be advertised in newspapers, in magazines, on CNBC/Financial News Network, or other TV or radio shows. Once you respond and receive the free literature, you are fair game.

• Cold calls by brokers are made at random. These calls typically come in the late afternoon or early evening—often at dinnertime. Frequently, a cold-calling broker will offer an enticing security, such as a tax-free bond that yields an unusually high return. Once you take the time to discuss your investment objectives or current portfolio with the caller, you are a hot prospect.

Before you turn your investment program over to stockbrokers, you need to understand how they work and their limitations. Following are a number of comments about stockbrokers that may seem harsh or unduly negative. But I am trying to get you to think in terms of probabilities rather than possibilities. I know from my experience as a licensed broker back in the 1960s and from my continued contact with brokers and their clients that, historically, brokers have not made money consistently for their clients.

The head of research for a major West Coast brokerage firm, who prefers to remain anonymous for obvious reasons, told me in strict confidence that the accounts handled by his firm's brokers earned an average of just over 5 percent compounded rate of return. Further, his firm's internal studies revealed less than 10 percent of the firm's clients earned more than T-bill rates.

I address meetings of certified public accountants (CPAs) at their invitation from time to time. I sometimes ask, "How many of you prepare tax returns for brokers?" A few hands go up. Then I ask, "How many of these brokers show profits from their personal market trading activities?" So far, none of the CPAs I have talked to can remember a broker who was successful in trading for his or her own account. I suspect brokers' big profits come from the sales of financial products to others rather than gains from their own investments.

Stockbrokers as Professionals

If "stockbroker" is a reasonable title for a person who buys and sells stocks for clients, why do so few claim that title? Instead you find such euphemisms as account executive, investment consultant, financial planner or vice president. Stockbroker, as a title, packs a lot of baggage.

A broker I worked with in the '60s at one of the major brokerages told me: "Brokers are not in business to make money for their clients; they are in business to create loyalty." Not in the business to make profits for clients? Was that your impression when you last talked with your broker? I have talked to many longtime unsuccessful investors who can't fire their broker because he is like a friend of the family. Now that's loyalty!

You may have read in *The Wall Street Journal* and various money and investment magazines about billionaire securities dealers, such as Michael Milken, the "junk bond king." Some of these news-making brokers or financial geniuses ended up in prison. Singularly lacking are stories about investors who had grown rich through the efforts of these Wall Street hotshots. The millions of dollars that ended up in the pockets of newly minted MBAs came from the pockets and financial resources of individuals—like you and the financial institutions and pension funds you may be counting on for your retirement. These highly visible characters may be unique, but the problems of dealing with an average stockbroker down the street are all too common.

Problem No. 1—Inherent Conflict of Interest

Critical in the client-broker relationship is a basic conflict of interest. What is good for the broker may or may not be good for you as an investor. Brokers, if they are to prosper, must sell something in good times and bad. If they don't sell, they don't earn a commission. And if they don't produce, they not only can't meet their financial obligations, but also their firm will fire them. Failure to produce—that is, to sell financial products that produce commissions—accounts for most of the 40 percent annual turnover of brokers.

A major dilemma for brokers is how their clients perceive the market. Bear markets cause major problems for brokers. Selling stocks one day can be difficult if clients believe the next day's prices may be lower. Few people can stomach continuing losses. In such an environment, investors fall back to a defensive position and keep their cash in T-bills or money market funds to protect capital.

How does a broker survive in this environment? Many don't. Others scrounge for business among new investors who may be inexperienced. Or they search out long-term investors who may be discouraged with their present broker. Unfortunately, many brokers cajole, bludgeon, intimidate, or pressure insecure investors into buying shares. Or they buy and sell shares in discretionary accounts where the investor either doesn't understand what is going on or is too busy to watch. The process is called *churning*. A broker who is churning an account sells stocks, it is hoped with at least a small profit, in order to buy others and, thereby, generate two commissions. If the process continues through both a bull and bear market, the capital value of an account can grind down to a fraction of its former total. Churning cases appear before arbitration boards every day.

Recognize that brokers are primarily salespersons. Please don't misunderstand me here. There is nothing wrong with being a salesperson. After all, the business day doesn't start until somebody sells something. But many brokers masquerade as financial analysts, financial planners, money managers, or consultants. Few are knowledgeable analysts who study companies' balance sheets, sales projections, and profit possibilities to seek out undiscovered companies with promising potentials. Analysis is the province of a back office specialist seldom seen by the public.

Problem No. 2—The Art of Touting

Originally a racetrack term, touting involves puffery or praise of a race horse—or a stock. The classic racetrack tout works the crowd at races by systematically whispering to bettors that a certain horse entered in the next race would likely win because he had talked with the jockey, knew something not generally known about the horse, or had inside information that the horse couldn't lose. The con is to give different horses to different people. By getting bettors to lay on bets for every horse in the race, the tout couldn't lose. After the race, the tout approaches the winning bettor to ask for a "tip," which the delighted bettor is only too happy to pay from his winnings. The winner of the last race is confident the tout has inside information and lays a bet on the next race according to the tout's recommendation. While all but one of the bettors lose, the tout has a sure thing.

Every stock has a "story." Brokers can always recommend stocks they consider to have good prospects for future profits. Even in down markets, a few stocks move up in price. Brokers hope to beat the odds by finding one or more of the 15 percent of stocks that rise in a bear market.

Most touting occurs in the large wire houses, those brokerages with many branch offices tied by telephone to the exchange floor in New York, to their own OTC market makers, or to their research departments. Two distinctly different types of touting occur:

Touting Initial Public Offerings.

Major brokerages on their own or as members of a selling group underwrite the issuance of new stock offerings. These initial public offerings (IPOs) enable small closely held corporations to expand into public ownership with three objectives:

- To gain access to more capital for future growth.
- To establish a value for the company's shares.
- To convert a portion of the owners' shares into cash.

As an underwriter, a brokerage agrees to sell the IPO and earn a fee and a commission for its efforts and the risks it assumes. With several million shares of a company not previously traded, the IPO manager sends out a message to his or her brokers to sell shares of the new corporation.

Brokers may have little voice in their decision to sell or not sell shares in an IPO. A former broker told me he left one of the major wire houses over this practice. "My manager would stop by my office and say, 'You've got 3,000 shares of XYZ Corp. to sell.' That was my quota. If I said I didn't want to push the issue, he repeated, 'You just bought 3,000 shares.' As part of my training, I was told that if I didn't like an issue, I should sell it to someone who had just made a profit on a trade. Investors are not very forgiving if they have to suffer two losing trades in a row."

Orders to Sell.   Another form of touting occurs during a frothy market when prices reach unsustainably high levels. For any of several reasons, the word from on high goes out along the wire to brokers in the branches to "sell PQR Corp."

If the shares of PQR Corp. have been rising steadily, the broker finds his or her sales efforts easier in response to a down-the-line call to sell PQR. The public loves to buy stocks that have already made major moves up in price.

If the shares of PQR Corp. have been declining, a broker must advance some reason for buying. The broker may indicate the company will be introducing a new product, the company is about to announce improved earnings, or a huge order is in the wind. The brokerage house may have acquired a large block of stock in some deal and wants to clear it out of its inventory. The new buyers may see share prices begin climbing as a the result of the many buy orders entering the market.

As the rising price appears to bear out the brokers' contentions, more investors climb on the bandwagon. Once the brokerage firm sells out its stock, it switches to a different issue, and the short-term game is over for the PQR Corp.

How can you avoid being savaged by a broker touting a specific stock? Follow the example of a new closed-end IPO. Closed-end funds are one of the biggest ripoffs in the business.

The New Iberia Fund, Germany Fund, Spain Fund, and numerous other single-country issues flooded the country in response to investors' interest in going international.

The manager of "One Country Fund," the new IPO, decides to issue 10 million shares. Money raised from the sale of the 10 million shares is to buy shares of companies operating in the one country. When the SEC approves, the brokerage sets a launch date and brokers begin calling clients. The initial offering may be sold out in a matter of days.

As an investor, you buy shares of a closed-end fund IPO at the introductory price, supposedly without a commission. You may think you are getting a bargain, but the managers typically set aside about 7 percent of the proceeds to pay brokers a commission. Thus, as an investor, you may pay $100 for $93 of security value. Typically, closed-end funds decline in share value by more than the 7 percent set-aside after several months. Reports of publicly traded (closed-end) funds appear Mondays in *The Wall Street Journal*.

The success of new closed-end funds is due entirely to the sales efforts of brokers. They know they are selling $93 worth of securities for $100, even if you don't. Closed-end mutual funds are popular with brokers for two major reasons—their upfront commissions and their resale potential. Investors tend to think of closed-end funds as stocks, so it is easy for brokers to persuade clients to move from one stock (closed-end fund) to another. Of course, there is a commission with each trade. If the client had purchased an open-end fund, a switch within the family would be commission-free—not a good deal for the broker looking to boost his or her income.

You can avoid the closed-end mutual fund IPO fiasco by not buying shares at the initial offering. Instead, wait a few weeks or months. If the fund's prospects appear worthwhile, buy the shares at a discount of as much as 25 to 30 percent below the original offering price.

Something you should know about IPOs—if your broker offers you as many shares as you want, the issue is a dog—avoid it. But if the IPO is a hot item, say a Microsoft, you won't be able to buy shares. When an IPO attracts wide attention, a demand for shares develops. Brokers known to be in the selling group may be swamped with demands for shares. An individual broker may be allotted 500 to 2,500 shares to be distributed among his or her clients. Who is likely to get a chance to buy these shares? Not you if you are a small client. The broker may offer a few hundred shares to several favored clients as a reward for their loyalty and past volume of business. Or brokers may offer a round lot of 100 shares to several prospects they have been trying to wean away from a competitor with the appeal, "I can let you have 100 shares of (supply the name of a hot new issue) if I can count on you as a regular client."

Problem No. 3—Misrepresenting Products

An obvious example of misrepresentation is the sale of no-load funds by brokers. This practice is closely related to the sale of closed-end funds as IPOs. Stung by the continued success of no-load funds, brokers began offering their own no-load funds. True, no-load funds sold by brokers exact no front-end commission (load). And, yes, all of your money goes into shares.

Why would brokers sell you no-load fund shares when they earn no commission? Actually, the mutual fund managing company pays brokers a commission, typically 4 to 6 percent of the invested funds. Commissions to brokers are reimbursed to the management company from 12b-1 fees charged against the fund's asset base. These fees may run from 0.25 percent to 1.5 percent of the fund's assets. The 12b-1 fees are charged every year to compensate the fund's managers for their marketing and distribution costs, including the 4 to 6 percent paid to brokers.

The important fact is that a 12b-1 fee is an expense above and beyond the regular expenses necessary to run a mutual fund. Any expense that is not associated with the operation is a "load." Both load and no-load funds may charge 12b-1 fees, sometimes referred to as hidden loads. The fund's prospectus notes the 12b-1 fees and includes them in the table of expenses now mandated by the SEC, but few investors read the prospectus, so the fees are called hidden charges in error.

"No-load" funds that pay brokers a commission expect to earn back the fees from 12b-1 charges. But the fund needs several years to recoup these payments. To permit the fund time to earn back the commissions, a fund may levy a contin-

TABLE 8A
Contingent Redemption Fee Schedule

Period Fund Shares Are Owned	Contingent Redemption Fee (% of NAV*)	Fee (on $10,000 Investment)
0–1 year	7%	$700
1–2 years	6	600
2–3 years	5	500
3–4 years	4	400
4–5 years	3	300
5–6 years	2	200
6–7 years	1	100
Over 7 years	0	

*Net asset value of shares owned.

gent redemption charge for early withdrawals. The contingency relates to how long you own the shares. A typical contingent redemption schedule might start at 7 percent of your investment if you withdraw funds within one year, then 6 percent for withdrawals after one year but before two years have elapsed, and so on until no redemption penalties would be charged for withdrawals after seven years (see Table 8A). Can you really call such a fund a no-load fund?

What disturbs me is that every 12b-1 fund investor I have talked to believed there would be no penalty if they held the fund six or more years. I have never heard of a broker who honestly told the client, "Whether you sell in the first year or the seventh, you will have to pay a penalty or a commission to buy this fund."

Brokers have been known to deliberately sell a 12b-1 fund to a large investor. This tactic may be the biggest ripoff of all. Here is what can happen. An investor wishes to put $1 million into a fund through a broker. That much cash generates a minimal 1 percent commission in many load funds. So the broker sells a 12b-1 fund with no front-end load to client instead and earns the same 4 to 6 percent commission from the fund as if the broker had sold a $10,000 investment. The investor is none the wiser until he or she tries to redeem the shares within a year or two of purchase. But even if the large investor holds the fund for seven years, he or she will have paid a huge annual 12b-1 fee that might not have been charged by regular front-end load fund.

Until 1989, reports of mutual funds in *The Wall Street Journal* and many metropolitan newspapers failed to distinguish between no-load funds with redemption penalties and/or 12b-1 fees and pure no-loads. A pure no-load fund charges no front- or rear-end loads and does not charge 12b-1 fees. Following a mandate from the SEC, these daily tables now carry footnotes to advise unwary investors about charges.

Problem No. 4—Questionable Broker Sales Practices

Brokers can always find an alternative product that has performed better than an investment you may own at the moment. Brokers are experts at making you feel insecure with your investment program. If you were happy with your results, they would have no reason to sell you a different product.

A broker may advise you on numerous occasions of a need to move your investments to take advantage of exciting new industries, changes in the global investment environment, or any of dozens of other reasons. One of the keynote speakers at a national mutual fund conference noted the brokerage industry's opposition to the concept of a "lifetime investment discipline." The brokers' opposition was obvious. If you could find an investment that would deliver reasonable returns and didn't require frequent switching to find the latest hot financial product, your one-decision program would take you out of the broker's commission base.

Another example of a broker exploiting a client's concern is the typical question fielded by many brokers. A client calls and asks, "What do you think of USX?" Immediately the broker senses the anger or concern in the client's voice and agrees that USX might be slipping. The old trick is to ask the obviously disgruntled investor if he had the cash would he invest in USX. The broker already knows the answer, "Hell no!" As the professional salesperson listens and feeds the concern back to the client, they agree to sell USX and buy something else; thus, generating two commissions for the broker. Professional salespersons know how to listen for clues of greed and fear and how to overcome objections.

Problem No. 5.—Not Understanding the Broker's Hidden Agenda

Most brokers learn, as part of their training, to minimize their risks. For example:

• An astute broker working with an issue he or she particularly likes limits future risks by putting no more than 10 to 15 percent of his or her clients into the stock. A broker who succeeds and survives recognizes that if only 10 or 15 percent of clients suffer from the miserable performance of a stock he or she recommended, the broker retains the other clients. Limiting the investment of an issue to a few clients is a form of damage control. While this tactic may be good strategy for the broker, it may not be good for you as one of the clients, another example of a conflict of interest. If your broker works with 400 to 500 clients, only 40 to 60 may get a chance to buy into an issue the broker really believes in.

• If the broker's research staff unearths a truly great stock, one that legitimately promises to double or triple in price over the next few years, the broker will probably call no more than 50 clients. The broker's time is limited and instincts are to limit the sales pitch to only a few clients. So who among the clients is the broker likely to select? Not the small investor who may buy 100 shares two or three times a year. Instead, the broker will likely call his or her best clients, those that invest substantial sums frequently. If your broker should get around to you, assuming you are a relatively small investor, the stock may have advanced above its attractive price during the days when other investors, alerted earlier to the prospects, bought shares.

Problem No. 6—Working with a Broker

Remember when you work with a broker, he or she is looking for a commission; you are looking for a profit sometime in the future.

Limitations affect you and your broker when buying or selling individual issues. Close to 90 percent of the shares traded on the floor of the New York Stock Exchange are between institutions. Big players include pension funds, accounts of major money managers, insurance companies, university endowment fund managers, and mutual funds. You can easily be the mouse in the elephant savannah—likely to be stomped on in the excitement. Trampling can take several forms, but mainly you operate at a significant time disadvantage. By the time any news, favorable or unfavorable, reaches you, the pros on the floor have already moved. You are too late. Your antidote for this potential poison is to join an institution—invest in a mutual fund. Now you are under the wing of one of the biggies. It's a case of "if you can't beat 'em, join 'em."

Another problem with investing in individual issues is the threatening volatility of program trading. Trading in the discrepancies between the prices for futures and the underlying securities, a big mover and shaker in the market throws tens of millions of dollars into the market in minutes. The effect on prices can be monumental, either up or down. Attempting to deal with such volatility can be unnerving at best and highly unprofitable at worst for you as an outsider. To deal with such activities, you would have to watch every minute and be prepared to jump in or out at a moment's notice. Most of us are ill prepared to operate in such an environment, including your broker.

One of the biggest traps in the securities industry is the salesperson's natural tendency to sell to the path of least resistance. All salespeople like "yes" and dislike "no." So they tend to sell you what you are most likely to say yes to. During the summer of 1987 brokers were encouraging clients to buy individual stocks and mutual funds that invested in stocks. The stock market was surging. If brokers don't make it in bull markets, they don't survive. Then in October, the DJIA fell 508 points during one momentous day. After the market fell from about 2,700 to 1,800 on the DJIA, the brokers emerged with an interesting recommendation. Buy bonds and bond funds, they said, or annuities, even CDs. Why would brokers encourage clients to buy stocks and stock mutual funds when the DJIA was at 2,700 and switch to bonds when the DJIA was at 1,800? Brokers are not in business to educate, they are in business to sell. So they sell what you will buy, and when investors wouldn't buy stocks, they sold them what they would buy—debt securities. As professional salespersons, they are adept at matching offerings to perceived desires.

Unsuitable investments can destroy the financial future for unsophisticated investors. I talked with a widow in Denver. Her total portfolio was in CDs from an insurance policy and her late husband's IRA. She had little income and was several years from retirement. Her friends assured her she could trust a certain broker with a major wire house. She contacted the broker for help. He recommended she put $10,000 of her cash into an annuity, $10,000 into a money market fund, and $10,000 into a commodity fund within an IRA. The annuity was inappropriate because she is in a very low tax bracket, the commodity fund for her IRA was obviously inappropriate, and the money market position was only there waiting for another high commission product. You don't hear these stories from your friends because they don't want to admit to their mistakes, assuming they realize they made them. I hear these stories weekly.

Who wins the prize? The brokerage industry is like any other; there are rewards for being the best. When brokerage firms hold their awards dinner, the broker who wins the prize or top honor is never the one who makes the most money for the client. The award goes to the broker who brought in the most commissions for the firm. Oscars awarded by the motion picture industry don't go to the picture that brought in the most cash. The Oscars go to the most talented people or at least to those people the judges perceive to be the most talented. It's the same in sports. The person who runs the fastest, jumps the farthest, or vaults the highest wins the gold medal. But not in the brokerage industry; there it is the person who brings in the most money for the firm.

Rosie is a friend who worked for a brokerage firm that was merged into a national wire house. She told me about a contest where the broker who sold the most dollar volume of an insurance product won a Mercedes-Benz. I asked Rosie, "Was it the best insurance product they could offer?"

"Absolutely not," she replied. Enough additional margin had been built into the price to pay for the Mercedes-Benz awarded to the top salesperson. You should know when you are helping to pay for someone's trip to the Caribbean.

One complaint about brokers is, "They always try to sell me something." Loren Dunton, the acknowledged father of financial planning and founder of the College for Financial Planning, answers by saying, "And isn't it a good thing for you that he does."

Investors tend to procrastinate. A broker may help them to make up their mind—to take action immediately. One broker-dealer tells his associates that a broker's duty is "to make up the client's mind for him." If a broker's telephone call jump-starts you into action, he or she may have helped keep your investment program moving. Procrastination, resulting mainly from a lack of confidence on your part, can devastate the best laid plans. How many times have you responded to a broker's call by saying, "Yeah, I've been meaning to do something like that. Go ahead, put me in for a hundred shares." The snap decision based on limited information may not be the best move for you, but it is a move. Controlling your natural bent to postpone decisions until you see the whole picture affords a better route to investment success, as you will see in Chapter 11.

HOW TO DEAL WITH YOUR BROKER

Your relationship with a broker begins with your first contact. Brokers are professionals. Expect them to control the relationship for their benefit if you let them. Some brokers I have known depend on intimidation to relegate you to the status of second-class citizen. Other brokers play a laid-back role, sort of a kindly friend of the family routine. Building confidence is their game. Whatever the broker's style, you can and should capture the initiative. Think or remember how a banker functions in similar positions.

When you approach bankers to ask for a loan, they ask questions. They may adopt a skeptical stance to put you on the defensive. What does the banker want to know? Anything and everything that affects your position as a borrower, including full disclosure of your financial position—in writing. You can apply these same techniques to set the tone as you deal with your broker. Ask questions, probe for information on his or her abilities, approach, and experience to be sure you are the one who will benefit from the relationship. You have every right to find out as much as you can about the broker. As you investigate your potential broker, ask these questions point-blank:

1. "What is your track record? How have the portfolios you manage or assist investors in managing performed?" Don't be put off with generalities; ask for specifics, in writing. Be aware, however, that brokers may disclose only limited and selected portions of their complete track records. The SEC requires mutual fund money managers to lay out their full record, but a broker may show you only the winners. If a potential broker refuses or hedges on this point, that's your cue to look elsewhere. Mutual funds not only disclose but also publish their track record, portfolio makeup, managers, and objectives in great detail. Expect no less from your broker. Thoroughly professional, caring, hardworking, honest brokers do business in every community. It's your job to find them, as they are probably too busy to look for you.

2. "What is your specialty as a broker?" We live in an age of specialization, and brokers are no different. Just as you would not ask a criminal attorney to write your will, don't ask a broker who specializes in municipal bonds to buy international stocks for you. If you are unsure about your own interests, the broker you contact will try to swing you around to his or her specialty. Thus, you need to define your goals and find a broker whose specialty serves your interests. You may need the services of a fee-only financial planner to help you identify what kind of securities should be in your portfolio. Only then are you prepared to find the broker who specializes in those areas.

3. Ask the National Association of Security Dealers (NASD) for a review of the broker's record. Have investors registered complaints about your broker? What were the charges and how were they resolved? Did the broker ever go bankrupt? The NASD maintains close surveillance over brokers to help preserve the integrity of the business. A call or letter to the NASD office in your area will disclose any information in the broker's file. The broker will be notified of your inquiry. In all my years in the industry, I have had only one person check this all-important record. Those who have a clean record welcome the scrutiny.

4. "What is your experience as a broker?" Unless a broker has been in the business for at least 10 years, I would be wary of his or her recommendations. One trap you should know about is the "broker of the day." This person, usually new to the staff of the broker-dealer, fields walk-ins and telephone inquiries from prospects who have no broker connections. The brokerage firm routinely rotates duty as broker of the day to new recruits to help them prospect for clients. I suggest you avoid such inexperienced brokers, as they have not had a chance yet to make mistakes and learn from them.

5. "How do you decide what to recommend to me and your other clients? Do you develop your own ideas or do you rely on others? Do you analyze potentials or take what the back office feeds you? If I ask specific questions about an investment or approach, will you investigate yourself or ask someone else to do the research?" Unless the broker can answer these questions specifically, look for someone else more capable and more willing to help you.

6. "What size accounts do you now manage?" If your broker works with clients whose accounts exceed $100,000 or $500,000, will he or she devote more than minimal attention to your $5,000 account? Brokers handle large accounts differently from small accounts. With large amounts of money to manage, they can diversify and balance risks. A broker who handles accounts similar to yours in size will probably do a better job for you.

7. "How often do you review client accounts? How often will we discuss the status of my account? What is the discipline you use to determine when we sell?" Most brokers are more active on the buying side and seldom recommend selling unless the cash is needed to buy into a different stock.

8. "Who handles my account when you are on vacation or not available?" Having a reliable backup could be important to you. Plan to meet the person who takes over when your broker is away, and ask him or her many of the same questions you ask your broker.

9. "How often do you trade?" Too many trades can cost you excess commissions. Get the broker's trading philosophy in writing; if he or she varies from that pattern later with your investments, call the broker on it.

10. "What backup services do you offer? Can I write checks on my credit balance? How much interest am I to be charged on margin credit? Will credit balances be swept into a money market fund to earn interest?" These questions not only tell you where you stand but also put the broker on notice that you are aware of these services.

11. "How much money are you willing to let me lose?" If you are a realistic investor, you recognize the potential for losses; not all of your investments will turn up roses. While you may be willing to risk a loss in order to gain a profit, how much are you willing to lose? Will the broker keep on top of your portfolio to minimize your losses? Determine as best you can his or her attitude toward losses and commitment to minimizing yours.

12. "What do you do with your own money?" Few brokers field this question gracefully. If your broker won't level with you about his or her own savings and investment program, be skeptical. If the broker candidly admits to an investment program radically different from one you envision, look elsewhere or understand why. Ideally, you would like your broker to invest in programs similar to yours—and to do well with them. You will get some interesting answers to this question.

13. "What are your credentials? Are you a certified financial planner (CFP) or member of some other professional group?" If your broker is not trained as a planner, you have a right to be skeptical of any planning advice he or she may give you. If the broker relies on someone else for financial planning advice, ask who it is and look into that person's credentials.

14. "Do you sell mainly the mutual funds and other products originated by your firm? Do you consider them to be the best? If you sell competing securities, how do you determine they are better than those offered by your firm?" Your question challenges the broker's loyalty to his or her firm, but your first priority is to protect your interests. One way to avoid a brokerage firm's proffered securities is to find a broker with a small, regional firm with more independence and no allegiance to an underwriting bureaucracy.

15. After you have interviewed your broker, establish a written set of guidelines and objectives. If the broker offers securities you believe are outside the guidelines, you can refer to the written record to remind him or her of your agreement.

16. Do not sign a discretionary agreement. Brokerage firms often try to sign clients to an agreement that authorizes the broker to buy or sell securities without the client's specific permission, that is, to exercise discretionary judgment. Avoid these agreements like the plague. A broker who knows he or she must get your permission exercises more caution than if acting alone. Requiring a broker to get your permission before any trade keeps the broker's feet to the fire.

17. I have saved the toughest question for last. "May I have a copy of your personal financial statement?" I have always offered to disclose my personal financial situation to prospective clients. If you ask to see a broker's financial statement and he or she refuses, walk away. Why would you do business with someone who is not completely open and straightforward with you? Put yourself in the position of a banker. A banker is not just interested in your balance sheet as an indication of your collateral. The balance sheet will reveal a lot about your financial character. A banker requires this information to limit risk. Why shouldn't you be given the same respect. After all, we are talking about your financial future.

Grilling a broker with these questions obviously takes time, yours and the broker's. But it's your money at stake. Make sure you know and believe in the person you expect to help you. If your prospective broker doesn't generate confidence, find someone or some institution that does. Brokers are not the only sources of help. I expect to help you find better ones.

WORKING WITH A FINANCIAL PLANNER

As financial activities have become more complicated, a new profession of financial planning has emerged. Control of financial planners has been rather loose, in contrast to the oversight and regulation of brokers. The title of registered investment advisor is conferred by registration with the Securities and Exchange Commission. With the exception of Washington state, no examination is required to be registered as a planner. A few states maintain registration and limited oversight of planners.

Two private organizations of financial planners attempt to

monitor operations and adherence to a code of ethics by their members.

• The College for Financial Planning (9725 E. Hampden Ave., Denver, CO 80231) offers on-site and correspondence instruction in six courses. Satisfactory completion of course materials and a passing grade on examinations permit a planner to use the initials CFP for certified financial planner after his or her name. Standards and ethics are monitored by a related non-profit organization, the International Board of Standards and Practices for Certified Financial Planners. At least 20,000 graduates are authorized to practice as certified financial planners.

• The American College (Bryn Mawr, PA 19010) offers degree courses leading to designations of chartered financial consultant (ChFC) and chartered life underwriter (CLU). About 15,000 graduates are authorized to use either of the two designations.

Three organizations of financial planners offer a variety of services to their members and attempt to raise and/or maintain standards for the profession:

• The International Association of Financial Planners (IAFP) maintains a "Registry of Financial Planning Practitioners," which is updated yearly. The list includes fewer than 1,000 planners whose qualifications are monitored by the IAFP. Address inquiries to Two Concourse Parkway, Suite 500, Atlanta, GA 30328 for a free copy of the list.

• The Institute of Chartered Financial Analysts includes about 9,000 members. For information and referrals, write to the Institute at P.O. Box 3668, Charlottesville, VA 22903.

• The Institute of Certified Financial Planners (Two Denver Highlands, 10065 East Harvard Ave., Denver, Co 80231) maintains a registry of approved planners but does not publish a list. Call 1-303-751-7600 or write for the names of approved planners in your area.

Financial planners may also function as stockbrokers, insurance agents, real estate agents, and bankers. Their specialty and professional alliance skews their recommendations at times. In any of your decision making, recognize the bias of the salesperson, planner, or advisor. Financial planners perform a needed service when they energize you to manage your financial affairs. When you meet with a professional planner, determine how he or she expects to be compensated. Typical prospecting tactics include but are not limited to the following.

A rewarding method of attracting your attention is to offer financial planning help—a review of your portfolio, for example. An experienced investor will likely spot the manipulations being used to restructure his or her holdings, possibly to sell everything and reinvest in more productive products. Recommendations invariably involve a commission on the sales of existing securities and new purchases. If you are not experienced, you may not recognize the underlying motive behind the self-serving advice.

I recently met with a teacher whose financial planner had moved her out of Oppenheimer Special mutual fund into a Security Ultra fund. The move was obvious to anyone in the industry, as the switch generated new commissions for the planner. If the planner had moved the teacher's money within the Oppenheimer family of funds, there would have been no commission—and results would probably have been similar.

Another ploy is less transparent. The planner may open with a question, "Do you believe we are headed toward inflation or deflation?" Your answer will likely be, "More inflation."

The planner then asks you to start with a clean piece of paper, even before he or she examines your portfolio. The planner asks you to divide the paper vertically, as in Chart 8A. As the planner mentions bonds and CDs, you will agree that these are deflationary hedges—good for you in case of a deflation. Under inflationary hedges, you will likely list stocks, real estate, oil and gas limited partnerships, coins, Chinese ceramics, and other collectibles. Inflationary hedges tend to include assets, while deflationary hedges are mainly IOUs—debt instruments.

Only then does the planner begin to examine your portfolio. Often he or she finds the majority of your portfolio in bonds, CDs, money market funds, and similar deflationary hedges. The planner asks, "If you believe we are headed for more inflation, why are you so heavily committed to deflationary hedges?" You are disarmed, and the planner proceeds to sell you a vari-

CHART 8A
Inflation and Deflation Hedges

Inflationary	Deflationary
Stocks Real estate Coins Oil & Gas LPs Collectibles	Bonds CDs T-bills Money market funds

ety of inflationary hedges on which he or she earns hefty commissions.

Financial planners may employ another ruse—a flat fee to prepare a detailed financial plan. The fee may be only $100 to $300, with no further commitment. What the planner has done is to create a bond, a feeling of understanding and commitment between the two of you. The planner will likely recommend buying stocks, bonds, or mutual funds to implement the plan. You can buy recommended stocks, bonds, or mutual funds from some other sources. But the planner is handy, and you trust him or her. So you agree to buy the products the planner recommends, and he or she earns a commission on the sales. Nothing is wrong, certainly nothing illegal, with this practice, but the planner should be up-front with you. An easy tipoff as to who the planner is really working for is found in the planner's mutual fund recommendations. If the planner does not recommend no-load mutual funds, you were not paying for a plan, you were paying for the right to buy commission products.

One answer to the planner dilemma is to seek a fee-only planner. This person is unlikely to be a broker or agent, as he or she earns compensation from the analysis of your financial situation plus recommendations for action. The planner does not earn commissions from products. With the fee the planner's only source of income, expect to pay $50 to $150 per hour for his or her time. Fee-only planners should recommend no-load funds as a low-cost product, so you regain some of the fee by avoiding commissions. But even fee-only planners may also have a gimmick. Your fee-only planner may charge a continuing annual fee of 1 to 2 percent of your assets under his or her management. The planner will review your portfolio regularly, possibly every quarter, and help you decide which funds, stocks, or bonds you should continue owning.

There is one problem with this approach—great investment disciplines are not viewed one quarter or one year at a time. But a planner can't justify the 1 or 2 percent fee unless he or she continues to move money around to create a sense of action. Such a program could be just as damaging to your assets as a commission-based planner.

One defense is to agree to a one-time investment program with the fee-only planner, and then do your own thing. Or you could ask the planner to come in once a year to review your portfolio, just as an accountant reviews your accounts at tax time. Plan on paying $100 to $200 per hour for the quick review. But the planner would not be getting 1 percent of your assets. After all, 1 percent of $100,000 is $1,000.

Several groups of purely fee-only advisors offer services free of the taint of selling financial products. The National Association of Personal Financial Advisors (1130 Lake Cook Road, Suite 105, Buffalo Grove, IL 60089) will provide a list of members for $1. Some of the members are CPAs; some are not. For a $75 finder's fee, the Licensed Independent Network of Certified Public Accountants (400 James Robertson Parkway, Suite 1200, Nashville TN, 37219) will find CPAs in your area who perform fee-only financial planning. Your $75 is refundable if none of them works out. I have attended national conferences with both of these groups and find their meetings oriented toward improving the quality of investment advice. Other organizations often have a heavy orientation toward building the profitability of the financial planning organization.

NEWSLETTERS

As many as 1,900 investment- or market-related newsletters were estimated to be in circulation before Black Monday, October 19, 1987. Many fell by the wayside, as investors lost confidence in the market and the advice they were getting from the so-called experts.

Most newsletters should be viewed as entertainment and not be confused with disciplined sources of investment advice. See Resources at the back of the book for access information. Newsletter writers communicate their information in any or all of three ways:

Monthly Newsletters

The time to compose, print, and distribute a newsletter of 4, 8, 12, 16, or more pages affects how up-to-date the information is. By the time a subscriber receives the newsletter, the information could easily be two weeks old. Operating in the stock market where major changes can occur in minutes with information that is two weeks old and is not updated more often than once a month can be frustrating.

Hot Line

To minimize the effect of time lost between analyzing data and publishing it in a newsletter, many newsletter publishers offer weekly, twice-weekly, or daily updates via a recorded message on the telephone. These numbers are typically not toll-free numbers, so you pay for the call. The newest gimmick is to use a 900 number where you are charged a connect fee to listen to the updated information. The major problem that afflicts hot lines is that you must initiate the contact. Even if you do keep up the discipline of calling every day, it is too easy for people to emotionally override the advice.

Overnight Messages

Federal Express, United Parcel Service, and others offer overnight delivery of letters to speed information to subscribers. Facsimile machines transmit special information following a major change in the market to subscribers with fax machines. Subscribers who wish to receive these special notices pay extra for the overnight or fax service. The advantage of these services over the telephone hot line is the recommendation to change sits on your desk and is more likely to be followed.

Newsletters suffer a number of other problems in accomplishing their mission of providing usable information that will improve subscribers' investment results.

You're one of a crowd as a subscriber to a high-circulation newsletter. Information that could be effective if acted on by an individual loses effectiveness when thousands of subscribers act. One of the most telling examples was the reaction of Fidelity to a switch signal from the *Telephone Switch Newsletter* (see Resources) in 1990. When the newsletter issued a switch signal to purchase Fidelity's Contrafund, the new money swamped the fund manager. The massive purchase caused Fidelity to issue a potential ban on market timers using telephone switching except under limited conditions. Ordinarily, market timers use so many different systems that produce switch signals at various times the massive movements in or out of the market are not a problem. Even so, you can still be one of a crowd, as your information is far from exclusive.

Responding to monthly newsletters and hot-line information can require considerable monitoring time. Further, unless you have a backup person available, you can lose contact with newsletter advisories if you travel either for business or for pleasure. Actively following a newsletter's advice may not be time-consuming, but tracking recommendations and keeping informed require a commitment of quality time.

MULTIPLE NEWSLETTERS

Diversification remains a major tool for reducing risk. If you plan to follow directions you receive via newsletters, use more than one. As many as four is desirable. Subscribing to four newsletters could cost $500 to $600 per year. While this expense is not unreasonable for a sizable portfolio, you need to follow a strict discipline to get your money's worth. For example, don't mix signals. If you subscribe to four newsletters, use the information to manage four separate portfolios. If you use Newsletter A to time 25 percent of your portfolio, follow directions exactly. Don't, for example, invest in Fund A according to a timing signal from Newsletter A and switch out of Fund A according to a timing signal from Newsletter B. Using four different timing signals, one for each 25 percent of our mutual funds, provides the risk-averting discipline we believe is important.

CONCLUSION

This chapter has been critical of several traditional sources of investment advice. I believe it is imperative that you become an effective boss in overseeing your "business"—your portfolio. Why should you be relegated to using less than the best in managing your-hard earned money. If you were going to buy a National Football League franchise, you would hire an experienced football coach, probably one who is experienced in the professional ranks rather than one who has been coaching high school football. Put the probabilities of success on your side and demand the best. If you have the opportunity to meet many successful businesspeople, you will not be surprised to find their success comes from their ability to surround themselves with the best advisors.

CHAPTER 9

COLLECTING CAPITAL

Investing is the fun part of managing money. Plans and strategies for making your dollars work harder and grow faster can be exciting. The usual investment program begins with the assumption that you will be investing $1,000—maybe only $100. Whatever the amount, the advice begins when you have capital to invest.

Question—where do you get the capital?

SOURCES OF CAPITAL

Individuals can seldom count on resources other than those they can do something about.

You could win a lottery, but your two chances are slim and none. A better choice is to drop the money you casually spend on lottery tickets into a cookie jar. Every so often extract the bills from the jar and deposit them into a savings account.

Betting at the races or taking a chance at the tables in Las Vegas can be a quick way to collect a stake. But chances are you will have a bit of fun and come out with less cash than you went in with.

That rich uncle of yours with the bad heart could die and leave you an inheritance. Your chances of acquiring investment capital through an estate settlement is infinitely greater than the chance of winning a lottery or a big stake at a gaming table, but you can't count on it. If you should receive a substantial inheritance, plan to invest it to achieve a specific objective. Don't spend it—at least don't spend all of it.

Savings, regular and consistent, represent your best chance to collect a beginning stake. Whether you earn $20,000 a year or $200,000—even $2 million—savings don't just happen. Somebody makes them happen. Since you are reading this book, that somebody could be you. Several systems will work, if you follow through. Collecting capital depends on an attitude, one that puts you first. Following are a few of the workable ways to collect cash for investment.

DEVELOP A SAVINGS HABIT

Many ideas for spending less than you earn surface and resurface regularly. Few are original, and they all work if you make them work. Developing a saving attitude is no small task. For years, you may have spent all you earned—possibly a little more. Changing an ingrained habit isn't easy because the habit itself resists change. It is hoped you can change a habit in less time than you spent developing it. Changing your behavior is the key. It's called behavior modification. Start with some small change, a trick that's easy:

Extra change at the end of the day can be collected in a cookie jar or teapot. At $1 per day, you could save as much as $365 per year—enough to take a long weekend vacation perhaps but scarcely enough to build a true investment account. Still, it's a start.

Savings from a habit change, such as the cash you save by stopping smoking can add up. If you smoked one pack of cigarettes a day and each pack cost $2, you could theoretically save $730 per year by not buying the cigarettes. If you were a smoker at one time and quit, did you save any money? Probably not. Instead, the money you didn't spend on cigarettes slipped into your spending stream and disappeared. For this tip to work, you need to slip $2 into the teapot every morning without fail on the same day you stop smoking. If you have been smoking two packs a day, deposit $4 in the teapot every morning. Since you were spending the $2 or $4 on cigarettes and you have stopped smoking, other spending is not affected.

Maybe you and your spouse have drifted into the habit of going out on Saturday nights, having a few drinks and socializing with friends. Total cost is $50 to $100 or more. Instead of going out, invite a few friends in, buy a couple of bottles of wine, broil hamburgers, and serve a pie you or your spouse bakes—total cost, $25 to $40. This saves you $25 to $60 for one Saturday. Your friends will probably reciprocate and you save the full $50 to $100 you formerly spent each week until it's your turn again—saving $100 to $200 each month.

Critical in these habit changes is keeping the money you don't spend out of your usual spending stream. Keep those funds separate and inviolable. Collecting $1,000 or $1,200 per year with one or more of these schemes is not out of the question—if you are committed.

My son and his wife found themselves short in saving for their goals. They elected to ask a fee-only financial planner to examine their spending and money management plans. They were shocked to find they were spending about $700 each month on dinners out and entertaining. Once they were aware of the problem, they were committed to changing their behavior pattern to channel cash savings into investments.

Use a lender's discipline to back up your commitment to collect a beginner's investment stake. If you work for a company or organization with a credit union, borrow $2,000 with an agreement to have the monthly payments plus interest deducted from your paycheck. Invest the $2,000 in a money market fund or one of the growth funds listed in Chapter 11. Two good things happen with this maneuver:

• After a few paychecks you adapt your spending habits to the smaller after-tax and after-deduction total. The working principle here is, "if you don't see it, you don't spend it." You have used this principle for years. You spend less than you make because your employer regularly withholds income tax payments. You have geared your lifestyle to the amount on your paycheck each pay period. Your deduction for the borrowed cash simply reduces the amount.

• After the year is up, the loan is paid in full and you are attuned to the lower paycheck amount. Continue the deduction to add the same amount to your savings each pay period. Only this time, your savings accumulate faster because no interest is deducted. If you should get a raise, ask the credit union to withhold the after-tax amount of the raise. You'll keep spending the old amount, and your balance in the credit union will rise even faster.

Another way to save is to pay yourself the payment on a car, furniture, appliances, or other big-ticket item when the contract is paid off. Suppose you financed a car over a four-year period and the payments are $200 per month. At the end of four years, you may be eager to replace the car and dance the payment polka again. Instead, take a year off. Drive your present car another year, possibly two. But, instead of letting the $200 slip into your spending stream, divert it immediately into a savings account. When the total reaches $1,000, pull it out and start a money market account in one of the major mutual fund families. Or you can start a money market fund immediately with 20th Century Cash Reserve; it has no minimum initial or continuing deposit limit. Since the $200 you have been paying to the auto finance company each month is from after-tax money, all of the $200 adds to your savings each month. Further, since car payment interest is no longer deductible, there is no impact on your income tax return. Ah, you say, driving the car another year decreases its trade-in value. Or the car needs maintenance and four new tires. These may be out-of-pocket costs, but they are far less than the depreciation charges the first year on a new car or younger used car. Studies have proved that total costs per mile decline each additional year you continue owning and driving a car.

Paying yourself first is a cliché you have heard before. The concept is sound; you and your family sit atop the priority totem pole. Because you are the most important, you deserve first crack at your financial resources. But what typically happens is you pay bills, and if you run out of cash, you use a credit card that shows up as a bigger bill next month. You promise yourself you will put whatever is left into a savings account. But at the end of the month, little, if anything, is left. Instead of you being at the top, you have relegated yourself to the bottom of the totem pole. Rather, as soon as you deposit your paycheck, write a check to a money market fund or savings account for 10 percent, 5 percent or whatever you decide is doable. Like the paycheck after a credit union deduction, what you have left is your spendable cash. If your attitude is right, you adapt your spending to the remaining total. It works, has worked for millions, and will work for you.

All of these ideas for saving may appear pompous, piddling, or patronizing. They are gimmicks, devices to trick you into spending less than you earn. A better way is to take a firm hold on your finances, decide how much you will spend and where, and deliberately plan to set aside a part of your earnings for the future. A goal, something you absolutely, positively must have, is your incentive. I have discussed numerous objectives (goals) elsewhere. The specifics of the goal are not as important here as having one you fervently believe in and committing yourself to achieve it.

One of the most practical systems I have seen for controlling spending and collecting capital for investments is one developed by my associate, Merle Dowd. He developed his "Personal Money Plan" while teaching a 10-week course in Personal Financial Planning at the University of Washington's evening school. He has given me permission to use it, and I heartily recommend it to you. For the complete Personal Money Plan, see Resources.

OBJECTIVES

Anyone who earns money and spends it can benefit from using the Personal Money Plan or Planner. Money is everyone's common denominator, only some have more than others. Some of us do a better job managing our money than others, but we must all use money in our daily living. The Planner aims to help you do a better job spending money for one big reason—those persons, single or married, who PLAN their spending get more for their money than those who don't. It's that simple. The emphasis is on spending effectively, because when you buy effectively, you have money left to invest. Too often individuals and couples spend impulsively with no goals in mind, and the money disappears.

The Planner's objectives are to help you manage your money like a small business, and like a business, to derive a profit. Individual or family "profit" can be defined as:

• Long-term financial security. Collecting the capital you need to begin and maintain an investment program is the first step on the road to achieving financial security for now and through retirement.

• Gaining a higher standard of living. You do this by reducing spending on nonessentials. With the money you save there, you buy the goods and services you really need and want. Developing a discipline with the Planner helps you make the important choices.

• Confidence in dealing with money matters. When your planning keeps you in control, you feel confident. Knowing where your money is coming from and where it is going keeps you in control.

GETTING STARTED

Your first objective is to save 10 percent of your current after-tax income through effective money management. If your current after-tax income is $20,000, a 10 percent savings rate will provide the $2,000 for your IRA (see Chapter 10). Consider the money you spend now; it's what's left after federal, state, and local taxes, including sales taxes, are extracted. You could easily have only $1 to $1.20 left from gross earnings of $2 after paying all those taxes. So, if you don't spend $2,000 of your current after-tax earnings, all $2,000 are yours to invest. Attempting to earn more to fund an investment program means you would have to earn $4,000, pay a total of about $2,000 in taxes, and have $2,000 left to invest. Further, you can implement your saving program at once; getting a raise or earning more money takes longer.

Don't expect $2,000 to drop into your lap without spending considerable time and effort. Work at reducing current spending like a part-time job. How much time must you spend to earn your $2,000 of after-tax income? That is, what rate per hour can you earn from your efforts to cut spending? Keeping records accounts for as much as a half-hour per week. That's 26 hours per year. Shopping in more stores could average another hour per week. Doing a few things for yourself to avoid buying from others takes another half-hour, so you may spend two hours per week cutting spending by $2,000 per year. That's 104 hours per year or $19.23 per hour to save $2,000—after taxes. Before taxes at an estimated 40 percent cumulative tax rate (federal, state, and local) you are earning an effective, before-tax rate of $32 an hour.

LEARNING TO CHOOSE

Most of us can't buy everything we want. So we must choose where we spend our money. Actually, we make two choices when we buy something. With the same decision, you also choose NOT to buy something else. For example, suppose you decide to buy a new car instead of driving your old one another year or two. By spending your cash or credit on the new car, you may also have decided not to take a ski vacation or pay off some old debts that keep dragging $40 to $50 out of each paycheck for nondeductible interest.

If you find too few dollars for spending on "fun," two routes are open to you:

1. Increase your income. But earning extra cash can be a tough assignment. Plus, for every dollar you earn, the tax collectors take their bites first.

2. Spend your present income more effectively. If you ruthlessly cut spending on unimportant goods and services, you end up with dollars to spend on goods and services that you really want, including dollars to invest for retirement or other major goals. So, when you pick and choose where to spend, fewer dollars dribble away.

Choosing effectively calls for examining alternatives and

picking the ones that satisfy your needs at the least cost. Your first task is to examine alternatives, a trait you can easily develop.

Suppose you decide to buy a car. New car or used? Small or big? Import or American? Red, black, two-tone? Stripped or loaded? Or—the choices run on and on. Look first at the alternatives of spending cash for a new car versus a used car. Driving a used car during its third or fourth years might cost $2,000 to $4,000 less than driving a new car during its first two years. As you dig into the differences in operating costs between a small car and a big "belchfire-8," you can sense the excitement of developing a range of alternatives before choosing. If you look at lower costs, include alternatives for spending the difference on a vacation trip or an IRA deposit. When you select the ONE course that offers the best combination of benefits from one batch of dollars, you begin to understand what effective money management is all about.

YOUR MONEY PLAN

Following is a step-by-step program that works to control your money and spend effectively:

Step 1: Compute Your Net Worth

Ask your bank for a net worth statement form; you may have filled one out if you ever applied for a loan. Or use a blank sheet with a line down the middle. Either way, list all of your assets on the left side. List your liabilities on the right side. That is, what you own on the left, what you owe on the right. Subtract your total liabilities from your total assets. The answer, and I hope it is a positive number, is your net worth.

Step 2: Set Out Your Goals

Work at a list over a period of a week or two. Otherwise, you may forget something. Let your subconscious mind flush good ideas to the surface over several days. If you are married, get the whole family involved in a brainstorming session. Once you have a list, attach dollar amounts to each item. Your first reaction may be a feeling of hopelessness—you could never achieve everything you really want. Possibly. But begin to prioritize the list. Top priority goals for goods and/or services you need right away come first. Others tail away to needs that seem far less important when you rate them against others. With price tags, you can play games where you might move up two less-pricey goals in place of one more costly goal. Going through this exercise of finding what's important to you and your family, of prioritizing your goals, is important. Don't skip it because it feeds directly into the next step.

Step 3: Develop a Spending Plan

You might call it a budget because it looks like a budget, but a spending plan has a positive image; we all prefer to spend rather than budget. Instead of a budget that tells you what you can't do, a spending plan tells you what you can spend your money on. It's a matter of semantics, but if it changes your mental approach, go for it.

The spending plan analysis in Chart 9A divides spending into 12 categories. It begins by organizing the money you spend now. You should be able to reconstruct your average weekly or monthly spending levels from credit card invoices, your check register, and memory. Try to account for at least 90 percent of your current spending and organize expenditures by category. If you pay for car insurance twice yearly, divide the total into 12 monthly pieces. Do the same with other big bills, such as house taxes. A monthly schedule works best because you pay many bills monthly. Your aim is to find an average monthly figure that when multiplied by 12 equals your gross income. Note there is a category for taxes.

When you have reconstructed average monthly spending levels, compare current spending in the 12 categories with your priority goals. How does your spending stack up? If you are spending more on housing or transportation, for example, look for places to cut spending. Few of us can get wildly excited about spending more dollars for fuel oil. If your cars are costing

CHART 9A
Spending Plan Analysis

SPENDING PLAN ANALYSIS WORKSHEET°

Spending Category	Current Spending		Desired Spending		%
	Weekly	Monthly	Weekly	Monthly	
MARKET Food, including quantity purchases					
Delivered milk and/or bread					
Nonfood items (paper, cleaning supplies, etc)					
Subtotal					
HOUSING Rent or mortgage payment					
Taxes					
Hazard Insurance					
Utilities (water, heat, electrical, etc.)					
Maintenance & repairs					
Home furnishings (Installment payments)					
Home equipment					
Subtotal					
TRANSPORTATION Car owning costs (payments, etc.)					
Car operating (gas oil, license)					
Car maintenance, repairs, & tires					
Car insurance					
Subtotal					
CLOTHING Purchases					
Cleaning & laundry					
Repair (shoe, etc.)					
Subtotal					
HUSBAND Recreation (movies, sports tickets, dinners out)					
Beverages (alcoholic & other)					
Cigarettes & tobacco					
Bus fares					
Personal care (haircuts, etc.)					
Newspapers, magazines, etc.					
Subtotal					
WIFE Personal care (beauty)					
Cigarettes					
Lunches					
Bus Fares					
Miscellaneous					
Subtotal					

(PERSONAL SPENDING)

CHART 9A *(continued)*

	Spending Category	Current Spending		Desired Spending		
		Weekly	Monthly	Weekly	Monthly	%
MEDICAL	Physicians' and dentists' visits ___					
	Hospitalization & medical ins. premiums ___					
	Drugs, prescriptions & other ___					
	Subtotal					
FAMILY BETTERMENT	Education ___					
	Club dues & other ___					
	Vacations ___					
	Sports (other than tickets) ___					
	Hobbies ___					
	Subtotal					
GIFTS & CONTRIB.	Birthday & Christmas gifts ___					
	Church and other contributions ___					
	Subtotal					
MISC.	Life insurance ___					
	Dues & occupational expenses ___					
SAVINGS OR DEBT PAYMENTS	Bank, savings ___					
	Credit union ___					
	Savings & loan ___					
	Other ___					
	Subtotal					
	TOTAL SPENDING ___					
TAXES	Social Security (FICA) ___					
	Income tax ___					
	Other ___					
	Subtotal					
	TOTAL INCOME					

too much, consider alternatives, such as riding the bus, not trading up as soon as your present car is paid for, or buying tires from a discount source instead of your corner service station. The concept here is to spend less on unimportant categories to free up more of your cash for "fun." Fun is an all-encompassing category that includes most of the things you like doing. Fun, in its broad definition, includes vacation trips, books and magazines, dinners out, contributions to your church, costs for educating children, and more.

If you find your actual spending patterns do not match your goals, ask yourself, "Why not?"

Restructure your spending plan as you would like it to realize your high-priority goals. Put more money into those categories that are important to you. Plan to spend less in those categories that are unimportant to you. Restructuring calls for more than simply putting different numbers into each category. You need to think about how you will spend less on housing, for example, if you plan to spend less there than you have been spending. Following are a few thoughts on how you can spend less.

• You can only save big money by attacking those categories where you are already spending major chunks of your income. Reducing a large expenditure by a small percentage is easier than reducing a small expenditure by a large percentage—and the actual number of dollars you save would be comparable. For example, you might pare 10 percent off your $500 bill for food and sundries at the market to save $50 each month. If you have been spending $100 each month for personal care (haircuts, face cream, and the like), you would have to cut that bill in half to save $50.

• A small reduction in frequent spending will account for a sizable amount over a long period, say a year.

• No spending category should escape critical scrutiny.

Consider food shopping for starters. Food buying accounts for a big chunk of your necessary spending and you buy food often. So it qualifies on both accounts—large expenditure and frequent expenditure. Aggressive shopping tactics can easily cut spending for food by 10 to 20 percent with little change in eating habits. If you eat to live rather than live to eat, gourmet meals will likely be less important than other defined goals. You may choose to gain further savings by changing your eating habits—fewer steaks grilled on the barbecue and more low-cost casseroles, for example. Money spent on food varies widely for families with about the same after-tax income. For detailed ideas on how to cut spending on housing, food, and other categories, see the books listed in Resources.

Other categories offer similar opportunities for changing spending patterns according to your own ideas of what is important and what is not important. All of us have certain "hot buttons," some things, services, or activities that are high on any priority list. You willingly spend more on hot-button goods and services than you do on others.

Changing spending patterns is not a one-night proposition. The more your mind tunes in to ways and means of changing your spending habits, the more opportunities open for you. What happens is like your interest in a new car. Suddenly you notice any number of similar cars as you drive around because it is in your mind. So it is with saving opportunities. Few major changes will be easy. You may slip or become discouraged. But remember, no beginning skier parallels down the fall line on his first try either.

Once you settle on a new "desired spending" plan, try it for at least six months. As you will see in the next step, you will need to track your spending. You may have planned wrong; one category may provide too little cash to meet your needs. If you have allocated all of your available income into the 12 categories, you can increase spending in one category only if you cut spending in another category by the same amount—or by going into debt. Because you are trying to collect capital to meet defined investment goals, slipping into deficit spending is strictly a no-no.

Step 4: Track Your Spending

Once you set up a new spending plan, how do you know your spending actually fits the plan? You won't know unless you keep records. The simplest system for tracking spending is with a series of "Howgozit Charts." You need a Howgozit Chart for

CHART 9B
Howgozit Chart for Market

Date	Item Description	Add	Subtract	Balance
Jan. 1	Transfer to Funds	$500.00		$500.00
2	Safeway		50.00	450.00
7	Giant Stores		100.00	350.00
10	Safeway		50.00	300.00
12	Price Store		25.00	275.00
14	Safeway		25.00	250.00
15	Safeway		50.00	200.00
20	Giant		100.00	100.00
28	Price Store		50.00	50.00
29	Safeway		100.00	(50.00)
Feb. 1	Transfer Funds	500.00		450.00

each category. Note the sample chart shown in Chart 9B and follow these steps:

Accounting forms with at least three columns on the right side are ideal, or you can rule the three columns on lined notebook paper. Label the heads of each column, Add, Subtract, and Balance. Accountants will blanch at not using credits and debits, but add and subtract are clearer.

Start each sheet by adding the amount you plan to spend on each category. For example, if you plan to spend $500 each month at the market, enter $500 in the Add column of the Howgozit Chart labeled "Market." Carry the $500 across to the Balance column. That is your starting point. If you write a check for the exact amount you spend at your supermarket for food, enter the amount on the next line under the Subtract heading. Suppose you spend $45.10. Enter that number in the Subtract column and reduce the amount in the Balance column to $454.90. The running balance adjusted for additions and checks written indicates the amount you have left to spend during that month.

You can use category balances as an incentive; if there is too little money available in a fund, don't buy something that will run the category account into the red. At the beginning of the next month, add another $500 to the Add column and adjust the balance accordingly. If you spent more than $500 at the market during the first month, figures in the balance column will be in red, indicating a deficit. At the beginning of the next month when you add $500, the balance will be less, as you deduct the deficit from the new $500 addition. If you spend more than $500 each month, the deficit continues to mount. At the end of six months, you might want to replan your spending because experience indicates your plan is unbalanced.

Some older readers may recognize this system as an alternative to the "envelope" plan. Years ago, before credit and checking accounts became so prevalent and some employers paid wages in cash, the family money manager would distribute the cash from wages into various envelopes labeled for food, rent, transportation, insurance, and other categories. When the shopper went to buy food, he or she spent money out of the envelope labeled "food." This system exacted a strict discipline. When there was no more money in the food envelope, the family ate out of its pantry. If the pantry was bare, one might borrow from another envelope, but that was only a last resort. If there was no money to borrow from other envelopes, they went hungry.

The Planner substitutes a number of categories for the envelopes. As you keep each Howgozit Chart up to date, the process is not unlike adding cash to or taking it out of an envelope. Breaking down spending into 12, possibly as few as 10 or as many as 16, categories makes money management practical. You can't make rational decisions strictly on a single balance in a checkbook.

After six months or a year, you may want to rebalance the spending plan. If you allocate all of your income to the 12 categories, including places for savings and taxes, you can recognize where all of your money is going. Setting up a miscellaneous category fails to develop discipline; it's too easy to slip something into miscellaneous. As you buy something, you must think which fund you will charge the purchase to. That thought at the moment of decision may prevent you from spending cash frivolously.

SPECIAL PROBLEMS

Few families or singles have enough cash in the bank to add the monthly allocation to each of the spending categories. That's the reason for the Allocation Fund shown in Chart 9C. The Allocation Fund accomplishes several functions:

1. It permits you to start using the Planner at any time, but preferably at the beginning of a month. Begin by noting the running balance in your check register in the Add column of the Allocation Fund and carrying that figure to the Balance column. Then deduct the total of the monthly allocations from the Spending Plan worksheet by entering the total in the Subtract column. Carrying over the amounts transferred will leave a large red total in the Balance column. That's OK. When you transfer the monthly allocation to each Hogozit Chart, your system will be in balance with your check register. The positive numbers in the 12 Howgozit Charts less the red balance in the Allocation Fund equals the balance in your check register.

CHART 9C
Allocation Chart

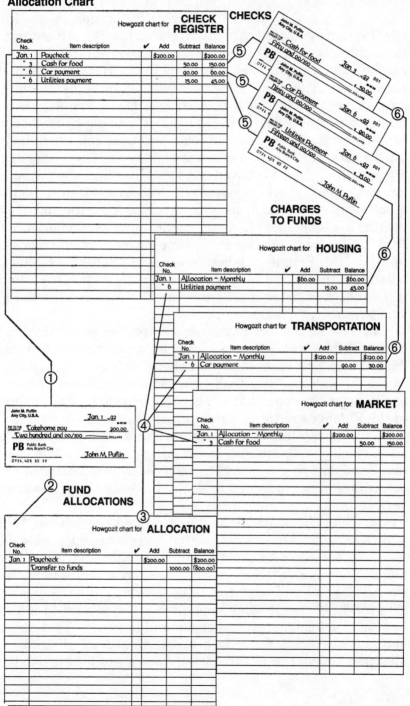

2. As you add deposits into your bank checking account and write checks against it, you first note each transaction in a check register. Repeat each transaction notation in the Planner. Deposits go to the Allocation Fund. Checks are entered in the Subtract columns of the Howgozit Chart affected. That is, a check to the supermarket is entered in the Howgozit Chart for market, etc. The check register is a tally of transactions and may be kept at the back of a book of check blanks. If both husband and wife write checks against a single bank checking account from different checkbooks, problems can arise, including overdrafts. A better system is to keep one check register at a home office desk or convenient location. Enter the payee and amount of each check, regardless of who wrote it, in the central check register. Do the same with deposits. After the end of each month, a single check register is easier to reconcile with the bank's statement. At the same time or more often, check the totals in the Planner. Balances of the 12 categories plus the balance in the Allocation Fund should always equal the balance in the check register if all transactions have been posted and your arithmetic is correct.

3. The Allocation Fund serves another purpose, that of collecting bits and pieces of income. If you are paid weekly, deposits are first entered in your check register and then added to the Allocation Fund under the Add column and carried to the Balance column. At the beginning of each month, amounts in the Planner are transferred to each Howgozit Chart and the total subtracted from the Allocation Fund. Any remaining balance, black or red, remains in the Allocation Fund. The Allocation Fund acts as a flywheel to keep the system balanced without adding dibs and dabs to each Howgozit Chart as income varies.

4. Note that two of the 12 categories are labeled "Wife" and "Husband." These Howgozit Charts represent personal allowances for each to avoid nickel and dime entries. For example, each month "Husband" receives a transfer of funds from the Allocation Fund according to the spending plan. Suppose he gets $200 per month (this amount is not intended to indicate how much a husband should be allowed to spend). That amount and the allowance for wife are determined as all income is allocated among the 12 categories. Allowances for husband and wife are 2 of the 12 categories. Each week he may write a check for $40 or $50 in cash. He may spend these dollars anyway he chooses—for coffee breaks, newspapers, lunch in town, a haircut, or whatever. Small out-of-pocket purchases are not distributed by category, as the quickest way to lose patience with a spending plan is to try to account for or track every penny. The wife handles her personal allowance the same way. Neither accounts to the other for how each spends the personal allowance for day-to-day needs.

5. Spending cash sometimes causes problems. For example, instead of writing a check for the exact amount of purchases in a supermarket, a wife may write a check for $10 to $25 over the amount. Using the market as a bank avoids stopping at the bank to cash a check. Deducting the full amount of a check written to acquire cash from "Market" skews the system. A simple solution is to charge the full amount of the check to the wife's personal allowance Howgozit Chart. Then, at the end of a week, total all purchases for cash and distribute the charges to market, house, transportation, or whatever. Keeping cash register tickets with the check register assures cash purchases are allocated to the proper category.

6. Some checks cover purchases in two or more categories. A check written to a bank credit card account, for example, may include amounts chargeable to several different Howgozit Charts. To assure proper distribution, divide the amounts according to category and charge each fund.

7. Using credit creates another set of problems. The Planner depends on using checks with provisions for charging various funds for cash purposes, as noted above. Thus, credit purchases do not enter the system until a check is written to pay for purchases charged earlier. A separate Howgozit Chart labeled "Credit" can be used to monitor credit obligations. Unlike the envelope system that stops a person from buying when the cash is used up, only large account limitations will stop credit buying. The Credit Howgozit Chart accumulates charged purchases and helps you monitor future payment obligations. It does not figure in the total numbers that balance with the check register. When you buy something and charge it on a MasterCard, VISA, or other general-purpose credit card, enter the purchase on the Credit Howgozit Chart in the Add column.

Carry the amount to the Balance. Enter other items as they are bought and charged to one or more cards, adjusting the balance accordingly. When you pay off a monthly bill from the credit card, subtract that amount from the balance carried in the Credit Howgozit Chart.

8. Managing your money effectively calls for not using credit to finance buying goods and services. Credit cards are convenient and often easier to use than writing personal checks. However, to avoid the onerous finance charges that range as high as 18 to 20 percent on outstanding balances, plan to pay off monthly balances in full. This way you avoid problems in allocating charges to the Howgozit Charts and you avoid paying interest. The whole point of using the spending plan and Howgozit Charts is to accumulate funds for investment. If you are not paying credit accounts off in full each month, your first investment opportunity is to pay credit accounts down to zero balances. Don't even attempt to collect cash for investing until all credit balances except the mortgage loan for your house are paid in full because no investment strategy will pay 18 to 20 percent consistently.

As part of your new spending discipline, plan to pay cash for everything you buy, including vacations and cars. Few investments return as much as financing charges cost. Further, consumer credit finance charges are no longer deductible when figuring taxable income. Paying cash provides a powerful discipline. One study found that restaurant patrons spent an average of 39 percent more when they charged meals and drinks to a credit card compared to those who paid cash. Learning to pay cash for everything except your house is a major step to managing your money effectively. Buying for cash, of course, includes writing checks and using credit cards when you pay all balances in full every month.

COLLECTING CASH RESERVES

Spending less than your after-tax income is the key to collecting funds for investment. Note that one of the 12 spending categories is "Savings or Debt Payment." You can plan for saving just as you plan to spend some of your income at the market. But don't let the balance in your Saving Howgozit Chart build up for long periods. Every month write a check for the planned saving amount and deposit it in a money market fund. There it will earn interest and be away from the temptation to spend it. Recognize two levels of cash accumulation:

• One is a rainy day fund that acts as a reserve. From your Planner, you can easily figure how much money would be needed to pay out-of-pocket expenses for three to six months. If your job is secure and includes a generous sick leave provision, a three-month reserve should be sufficient. If you are self-employed or earn a variable income as a salesperson or for some other reason, a six-month reserve would provide a higher level of comfort. However, instead of stashing the reserve cash in a bank, invest it separately in a money market fund or short-term bond fund. If you don't need the money for an emergency, you have a beginning on another investment cache of capital.

• Another is the cash you expect to invest to achieve one or more of the long-term goals noted in Chapters 1 and 11. Keep these funds moving into one or more of the investments noted in Chapter 11. After all, the whole point of accumulating capital through effective spending is to invest it for the future or to achieve defined goals. At least once a month make a new payment on your future by transferring the cash from the saving category to an investing category.

CONCLUSION

Accumulating capital for investment is a challenging assignment. If you muff this opportunity, the other chapters in this book might provide interesting reading but will not help you achieve your financial goals. Accumulating capital is crucial.

CHAPTER 10

IRA STRATEGIES FOR MAXIMUM RETIREMENT AND NONRETIREMENT BENEFITS

Individual Retirement Accounts, usually referred to as IRAs, offer the best and most flexible opportunities for accumulating wealth—for whatever purpose you have in mind. IRAs are not investments; they merely hold a tax-deferral umbrella over whatever investment vehicle you choose. Other tax-advantaged plans, such as 401(k) deferred income plans, 403(b) plans for nonprofit organization and government employees, and SEP-IRA plans offer similar advantages to the IRA, namely tax deferral of income until withdrawal. The one advantage of an IRA over other tax-advantaged plans is individual choice. To participate in a 401(k), 403(b), or SEP-IRA, the company or organization you work for must offer the option; you cannot unilaterally set up and participate in a 401(k), 403(b), or SEP-IRA. Not so with an IRA. You can not only initiate your own IRA, but you can also control the investments under it. With a 401(k) or 403(b) plan you have limited choices, if any, depending on the structure of the plan.

Anyone with earned income can set aside savings and manage investments under an IRA with the following rules.

Individuals with at least $2,000 of earned income can deposit up to $2,000 per year in an IRA. Note the "up to" qualification. If you say, "I can't afford an IRA," start with whatever you can afford. Many mutual funds will open an IRA with an initial investment of as little as $250, some for as little as $100, and 20th Century Funds have no minimum. You need not contribute the full $2,000 to an IRA; that is only the maximum. If you think such small investments aren't worth the trouble, think again. Just $250 invested annually for 25 years, a total investment of only $6,250, will grow to $37,333 at a 12 percent compound rate of return (CRR).

You can contribute to your IRA anytime during the tax year and up to April 15 of the following year. Depositing contributions on the first available day of each new year boosts the end value of the IRA because your investments earn tax-deferred income over longer periods.

Contributions to IRAs are deductible from adjusted gross income for each tax year under various conditions:

• If you or your spouse do not participate in a pension or profit sharing plan where you work, all contributions to IRAs are tax deductible—even if you make $100,000 a year.

• If either you or your spouse is an active participant in a pension or profit-sharing plan at work and your total gross income does not exceed $40,000, all contributions to your IRAs are deductible. If your gross income exceeds $50,000, none of your IRA contributions is deductible. Between $40,000 and $50,000 deductibility is proportioned to income. If total income is $45,000, for example, only half of IRA contributions is deductible. Similar numbers for single taxpayers who participate in a pension or profit-sharing plan are fully deductible if adjusted gross income is less than $25,000 with no deductibility for adjusted gross income of $35,000 or more. The deductibility is phased out between $25,000 and $35,000 for single persons.

• If you are married and your spouse does not work outside the home, you are entitled to contribute up to $2,250 into a spousal IRA. The $2,250 may be divided equally, with $1,125 being deposited in the spousal IRA and $1,125 in your IRA, or the $2,250 may be divided in any other way you may select as long as neither spouse's contribution exceeds $2,000 per year. I recommend putting the maximum $2,000 into the younger person's IRA to permit it to grow tax-deferred for a longer period.

Nondeductible contributions of as much as $2,000 from after-tax earnings may be deposited in IRAs each year. Once deposited in an IRA, earnings are free of taxes until both contributions and earnings are withdrawn. Tax-deferred earnings within an IRA open a number of strategies for accumulating wealth without the tax man taking his bite each year. More on nondeductible IRA strategies later in this chapter.

Once deposited in an IRA, whether deductible or nondeductible, funds may not be withdrawn without penalty until you reach age 59 1/2 with one exception. If you elect to withdraw funds from an IRA on an annuitized basis, you can withdraw from an IRA earlier than 59 1/2 without penalty if you abide by the rules. The annuitized plan, once started, must continue for a minimum of five years and until you reach 59 1/2. The amount that may be withdrawn under an annuitized plan depends on your life expectancy and how much you have accumulated in your IRA. You pay taxes on all withdrawals from IRAs except contributions from after-tax income. Withdrawals must begin in the year you reach 70 1/2, although the initial withdrawal may be postponed until April 1 of the year following the year you reach 70 1/2. Annual withdrawals must be scheduled to exhaust your IRA account within your expected lifetime or the joint life expectancy of you and your spouse or other person. If the other person is younger than you, a maximum of 10 years difference in ages is allowed. Your life expectancy and the minimum amounts you must withdraw may be refigured each year, as the longer you live, the longer you can expect to live. More details on minimum withdrawal amounts and regulations are included in IRS Publication 590 *Individual Retirement Arrangements*, free from IRS offices or Document Distribution Centers.

IRAs are administered through a trust with the trustee holding securities as custodian. Various trust arrangements are available. The simplest IRA permits you to contribute annual deposits to a bank or other institution that manages the trust at its discretion for your benefit. Self-directed trusts permit you to direct the trustee on where and how to invest your funds. You may set up a self-directed IRA with a broker who keeps your funds in trust, usually with a bank. You may tell your broker to buy stock, bonds, or mutual fund shares, and the broker buys them in the name of the trust. A less expensive alternative is to set up your IRA with a mutual fund that also acts as the trustee. You may still direct the mutual fund's activities, including switching into a money market fund, if you follow a market timing program. A small fee, typically $10 per year, is charged to each IRA in mutual funds. Brokers and banks typically charge several times that amount for administering an IRA. You may have as many separate IRAs as you wish, but more than five or six can unnecessarily increase your accounting activities and administration charges.

MYTHS ABOUT IRAS

Despite the simple rules, congressional tinkering and a lack of governmental promotion have fostered numerous misconceptions about IRAs. A few of these myths that need to be debunked are:

• "I don't qualify for an IRA." I recently had lunch with two people whose CPA told them they didn't qualify. But they did, and you probably do too. No matter how much you earn, you qualify for an IRA as long as your income is documented by IRS Form W-2. Questions about qualification usually concern whether an IRA is deductible or not. But deductible or nondeductible, IRAs defer income from taxes until withdrawn, as noted elsewhere in this chapter. So IRAs are available to anyone with income earned from personal services.

• "I can't afford $2,000 for an IRA." Another misconception is that you must have $2,000 to qualify. Nonsense, $2,000 is the maximum, but you can put $10 in an IRA if that's all you earned. Most mutual funds accept smaller initial and continuing contributions to IRAs than non-IRA accounts. Many will open accounts for as little as $100 or $250.

- "Variable annuities are as good as an IRA." Rarely, if ever, is this true. Fees associated with annuities eat a big hole in earnings. IRAs in no-load mutual funds are almost certain to produce higher earnings over the long term.
- "A bank is the best place to invest my IRA." Again, rarely is this the case. Banks may be safe, although recent events cast shadows on this onetime certainty, but they make their money by paying customers low returns. When I talk to retirees, they almost always tell me they want to live on their interest, dividends, and capital gains and not touch their principal. Low accumulation rates and low interest rates paid on accumulated balances mean your lifestyle will be severely restricted if you stick with banks. Details are noted elsewhere in this chapter.
- "The most I can invest for my nonworking spouse is $250." The law says a married couple filing jointly, only one of which works outside the home, can contribute a maximum of $2,250 to their IRAs and a maximum of $2,000 to either one of them. That means you can set up equal IRAs of $1,125 each or split the dollars any other way you like, as long as you observe the $2,000 maximum. If you participate in a company 401(k) or profit-sharing plan, you might want to contribute $250 to your IRA and $2,000 to your nonworking spouse's IRA.

The basics noted above are not intended to be a rigorous explanation of IRA rules, but they will help you to understand the following strategies.

IRA FOR RETIREMENT

Congress established IRAs to encourage individuals to save for their retirement, and incidentally provide a pool of savings from which they could borrow to finance the senators' and representatives' reckless spending habits. Congress knows Social Security provides only subsistence, if that. Social Security benefits were never intended to provide for a lifestyle most of us have grown accustomed to.

Only about half of the workers in the United States participate in some form of pension or profit-sharing plan. So if you are planning to retire with a comfortable income from investments plus Social Security and possibly a pension, you need your own savings and investment plan. The simplest, easiest, and least expensive plan for generating capital to support a more affluent lifestyle in retirement is the IRA. The following are key elements of a productive IRA:

Start Early

Compound interest, where interest is paid on interest without taxation, can be a powerful tool for building retirement assets. But compound interest needs time to work. Table 10A clearly spells out the advantages of starting early. In the three scenarios, $2,000 is invested in an IRA for 15 years; total contributions equal $30,000 for each. In the first scenario, contributions begin at 30 and continue through age 44; then contributions stop but accumulated assets continue to earn tax-deferred income. Once under the umbrella of an IRA, all funds earn an assumed steady 10 percent income. The income is added to the annual contributions and continues to compound. At age 65, the total is $517,273—all of which will be taxable when withdrawn if original contributions were deducted.

In the second scenario, contributions do not begin until age 40; they continue until age 54. Total contributions are the same at $30,000. But with less time for earnings to compound, the total at 65 reaches only $199,431.

In the third scenario, contributions do not begin until age 51 and continue to age 65—$30,000 in all. At age 65, the total is only $69,899. The only difference between the three scenarios is the starting time; $30,000 were invested in all three scenarios and earnings for all averaged 10 percent. Starting early at age 30 produced more than seven times the total of contributions that began at age 51. Rather than stop after contributing $2,000 per year for 15 years, you would likely continue until you reach 65, possibly even 70 1/2 when you may no longer add to an IRA.

But, if you do not start early, you do not have the option of continuing contributions for many years and for compound interest to work its magic over a longer period. Also, those who

TABLE 10A
Effect of Time Value of Retirement Fund

Begin Age	Amount Contrib- uted	Total	Annual Earnings at 10%	End-of- Year Total	Amount Contrib- uted	Total
30	$2,000	$2,000	$200	$2,200		
31	2,000	4,200	420	4,620		
32	2,000	6,620	662	7,282		
33	2,000	9,282	928	10,210		
34	2,000	12,210	1,221	13,431		
35	2,000	15,431	1,543	16,974		
36	2,000	18,974	1,897	20,872		
37	2,000	22,872	2,287	25,159		
38	2,000	27,159	2,716	29,875		
39	2,000	31,875	3,187	35,062		
40	2,000	37,062	3,706	40,769	$2,000	$2,000
41	2,000	42,769	4,277	47,045	2,000	4,200
42	2,000	49,045	4,905	53,950	2,000	6,620
43	2,000	55,950	5,595	61,545	2,000	9,282
44	2,000	63,545	6,354	69,899	2,000	12,210
45		69,899	6,990	76,889	2,000	15,431
46		76,889	7,689	84,578	2,000	18,974
47		84,578	8,458	93,036	2,000	22,872
48		93,036	9,304	102,340	2,000	27,159
49		102,340	10,234	112,574	2,000	31,875
50		112,574	11,257	123,831	2,000	37,062
51		123,831	12,383	136,214	2,000	42,769
52		136,214	13,621	149,836	2,000	49,045
53		149,836	14,984	164,819	2,000	55,950
54		164,819	16,482	181,301	2,000	63,545
55		181,301	18,130	199,431		69,899
56		199,431	19,943	219,374		76,889
57		219,374	21,937	241,312		84,578
58		241,312	24,131	265,443		93,036
59		265,443	26,544	291,987		102,340
60		291,987	29,199	321,186		112,574
61		321,186	32,119	353,305		123,831
62		353,305	35,330	388,635		136,214
63		388,635	38,864	427,499		149,836
64		427,499	42,750	470,249		164,819
65		470,249	47,025	517,273		181,301

TABLE 10A *(Continued)*

Total	Annual Earnings at 10%	End-of-Year Total	Amount Contrib-uted	Total	Annual Earnings at 10%	End-of-Year Total
$2,000	$200	$2,200				
4,200	420	4,620				
6,620	662	7,282				
9,282	928	10,210				
12,210	1,221	13,431				
15,431	1,543	16,974				
18,974	1,897	20,872				
22,872	2,287	25,159				
27,159	2,716	29,875				
31,875	3,187	35,062				
37,062	3,706	40,769				
42,769	4,277	47,045	$2,000	$2,000	$200	$2,200
49,045	4,905	53,950	2,000	4,200	420	4,620
55,950	5,595	61,545	2,000	6,620	662	7,282
63,545	6,354	69,899	2,000	9,282	928	10,210
69,899	6,990	76,889	2,000	12,210	1,221	13,431
76,889	7,689	84,578	2,000	15,431	1,543	16,974
84,578	8,458	93,036	2,000	18,974	1,897	20,872
93,036	9,304	102,340	2,000	22,872	2,287	25,159
102,340	10,234	112,574	2,000	27,159	2,716	29,875
112,574	11,257	123,831	2,000	31,875	3,187	35,062
123,831	12,383	136,214	2,000	37,062	3,706	40,769
136,214	13,621	149,836	2,000	42,769	4,277	47,045
149,836	14,984	164,819	2,000	49,045	4,905	53,950
164,819	16,482	181,301	2,000	55,950	5,595	61,545
181,301	18,130	199,431	2,000	63,545	6,354	69,899

start early are more likely to invest in securities that offer
higher returns. Older investors are more likely to invest in
more conservative securities that produce lower returns. The
average of 10 percent assumed in Table 10A is conservative for
long-term investors.

Invest Aggressively

IRA investments are long-term commitments. You can expect
them to generate substantial capital over those years, including the down years. You can also expect inflation to eat away at
the buying power of your growing capital. From the data on
inflation risk from Chapter 2, you will remember that the increase in the Ibbotson index after taxes and after inflation varied from 1.40 for T-bills to 171.15 for small-company stocks.
Investing in small companies involved more risk. But over long
periods, losses, and you are guaranteed to have some, are overcome by large increases during bull markets. The period covered by the Ibbotson data included the major bear markets of
the 1930s, 1968–74, 1980–82, 1987, and several minor reces-
sions in other years. But at the end, small-company stocks
were far ahead of other investments—and inflation.

I suggest shooting for at least a 12 percent gross return in
your IRA. Investing in aggressive growth stock funds exposes
your IRA to wide swings in value, volatility that may cause you
to swallow hard and wonder at times. As noted early, market
timing can reduce the emotional impact of volatility and at the
same time increase overall gains by moving you out of the
market during major portions of bear markets.

Table 10B explores the after-inflation benefit of investing
aggressively. If inflation were to continue at an average of 5
percent, you can expect the general level of prices to double in
15 years using the "rule of 72." This mathematical anomaly is a
quick way to calculate how many years are needed to double
your money when you know the average interest rate. For example, if interest rates average 5 percent, divide 5 into 72 and
find the answer—just under 15; that is, if your money com-
pounds annually at 5 percent, it will double in 15 years without
considering taxes. The "rule of 72" works in reverse, too. If you

want to know what rate of return is needed to double your money in 9 years, divide 9 into 72 and the answer is 8 percent. The "rule of 72" can be applied to inflation; 5 percent average inflation doubles prices every 15 years. Thus, if a loaf of bread costs $1 today and inflation averages 5 percent, a loaf of bread can be expected to cost $4 in 30 years—two doublings of 15 years each.

If your IRA earns an average of 5 percent and inflation averages 5 percent, you remain even before taxes. If your IRA earns an average of 6 percent, you gain 1 percent in purchasing power before taxes. If your IRA averages 10 percent, the after-inflation buildup of assets is double the inflation rate before taxes. Considering taxes at 28 percent, your IRA must earn 6.94 percent just to stay even with 5 percent inflation after taxes. For this reason alone, you should shoot for a high earnings rate by investing aggressively in your IRA. Don't speculate or take excessive risks, but don't be too conservative either. A middle-of-the-road approach will produce the best results and will be within the risk-tolerance level of most investors.

Table 10B looks at what happens if your IRA investments average 12 percent annually. If you were to start at age 36 equivalent to Year No. 1, as noted in the table, and contribute $2,000 each year until age 65, you can expect to attain the numbers noted in Table 10B. The $2,000 may be from before-tax or after-tax dollars. The only difference will be the tax consequences for withdrawals. You will not be required to pay taxes again on contributions of original after-tax dollars—only on the tax-deferred earnings over the 30 years. To assure the IRS knows your contributions are from after-tax dollars, you must file Form 8606, Nondeductible IRA Contributions, each year. Keep a copy of this form for as long as you maintain an active IRA, because the IRS could ask you for proof of the after-tax contributions when you begin withdrawals from your IRA.

At the end of the year you reach 65, your IRA(s) will total $540,585. Total contributions are $60,000. While $540,585 is almost a 10-fold increase, you must not ignore inflation. If you assume an average inflation rate of 5 percent, your effective purchasing power at age 65 will be $131,333 in constant dollars. That is, your $540,585 will buy as many goods and ser-

TABLE 10B
Aggressive Investing and Inflation

Year Number	Balance	Balance with $2,000 Annual Contribution	Total Return at 12%	New Total
1	0	$2,000	$240	$2,240
2	$2,240	4,240	509	4,749
3	4,749	6,749	810	7,559
4	7,559	9,559	1,147	10,706
5	10,706	12,706	1,525	14,230
6	14,230	16,230	1,948	18,178
7	18,178	20,178	2,421	22,599
8	22,599	24,599	2,952	27,551
9	27,551	29,551	3,546	33,097
10	33,097	35,097	4,212	39,309
11	39,309	41,309	4,957	46,266
12	46,266	48,266	5,792	54,058
13	54,058	56,058	6,727	62,785
14	62,785	64,785	7,774	72,559
15	72,559	74,559	8,947	83,507
16	83,507	85,507	10,261	95,767
17	95,767	97,767	11,732	109,499
18	109,499	111,499	13,380	124,879
19	124,879	126,879	15,226	142,105
20	142,105	144,105	17,293	161,397
21	161,397	163,397	19,608	183,005
22	183,005	185,005	22,201	207,206
23	207,206	209,206	25,105	234,310
24	234,310	236,310	28,357	264,668
25	264,668	266,668	32,000	298,668
26	298,668	300,668	36,080	336,748
27	336,748	338,748	40,650	379,398
28	379,398	381,398	45,768	427,166
29	427,166	429,166	51,500	480,665
30	480,665	482,665	57,920	540,585

TABLE 10B *(continued)*

Inflation Index	Annual Rate at 5%	Balance after 28% Tax	After Inflation and after Tax	After Inflation Only
1.00	1.05	$1,613	$1,613	$2,240
1.05	1.10	3,419	3,256	4,523
1.10	1.16	5,442	4,936	6,856
1.16	1.22	7,708	6,659	9,248
1.22	1.28	10,246	8,429	11,707
1.28	1.34	13,088	10,255	14,243
1.34	1.41	16,272	12,142	16,864
1.41	1.48	19,837	14,098	19,580
1.48	1.55	23,830	16,129	22,402
1.55	1.63	28,303	18,244	25,339
1.63	1.71	33,312	20,451	28,403
1.71	1.80	38,922	22,757	31,607
1.80	1.89	45,205	25,172	34,961
1.89	1.98	52,243	27,705	38,480
1.98	2.08	60,125	30,367	42,176
2.08	2.18	68,952	33,167	46,066
2.18	2.29	78,840	36,117	50,163
2.29	2.41	89,913	39,229	54,484
2.41	2.53	102,316	42,514	59,048
2.53	2.65	116,206	45,987	63,870
2.65	2.79	131,764	49,660	68,973
2.79	2.93	149,188	53,550	74,375
2.93	3.07	168,704	57,671	80,099
3.07	3.23	190,561	62,041	86,168
3.23	3.39	215,041	66,677	92,607
3.39	3.56	242,459	71,599	99,443
3.56	3.73	273,166	76,826	106,702
3.73	3.92	307,559	82,379	114,416
3.92	4.12	346,079	88,283	122,615
4.12	4.32	389,221	94,560	131,333

vices at price levels 30 years from now as $131,333 would buy at today's price levels.

If you elect to withdraw your IRA total over a 20-year joint life expectancy period, you may consider switching your total into a capital-conserving bond fund that pays an average 8 percent. At that rate, you could withdraw $8.19 per month for each $1,000 of assets. This number comes from a table of annuitized capital withdrawal amounts that are dependent on earning rate and the number of years for withdrawal (see Resources, Capital Withdrawal Chart). Multiplying $8.19 by 131.333 (thousands), you could withdraw $1,076 ($8.19 x 131.333) per month, equal to $12,907 per year. After taxes at 28 percent, spendable income would be the equivalent of $9,293 in today's dollars. Actual dollars projected 30 years hence will be substantially larger, but this scenario accounts for inflation and taxes at current rates. Thus, you can project the spending value at retirement in terms of what goods and services cost today. If you continue to manage your IRA more aggressively than leaving it in a bond fund and gain a 9 to 12 percent total return, spendable dollars will be higher.

If you should elect a conservative investment for your IRA, such as blue-chip stock funds for an average return of 10 percent, you can expect the results displayed in Table 10C. After 30 years, your annual contributions of $2,000 will have grown to $361,887, about two thirds as much as your contributions invested at 12 percent. After inflation at an assumed average annual rate of 5 percent, your accumulation totals $87,919 in constant dollars. For the same 20-year withdrawal pattern, monthly before-tax withdrawals would be the same $8.19 per $1,000 of assets or $720.06 ($8.19 x 87.919) before taxes. After taxes at 28 percent, the monthly withdrawal amounts to $518.44 or $6,221.32 for each year—quite a difference from the $9,293 noted above. The $6,221.32 also represents effective purchasing power 30 years ahead at today's prices with inflation projected to average 5 percent per year. Unfortunately, over 25 percent of IRA investors are placing their IRA investments in CDs earning less than 8 percent.

Older people tend to think differently than those in their middle and most productive years. Oldsters tend to think of spending income only from whatever invested funds they may have. Two factors affect the level of their spendable dollars: (1) The size of the lump sum of savings available, and (2) the rate of earnings from that lump sum. Investing more aggressively over a long period will likely produce a bigger lump sum at retirement than a less aggressive program of sticking only with bank instruments. Obviously, with a bigger lump sum at retirement, more options are available to generate the income that permits a lively lifestyle that includes travel and a higher level of financial security.

Invest in Your IRA at the Beginning of the Year

You are always better off investing on the first business day of the year rather than at year end—or on April 15 of the following year. Without detailing the year-by-year difference, consider this scenario. You invest $2,000 each year for 25 years. The compound rate or return (CRR) is an achievable 15 percent. After 25 years, your IRA would be worth $491,424 if you deposited your $2,000 annual contribution on the first business day of the year. If you waited until the last business day of the year, your $50,000 of annual contributions would have grown to $425,586—$65,838 less. If you prefer to consider a 12 percent CRR, the difference is $34,000—and that's not peanuts either. A longer contribution period, say 40 years instead of 25 years, would only increase the difference. Yet, banks and mutual funds actively promote IRA investments in the two months before the April 15 tax filing deadline. Why? Because most investors are more concerned about a $2,000 deduction from income taxes than the long-term buildup of assets from tax-deferred earnings. As an astute investor, I expect you to contribute to your IRA early in the year, now that you know it makes a real difference.

DOLLAR-COST AVERAGING

Dollar-cost averaging is known as a "mechanical" system for investing. That means you use a system that requires no forecast of market or stock trends. Dollar-cost averaging (DCA) has proved successful for many investors for years in both up and

TABLE 10C
Conservative Investing and Inflation

Year Number	Balance	Balance with $2,000 Annual Contribution	Total Return at 10%	New Total
1	0	$2,000	$200	$2,200
2	$2,200	4,200	420	4,620
3	4,620	6,620	662	7,282
4	7,282	9,282	928	10,210
5	10,210	12,210	1,221	13,431
6	13,431	15,431	1,543	16,974
7	16,974	18,974	1,897	20,872
8	20,872	22,872	2,287	25,159
9	25,159	27,159	2,716	29,875
10	29,875	31,875	3,187	35,062
11	35,062	37,062	3,706	40,769
12	40,769	42,769	4,277	47,045
13	47,045	49,045	4,905	53,950
14	53,950	55,950	5,595	61,545
15	61,545	63,545	6,354	69,899
16	69,899	71,899	7,190	79,089
17	79,089	81,089	8,109	89,198
18	89,198	91,198	9,120	100,318
19	100,318	102,318	10,232	112,550
20	112,550	114,550	11,455	126,005
21	126,005	128,005	12,800	140,805
22	140,805	142,805	14,281	157,086
23	157,086	159,086	15,909	174,995
24	174,995	176,995	17,699	194,694
25	194,694	196,694	19,669	216,364
26	216,364	218,364	21,836	240,200
27	240,200	242,200	24,220	266,420
28	266,420	268,420	26,842	295,262
29	295,262	297,262	29,726	326,988
30	326,988	328,988	32,899	361,887

TABLE 10C (*continued*)

Inflation Index	Annual Rate at 5%	Balance after 28% Tax	After Inflation and after Tax	After Inflation Only
1.00	1.05	$1,584	$1,584	$2,200
1.05	1.10	3,326	3,168	4,400
1.10	1.16	5,243	4,756	6,605
1.16	1.22	7,351	6,350	8,820
1.22	1.28	9,670	7,956	11,050
1.28	1.34	12,222	9,576	13,300
1.34	1.41	15,028	11,214	15,575
1.41	1.48	18,114	12,874	17,880
1.48	1.55	21,510	14,559	20,220
1.55	1.63	25,245	16,273	22,601
1.63	1.71	29,353	18,020	25,028
1.71	1.80	33,873	19,805	27,506
1.80	1.89	38,844	21,630	30,041
1.89	1.98	44,312	23,500	32,639
1.98	2.08	50,328	25,419	35,304
2.08	2.18	56,944	27,391	38,043
2.18	2.29	64,223	29,421	40,863
2.29	2.41	72,229	31,513	43,768
2.41	2.53	81,036	33,672	46,767
2.53	2.65	90,724	35,902	49,864
2.65	2.79	101,380	38,209	53,068
2.79	2.93	113,102	40,597	56,385
2.93	3.07	125,996	43,072	59,822
3.07	3.23	140,180	45,639	63,387
3.23	3.39	155,782	48,303	67,087
3.39	3.56	172,944	51,071	70,932
3.56	3.73	191,822	53,948	74,928
3.73	3.92	212,589	56,941	79,085
3.92	4.12	235,431	60,057	83,413
4.12	4.32	260,559	63,302	87,919

down markets and can be particularly useful over the long periods expected in an IRA. DCA is particularly useful when investing in mutual funds because you can add small amounts regularly with minimum transaction costs. Further, by buying into a mutual fund, you achieve ready-made diversification— something you would have great difficulty doing if you were to invest directly in stocks with DCA.

Over the years, this automatic system works best in markets that move up and down rather than markets that trend upward or downward for long periods. Its more apparent advantage is that it requires no foresight. Follow the system automatically and your average price for mutual fund shares acquired will be less than the average prices paid, as in the example in Table 10D.

To practice DCA, plan to invest a specific dollar amount on a regular schedule. For example, once a month on the 17th day by the calendar, you decide to buy $500 worth of shares in the XYZ no-load growth mutual fund. Since a mutual fund will accept specific dollar amounts and issue fractional shares, you need not worry about rounding the number of shares up or down to an even number to make a purchase. The important thing to remember is to invest a specific number of dollars. Do not attempt to buy a specific and regular number of shares. If the 17th day of the month falls on a Saturday, buy the shares on the preceding 16th. If the 17th falls on a Sunday, invest your $500 on the following Monday. As share prices move up and down, your $500 buy a different number of shares each time. This is the "secret" of the system.

You must not deviate from your plan. Do not attempt to tailor your purchases to your perception of where you think the market may be headed. Let the system work.

Table 10D illustrates how DCA works with $1,000 invested for each period. This number was used to simplify the arithmetic. The period is not important either. You could use a monthly plan as indicated earlier. Or you might prefer to invest a lesser amount more often, say every Thursday. You could invest once a quarter. But whatever period you select, keep it even—always the same date each month or quarter or the same day each week. Regularity and consistency are critical to the success of the system.

TABLE 10D
Dollar-Cost Averaging

Investment	Price/Share	Number of Shares
$1,000	$7.50	133
1,000	7.00	143
1,000	6.00	167
1,000	4.50	222
1,000	3.50	286
1,000	4.00	250
1,000	5.00	200
1,000	6.50	154
1,000	7.50	133
1,000	8.50	118
$\dfrac{\$10,000}{1,801} = \$5.55$	$\dfrac{\$60.00}{10} = \$6/\text{share}$	1,801

$$\frac{\$6.00 - \$5.55}{\$5.55} = 0.81 \text{ or } 8.1\%$$

From Table 10D note that in the first column, the total investment adds to $10,000. The number of shares purchased during the 10 periods totaled 1,801. The average of the share prices is the total ($60,000) divided by the number of different prices (10) for an average of $6 per share. The average price of the shares actually purchased is the amount invested ($10,000) divided by the total number of shares purchased (1,801) for an average price of $5.55 per share. The difference between the average of the share prices ($6.00) and the average price of shares ($5.55) is 8.1 percent—the advantage gained from DCA in this example.

As does every system, dollar-cost averaging comes with a risk. The emphasis is on buying over an extended period. At no time are accumulated shares sold. The lack of a sell discipline could leave you at a disadvantage if, after years of accumulating assets, you needed cash at a time when market prices were depressed. If you arrive at retirement, for example, after years of DCA, you could find the shares of your mutual fund valued at less than the average price of shares. You could end up spending less than you anticipated. While the opposite is more likely to occur due to the upward bias of the stock market, the risk remains.

Dollar-cost averaging is a simple system, but it seldom works as promised because investors fail to follow through with disciplined, regular investments on a rigid schedule. The tendency is to hesitate if the market has been moving down either because the investors may think they can buy shares cheaper later or because they have lost confidence in the market. The investors may believe they are foolish by throwing money into a declining market.

When the market is moving down is exactly the time you should continue buying shares regularly. DCA benefits depend on your set amount buying shares on a regular schedule. When prices are down, your $500 buys more shares than when prices are higher. If you elect to invest with DCA, plan to invest regularly without regard to what the market may be doing.

NONDEDUCTIBLE IRA VERSUS NONDEFERRED INVESTMENT

If you are eligible, a deductible IRA is always preferable to a nondeductible IRA. But if you are not eligible for any of the reasons noted above, should you set up an IRA anyway?

Recognize that the U.S. government has no interest in promoting a nondeductible IRA, even though you can expect to benefit. In fact, the U.S. government would prefer that you did not use either a deductible or nondeductible IRA because putting aside your cash in a tax-deferred IRA removes that cash from taxable income. The government loses current revenue when you remove $2,000 a year from your adjusted gross income (if your IRA is deductible) and from all the earnings from your IRA until years later when you withdraw the funds. If the U.S. Treasury really had your best interests at heart, it would promote deductible and nondeductible IRAs with the same aggressiveness it uses to promote the sale of low-paying Series EE savings bonds. If all of the Treasury's borrowing needs could be filled from the sale of EE bonds, interest costs to the U.S. Treasury would be billions less each year. And if no one set aside $2,000 in an IRA every year, more taxes would flow into the Treasury's vaults. So don't depend on the U.S. government to look after your long-term retirement interests. That's your job. If your income level prevents deducting your annual IRA contributions, setting up an IRA still makes sense.

A nondeductible IRA begins with after-tax dollars. That is, if your marginal tax rate is 28 percent, federal only, your gross earnings will be $2,817, from which you pay $817 in federal taxes and have $2,000 to deposit in your IRA. Once under the protective umbrella of an IRA, your earnings are tax-deferred until withdrawal. With a non-IRA investment, you would start with the same after-tax dollars. When withdrawals begin, the dollars you deposited in your IRA from after-tax income are returned to you without further taxes, because the IRS gets only one bite. If you were to invest in a program without deferring taxes, you would pay taxes on the earnings each year.

Table 10E shows how a nondeductible IRA grows relative to similar annual investments of $2,000 without the benefit of tax deferral. Note how much tax is taken out of the investment pool each year in the program unprotected by the IRA umbrella. A marginal tax rate of 28 percent is assumed for both the IRA and non-IRA program. An average annual total return of 12 percent is assumed in calculating the values of Table 10E.

The numbers from Table 10E point up the major benefits from investing under the IRA umbrella even though annual contributions are from before-tax dollars. The comparison assumes you start contributing to your IRA at the beginning of the year you are 25 and continue through age 65. Total contributions from after-tax earnings are $82,000—$2,000 per year for 41 years. At the end of the year you reach 65, the total in the non-IRA account is $726,624 and no additional taxes are due because earnings were not deferred. The total in the IRA account is $1,926,719, all of which is taxable except for the $82,000 in contributions from after-tax dollars. Taxes on the $1,844,719 of deferred interest ($1,926,719 − $82,000) at 28 percent would be $516,521, leaving $1,328,198 after taxes. Adding in the $82,000 in after-tax contributions amounts to a total of $1,410,198 compared to the $726,624 total from the non-IRA account—an increase of 94 percent. If you were to withdraw all of the $1,410,198 of deferred income in one year, you would pay more than the midrange marginal tax rate of 28 percent. How-

TABLE 10E
Nondeductible IRA versus Non-Ira Investment

Year Number	Beginning Total	Amount Contrib- uted	New Total	Interest Earned at 12%	Federal Tax at 28%
1	0	$2,000	$2,000	$240	$67
2	$2,173	2,000	4,173	501	140
3	4,533	2,000	6,533	784	220
4	7,098	2,000	9,098	1,092	306
5	9,884	2,000	11,884	1,426	399
6	12,911	2,000	14,911	1,789	501
7	16,199	2,000	18,199	2,184	611
8	19,771	2,000	21,771	2,613	732
9	23,652	2,000	25,652	3,078	862
10	27,869	2,000	29,869	3,584	1,004
11	32,449	2,000	34,449	4,134	1,157
12	37,422	2,000	39,426	4,731	1,325
13	42,832	2,000	44,832	5,380	1,506
14	48,706	2,000	50,706	6,085	1,704
15	55,087	2,000	57,087	6,850	1,918
16	62,019	2,000	64,019	7,682	2,151
17	69,550	2,000	71,550	8,586	2,404
18	77,732	2,000	79,732	9,568	2,679
19	86,621	2,000	88,621	10,635	2,978
20	96,278	2,000	98,278	11,793	3,302
21	106,769	2,000	108,769	13,052	3,655
22	118,167	2,000	120,167	14,420	4,038
23	130,549	2,000	132,549	15,906	4,454
24	144,001	2,000	146,001	17,520	4,906
25	158,616	2,000	160,616	19,274	5,397
26	174,493	2,000	176,493	21,179	5,930
27	191,742	2,000	193,742	23,249	6,510
28	210,481	2,000	212,481	25,498	7,139
29	230,840	2,000	232,840	27,941	7,823
30	252,957	2,000	254,957	30,595	8,567
31	276,985	2,000	278,985	33,478	9,374
32	303,090	2,000	305,090	36,611	10,251
33	331,449	2,000	333,449	40,014	11,204
34	362,259	2,000	364,259	43,711	12,239
35	395,731	2,000	397,731	47,728	13,364
36	432,095	2,000	434,095	52,091	14,586
37	471,601	2,000	473,601	56,832	15,913
38	514,520	2,000	516,520	61,982	17,355
39	561,148	2,000	563,148	67,578	18,922
40	611,804	2,000	613,804	73,656	20,624
41	666,836	2,000	668,836	80,260	22,473
Totals		$82,000		$895,311	$250,687

TABLE 10E *(continued)*

Net Total	Tax-Deferred Total	Amount Contrib-uted	Interim Total	Interest Earned at 12%	Total
$2,173	0	$2,000	$2,000	$240	$2,240
4,533	$2,240	2,000	4,240	509	4,749
7,098	4,749	2,000	6,749	810	7,559
9,884	7,559	2,000	9,559	1,147	10,706
12,911	10,706	2,000	12,706	1,525	14,230
16,199	14,230	2,000	16,230	1,948	18,178
19,771	18,178	2,000	20,178	2,421	22,599
23,652	22,599	2,000	24,599	2,952	27,551
27,869	27,551	2,000	29,551	3,546	33,097
32,449	33,097	2,000	35,097	4,212	39,309
37,426	39,309	2,000	41,309	4,957	46,266
42,832	46,266	2,000	48,266	5,792	54,058
48,706	54,058	2,000	56,058	6,727	62,785
55,087	62,785	2,000	64,785	7,774	72,559
62,019	72,559	2,000	74,559	8,947	83,507
69,550	83,507	2,000	85,507	10,261	95,767
77,732	95,767	2,000	97,767	11,732	109,499
86,621	109,499	2,000	111,499	13,380	124,879
96,278	124,879	2,000	126,879	15,226	142,105
106,769	142,105	2,000	144,105	17,293	161,397
118,167	161,397	2,000	163,397	19,608	183,005
130,549	183,005	2,000	185,005	22,201	207,206
144,001	207,206	2,000	209,206	25,105	234,310
158,616	234,310	2,000	236,310	28,357	264,668
174,493	264,668	2,000	266,668	32,000	298,668
191,742	298,668	2,000	300,668	36,080	336,748
210,481	336,748	2,000	338,748	40,650	379,398
230,840	379,398	2,000	381,398	45,768	427,166
252,957	427,166	2,000	429,166	51,500	480,665
276,985	480,665	2,000	482,665	57,920	540,585
303,090	540,585	2,000	542,585	65,110	607,695
331,449	607,695	2,000	609,695	73,163	682,859
362,259	682,859	2,000	684,859	82,183	767,042
395,731	767,042	2,000	769,042	92,285	861,327
432,095	861,327	2,000	863,327	103,599	966,926
471,601	966,926	2,000	968,926	116,271	1,085,197
514,520	1,085,197	2,000	1,087,197	130,464	1,217,661
561,148	1,217,661	2,000	1,219,661	146,359	1,366,020
611,804	1,366,020	2,000	1,368,020	164,162	1,532,183
666,836	1,532,183	2,000	1,534,183	184,102	1,718,285
726,624	1,718,285	2,000	1,720,285	206,434	1,926,719
		$82,000		$1,844,719	

ever, 5-year averaging and programmed withdrawals over a joint life expectancy period would keep much of the tax-deferred income out of the 31 percent top tax rate.

What accounts for the huge difference? Tax-deferred compounding amounts to a humongous benefit compared to the after-tax compounding for the non-IRA program. You must look at the boxcar numbers to appreciate the difference tax-deferred compounding makes for serious savers. Originally, IRAs were fully deductible and compounded at tax-deferred rates—two major benefits. When Congress took away the deductibility of IRA contributions for some persons, it left tax-deferred compounding. Of the two benefits, tax-deferred compounding is by far the best—and it remains available to every taxpayer regardless of earned income or other retirement accounts.

The figures in Table 10E assume a 12 percent average total return annually. If your investments were to earn 8 percent, you can compare the differences in Table 10F with those in Tables 10E and 10G. If your investments were to earn 15 percent, you can compare the differences in Table 10G with those in Tables 10E and 10F.

MUNICIPAL BONDS VERSUS NONDEDUCTIBLE IRA

Another possibility for accumulating wealth over the long term is to invest after-tax savings in tax-free municipal bonds (muni-bonds) or a tax-free bond mutual fund. Interest from muni-bonds is totally tax free at the federal level. Income from a nondeductible IRA is only tax-deferred. How would a regular investment of $2,000 after-taxes grow if invested in muni-bonds versus a nondeductible IRA? Assuming the same interest rate for both investments is not realistic, as tax-free rates factor in their tax-free status. Table 10H computes the accumulation from an average tax-free interest rate applied to an annual contribution of $2,000.

Investing in muni-bonds or a tax-free mutual fund does have one advantage over the IRA—you are not limited to $2,000 in contributions each year. You could, for example, invest the maximum $2,000 in an IRA and invest other available after-tax income in a muni-bond mutual fund. If you elect to do both, invest in a nondeductible IRA up to $2,000 per year before any other investments. Invest another amount regularly in tax-exempt bond funds. Select aggressive mutual funds for your IRA. This mix of conservative and aggressive investments allows all your investments to grow tax advantaged with a portion positioned for appreciation and a portion invested with a goal of capital preservation. If you are an ultraconservative investor, a tax-exempt bond fund is better than putting nondeductible IRA contributions into bank CDs.

NONDEDUCTIBLE IRA VERSUS VARIABLE TDA

Tax-deferred annuities (TDAs), variable or fixed, are similar in many ways to an IRA and have one major advantage—they are not limited to $2,000 annually. However, TDAs come with an extra level of costs that you don't pay with a no-load fund under the IRA umbrella. Extra costs associated with the TDA result from the need to establish insurance coverage to qualify for the deferral of taxes. Penalties for withdrawal before age 59 1/2 also apply to the TDA. With Congress hungrily looking for additional tax revenue, the future of tax-deferred annuities may be in doubt. Generally, I believe insurance should be considered separately from investing. Commingling the two is not good business. I prefer to buy term insurance and invest the difference in a no-load mutual fund, with at least $2,000 each year under an IRA umbrella. If you should elect to invest in a TDA, do so only after you have funded your IRA to the maximum of $2,000 each year whether the IRA is deductible or not. Also, fully fund any 401(k) plan for which you may be eligible before investing in a TDA.

EARLY START FOR KIDS' IRAS

Many of us want to help our children get a firm start toward a secure financial future. One helping aid is what I call the "incentive IRA." Several strategies can get children started right depending on their age and circumstances.

Working teenagers are eligible to start an IRA, as long as

TABLE 10F
Nondeductible IRA versus Non-IRA Investment at 8 Percent

Year Number	Beginning Total	Amount Contrib- uted	New Total	Interest Earned at 8%	Federal Tax at 28%
1	0	$2,000	$2,000	$160	$45
2	$2,115	2,000	4,115	329	92
3	4,352	2,000	6,352	508	142
4	6,718	2,000	8,718	697	195
5	9,220	2,000	11,220	898	251
6	11,867	2,000	13,867	1,109	311
7	14,665	2,000	16,665	1,333	373
8	17,625	2,000	19,625	1,570	440
9	20,756	2,000	22,756	1,820	510
10	24,066	2,000	26,066	2,085	584
11	27,568	2,000	29,568	2,365	662
12	31,271	2,000	33,271	2,662	745
13	35,187	2,000	37,187	2,975	833
14	39,329	2,000	41,329	3,306	926
15	43,710	2,000	45,710	3,657	1,024
16	48,343	2,000	50,343	4,027	1,128
17	53,242	2,000	55,242	4,419	1,237
18	58,424	2,000	60,424	4,834	1,354
19	63,905	2,000	65,905	5,272	1,476
20	69,701	2,000	71,701	5,736	1,606
21	75,831	2,000	77,831	6,226	1,743
22	82,314	2,000	84,314	6,745	1,889
23	89,171	2,000	91,171	7,294	2,042
24	96,422	2,000	98,422	7,874	2,205
25	104,091	2,000	106,091	8,487	2,376
26	112,202	2,000	114,202	9,136	2,558
27	120,780	2,000	122,780	9,822	2,750
28	129,852	2,000	131,852	10,548	2,953
29	139,447	2,000	141,447	11,316	3,168
30	149,594	2,000	151,594	12,128	3,396
31	160,326	2,000	162,326	12,986	3,636
32	171,676	2,000	173,676	13,894	3,890
33	183,680	2,000	185,680	14,854	4,159
34	196,375	2,000	198,375	15,870	4,444
35	209,801	2,000	211,801	16,944	4,744
36	224,001	2,000	226,001	18,080	5,062
37	239,018	2,000	241,018	19,281	5,399
38	254,901	2,000	256,901	20,552	5,755
39	271,699	2,000	273,699	21,896	6,131
40	289,464	2,000	291,464	23,317	6,529
41	308,252	2,000	310,252	24,820	6,950
Totals		$82,000		$341,837	$95,714

TABLE 10F *(continued)*

Net Total	Tax-Deferred Total	Amount Contrib-uted	Interim Total	Interest Earned at 8%	Total
$2,115	0	$2,000	$2,000	$160	$2,160
4,352	$2,160	2,000	4,160	333	4,493
6,718	4,493	2,000	6,493	519	7,012
9,220	7,012	2,000	9,012	721	9,733
11,867	9,733	2,000	11,733	939	12,672
14,665	12,672	2,000	14,672	1,174	15,846
17,625	15,846	2,000	17,846	1,428	19,273
20,756	19,273	2,000	21,273	1,702	22,975
24,066	22,975	2,000	24,975	1,998	26,973
27,568	26,973	2,000	28,973	2,318	31,291
31,271	31,291	2,000	33,291	2,663	35,954
35,187	35,954	2,000	37,954	3,036	40,991
39,329	40,991	2,000	42,991	3,439	46,430
43,710	46,430	2,000	48,430	3,874	52,304
48,343	52,304	2,000	54,304	4,344	58,649
53,242	58,649	2,000	60,649	4,852	65,500
58,424	65,500	2,000	67,500	5,400	72,900
63,905	72,900	2,000	74,900	5,992	80,893
69,701	80,893	2,000	82,893	6,631	89,524
75,831	89,524	2,000	91,524	7,322	98,846
82,314	98,846	2,000	100,846	8,068	108,914
89,171	108,914	2,000	110,914	8,873	119,787
96,422	119,787	2,000	121,787	9,743	131,530
104,091	131,530	2,000	133,530	10,682	144,212
112,202	144,212	2,000	146,212	11,697	157,909
120,780	157,909	2,000	159,909	12,793	172,702
129,852	172,702	2,000	174,702	13,976	188,678
139,447	188,678	2,000	190,678	15,254	205,932
149,594	205,932	2,000	207,932	16,635	224,566
160,326	224,566	2,000	226,566	18,125	244,692
171,676	244,692	2,000	246,692	19,735	266,427
183,680	266,427	2,000	268,427	21,474	289,901
196,375	289,901	2,000	291,901	23,352	315,253
209,801	315,253	2,000	317,253	25,380	342,634
224,001	342,634	2,000	344,634	27,571	372,204
239,018	372,204	2,000	374,204	29,936	404,141
254,901	404,141	2,000	406,141	32,491	438,632
271,699	438,632	2,000	440,632	35,251	475,882
289,464	475,882	2,000	477,882	38,231	516,113
308,252	516,113	2,000	518,113	41,449	559,562
328,123	559,562	2,000	561,562	44,925	606,487
		$82,000		$524,487	

TABLE 10G
Nondeductible IRA versus Non-Ira Investment at 15 Percent

Year Number	Beginning Total	Amount Contrib- uted	New Total	Interest Earned at 15%	Federal Tax at 28%
1	0	$2,000	$2,000	$300	$84
2	2,216	2,000	4,216	632	177
3	4,671	2,000	6,671	1,001	280
4	7,392	2,000	9,392	1,409	394
5	10,406	2,000	12,406	1,861	521
6	13,746	2,000	15,746	2,362	661
7	17,447	2,000	19,447	2,917	817
8	21,547	2,000	23,547	3,532	989
9	26,090	2,000	28,090	4,213	1,180
10	31,124	2,000	33,124	4,969	1,391
11	36,701	2,000	38,701	5,805	1,625
12	42,881	2,000	44,881	6,732	1,885
13	49,728	2,000	51,728	7,759	2,173
14	57,314	2,000	59,314	8,897	2,491
15	65,720	2,000	67,720	10,158	2,844
16	75,034	2,000	77,034	11,555	3,235
17	85,354	2,000	87,354	13,103	3,669
18	96,788	2,000	98,788	14,818	4,149
19	109,457	2,000	111,457	16,719	4,681
20	123,494	2,000	125,494	18,824	5,271
21	139,048	2,000	141,048	21,157	5,924
22	156,281	2,000	158,281	23,742	6,648
23	175,375	2,000	177,375	26,606	7,450
24	196,532	2,000	198,532	29,780	8,338
25	219,973	2,000	221,973	33,296	9,323
26	245,946	2,000	247,946	37,192	10,414
27	274,725	2,000	276,725	41,509	11,622
28	306,611	2,000	308,611	46,292	12,962
29	341,941	2,000	343,941	51,591	14,446
30	381,086	2,000	383,086	57,463	16,090
31	424,460	2,000	426,460	63,969	17,911
32	472,517	2,000	474,517	71,178	19,930
33	525,765	2,000	527,765	79,165	22,166
34	584,764	2,000	586,764	88,015	24,644
35	650,134	2,000	652,134	97,820	27,390
36	722,565	2,000	724,565	108,685	30,432
37	802,818	2,000	804,818	120,723	33,802
38	891,738	2,000	893,738	134,061	37,537
39	990,262	2,000	992,262	148,839	41,675
40	1,099,426	2,000	1,101,426	165,214	46,260
41	1,220,380	2,000	1,222,380	183,357	51,340
Totals		$82,000		$1,767,219	$494,821

TABLE 10G *(continued)*

Net Total	Tax-Deferred Total	Amount Contrib-uted	Interim Total	Interest Earned at 15%	Total
$2,216	0	$2,000	$2,000	$300	$2,300
4,671	2,300	2,000	4,300	645	4,945
7,392	4,945	2,000	6,945	1,042	7,987
10,406	7,987	2,000	9,987	1,498	11,485
13,746	11,485	2,000	13,485	2,023	15,507
17,447	15,507	2,000	17,507	2,626	20,134
21,547	20,134	2,000	22,134	3,320	25,454
26,090	25,454	2,000	27,454	4,118	31,572
31,124	31,572	2,000	33,572	5,036	38,607
36,701	38,607	2,000	40,607	6,091	46,699
42,881	46,699	2,000	48,699	7,305	56,003
49,728	56,003	2,000	58,003	8,701	66,704
57,314	66,704	2,000	68,704	10,306	79,009
65,720	79,009	2,000	81,009	12,151	93,161
75,034	93,161	2,000	95,161	14,274	109,435
85,354	109,435	2,000	111,435	16,715	128,150
96,788	128,150	2,000	130,150	19,523	149,673
109,457	149,673	2,000	151,673	22,751	174,424
123,494	174,424	2,000	176,424	26,464	202,887
139,048	202,887	2,000	204,887	30,733	235,620
156,281	235,620	2,000	237,620	35,643	273,263
175,375	273,263	2,000	275,263	41,289	316,553
196,532	316,553	2,000	318,553	47,783	366,336
219,973	366,336	2,000	368,336	55,250	423,586
245,946	423,586	2,000	425,586	63,838	**489,424**
274,725	489,424	2,000	491,424	73,714	565,138
306,611	565,138	2,000	567,138	85,071	652,208
341,941	652,208	2,000	654,208	98,131	752,339
381,086	752,339	2,000	754,339	113,151	867,490
424,460	867,490	2,000	869,490	130,424	999,914
472,517	999,914	2,000	1,001,914	150,287	1,152,201
525,765	1,152,201	2,000	1,154,201	173,130	1,327,331
584,764	1,327,331	2,000	1,329,331	199,400	1,528,731
650,134	1,528,731	2,000	1,530,731	229,610	1,760,340
722,565	1,760,340	2,000	1,762,340	264,351	2,026,691
802,818	2,026,691	2,000	2,028,691	304,304	2,332,995
891,738	2,332,995	2,000	2,334,995	350,249	2,685,244
990,262	2,685,244	2,000	2,687,244	403,087	3,090,331
1,099,426	3,090,331	2,000	3,092,331	463,850	3,556,181
1,220,380	3,556,181	2,000	3,558,181	533,727	4,091,908
1,354,398	4,091,908	<u>2,000</u>	4,093,908	<u>614,086</u>	4,707,994
		$82,000		$4,625,994	

TABLE 10H
Nondeductible IRA versus Tax-Free Bond Fund

Year Number	Beginning Total	Amount Contrib- uted	New Total	Interest Earned at 12%	Net Total
1	0	$2,000	$2,000	$240	$2,240
2	2,240	2,000	4,240	509	4,749
3	4,749	2,000	6,749	810	7,559
4	7,559	2,000	9,559	1,147	10,706
5	10,706	2,000	12,706	1,525	14,230
6	14,230	2,000	16,230	1,948	18,178
7	18,178	2,000	20,178	2,421	22,599
8	22,599	2,000	24,599	2,952	27,551
9	27,551	2,000	29,551	3,546	33,097
10	33,097	2,000	35,097	4,212	39,309
11	39,309	2,000	41,309	4,957	46,266
12	46,266	2,000	48,266	5,792	54,058
13	54,058	2,000	56,058	6,727	62,785
14	62,785	2,000	64,785	7,774	72,559
15	72,559	2,000	74,559	8,947	83,507
16	83,507	2,000	85,507	10,261	95,767
17	95,767	2,000	97,767	11,732	109,499
18	109,499	2,000	111,499	13,380	124,879
19	124,879	2,000	126,879	15,226	142,105
20	142,105	2,000	144,105	17,293	161,397
21	161,397	2,000	163,397	19,608	183,005
22	183,005	2,000	185,005	22,201	207,206
23	207,206	2,000	209,206	25,105	234,310
24	234,310	2,000	236,310	28,357	264,668
25	264,668	2,000	266,668	32,000	298,668
26	298,668	2,000	300,668	36,080	336,748
27	336,748	2,000	338,748	40,650	379,398
28	379,398	2,000	381,398	45,768	427,166
29	427,166	2,000	429,166	51,500	480,665
30	480,665	2,000	482,665	57,920	540,585
31	540,585	2,000	542,585	65,110	607,695
32	607,695	2,000	609,695	73,163	682,859
33	682,859	2,000	684,859	82,183	767,042
34	767,042	2,000	769,042	92,285	861,327
35	861,327	2,000	863,327	103,599	966,926
36	966,926	2,000	968,926	116,271	1,085,197
37	1,085,197	2,000	1,087,197	130,464	1,217,661
38	1,217,661	2,000	1,219,661	146,359	1,366,020
39	1,366,020	2,000	1,368,020	164,162	1,532,183
40	1,532,183	2,000	1,534,183	184,102	1,718,285
41	1,718,285	2,000	1,720,285	206,434	1,926,719
Totals		$82,000		$1,844,719	

TABLE 10H *(continued)*

Beginning Total	Amount Contrib- uted	New Total	Interest Earned at 7%	Net Total
0	$2,000	$2,000	$140	$2,140
$2,140	2,000	4,140	290	4,430
4,430	2,000	6,430	450	6,880
6,880	2,000	8,880	622	9,501
9,501	2,000	11,501	805	12,307
12,307	2,000	14,307	1,001	15,308
15,308	2,000	17,308	1,212	18,520
18,520	2,000	20,520	1,436	21,956
21,956	2,000	23,956	1,677	25,633
25,633	2,000	27,633	1,934	29,567
29,567	2,000	31,567	2,210	33,777
33,777	2,000	35,777	2,504	38,281
38,281	2,000	40,281	2,820	43,101
43,101	2,000	45,101	3,157	48,258
48,258	2,000	50,258	3,518	53,776
53,776	2,000	55,776	3,904	59,680
59,680	2,000	61,680	4,318	65,998
65,998	2,000	67,998	4,760	72,758
72,758	2,000	74,758	5,233	79,991
79,991	2,000	81,991	5,739	87,730
87,730	2,000	89,730	6,281	96,011
96,011	2,000	98,011	6,861	104,872
104,872	2,000	106,872	7,481	114,353
114,353	2,000	116,353	8,145	124,498
124,498	2,000	126,498	8,855	135,353
135,353	2,000	137,353	9,615	146,968
146,968	2,000	148,968	10,428	159,395
159,395	2,000	161,395	11,298	172,693
172,693	2,000	174,693	12,229	186,922
186,922	2,000	188,922	13,225	202,146
202,146	2,000	204,146	14,290	218,436
218,436	2,000	220,436	15,431	235,867
235,867	2,000	237,867	16,651	254,518
254,518	2,000	256,518	17,956	274,474
274,474	2,000	276,474	19,353	295,827
295,827	2,000	297,827	20,848	318,675
318,675	2,000	320,675	22,447	343,122
343,122	2,000	345,122	24,159	369,281
369,281	2,000	371,281	25,990	397,270
397,270	2,000	399,270	27,949	427,219
427,219	2,000	429,219	30,045	459,264
	$82,000		$377,264	

they have earned income from personal services. But a teen-ager, particularly those aiming for college, will not be inter-ested in socking away $1,000, $1,500, or the maximum $2,000 in a saving and investment program that they can't touch with-out penalty for almost 50 years. If you are so inclined, you can match their earned income with annual gifts. Your children don't even need to know you are setting up an IRA in their name. Even with the penalty, they may be tempted to with-draw the funds if they know. What a surprise it would be to your children if they were to turn 60 and discover they had an extra $1 million in an account in their name. You can leave word with a friend or in your will about the IRA established for your children.

But let's assume you're going to tell your child about the IRA and your child earned $1,500 working part time. You agree to match the $1,500 and invest it under an IRA umbrella. From age 16 through age 60, that $1,500 would grow to more than $245,981 at an average tax-deferred rate of 12 percent—even if no additional money is contributed to your child's IRA. One restraint—your child can't touch the money until age 59 1/2 without paying the 10 percent penalty. Later, if Congress should liberalize regulations to permit using the IRA resources to buy a first home or for catastrophic medical expenses, the money could be used before retirement.

Incentive IRAs are perfectly legal. The only requirement is earned income, substantiated by a Form W-2. The dollars your son or daughter earns from flipping hamburgers or other jobs need not be invested. You can give equivalent dollars on condi-tion they promise to invest your cash in an IRA. One problem could arise. Mutual fund custodial banks may not knowingly open accounts for minors, as they cannot legally enter into contractual agreements. Mutual fund managers are afraid of their potential liability if a minor's account should decline in value. The minor could simply back out, asserting he or she was not legally able to sign the contract to open the account. Banks will open accounts for minors to be put into CDs because they cannot lose capital value. So, until your son or daughter reaches the legal age in your state, start the IRA with a bank, even though the earnings rate will be less than is available in mutual funds. When he or she reaches legal age, transfer the IRA account to a mutual fund and teach your child to manage it using the strategies noted in other parts of this book.

Another plan offers a further incentive. You could agree to continue contributions to an IRA after they begin their careers as long as they do not touch the capital in their IRA. How do you keep them from dipping into the gifted IRA prematurely? The arrangement I have with my two children is, if they tap into the IRA, my annual gifts stop and they receive no more money from me. And they know I mean it! I direct the mutual fund to send all confirmations to my address to avoid tempting them. Such a plan can be a powerful incentive for your children to get an early start on a long-term capital acquisition plan, as early IRAs allow compound interest to work its magic over longer periods. Plus, your gift to your child's IRA may mean a tax refund for the child.

Many parents will not approve gifting IRA contributions. Instead of simply giving a child who is working and earning income up to $2,000 to set aside in an IRA, agree to match contributions. If your child is just starting on a career and is newly married, he or she may not be terribly interested in looking ahead 40 years to retirement. There will likely be higher priority needs for cash. But to encourage your children to think about saving and investing, agree to a "cooperative" IRA. For every $1 they may put into an IRA, you could match the contribution with another $1. Thus, for every $1,000 they set aside, you could put up another $1,000 for the maximum $2,000 per year contribution. There's nothing sacred about the 1-for-1 match. You could put up $2 for every $1 they contribute—or some other ratio. You can agree to continue contributions as long as they do not touch the cash. Important in a cooperative IRA is the realization by young adults that they can carve out a few bucks from their income to set aside for the future. They might not do it on their own, but with the idea that $1 will get them $2, you can build a partnership that assures their financial future.

A leveraged IRA can jump-start your children into investing without your gifts of cash. Leverage within an IRA is illegal, and your broker can't put stocks purchased on margin into your IRA. Also, you cannot use IRA funds as collateral for a loan. But you can leverage your cash when you act as the bank. In a margin account, you borrow some of the money you want to invest, usually from your broker. Your margin limit is 50 percent; that is, if you put up $1,000 to buy stock, your broker can lend you no more than $1,000 on margin—50 percent to buy more shares. Leverage investing depends on earning a higher rate of return than the interest you pay on the money you borrowed.

Applying this same logic to an IRA can help you start your children on the road to investing and teach them about the basics of business. You can develop a business plan with your children involving borrowed capital and interest. Further, your young adult children learn the responsibility for saving on their own. You also gain from the transaction, because your loan will be earning interest equivalent to that of a bond or money market fund. The procedure is a bit more complicated than simply giving your children the money to start their IRA. Here's how it could work:

Each year you lend each of your children the full $2,000 with the agreement that they pay you interest only for five years and that they use the money to set up IRAs. Table 10J details the money flows in this family business plan. Of course, your children must earn $2,000 to establish eligibility. Assume your children pay federal income taxes at the marginal rate of 28 percent. By putting $2,000 in the IRA the first year, your children each save $560 on taxes. But instead of spending it, they put the $560 into a reserve account in a bank or money market fund to earn interest at an assumed rate of 6 percent.

At the beginning of the second year, before you loan your children another $2,000, they pay you $160 interest at the rate of 8 percent on the first year's $2,000 contribution out of the reserve account. That leaves $425.20 in the reserve account. The second year your children save another $560, boosting the reserve account to $985.20. At the end of the second year, they pay you $320 interest on the outstanding $4,000 loan. The process continues each year. After five years, interest on the growing loan principal nearly depletes the reserve account that has been replenished from the tax savings. At this point, your children have not put up as much as a penny of their own money.

TABLE 10J
Leveraged IRA Business Plan for Son or Daughter

Year Number	Loan Amount	Income Tax Refund	Interest Earned on Refund + Reserve	Reserve Account Total	Interest Payable on Loan
1—Start	$2,000	$560		$560.00	
End	2,000		$25.20	425.20	$160
2—Start	4,000	$560		985.20	
End	4,000		50.70	614.50	320
3—Start	6,000	$560		1,174.40	
End	6,000		62.07	632.33	380
4—Start	8,000	$560		1,192.33	
End	8,000		63.13	489.20	640
5—Start	10,000	$560		1,049.20	
End	10,000		54.55	194.65	800

At the beginning of the sixth year, the program changes. Each of your children owes you $10,000 less the $194.65 remaining in the reserve fund, but they are unlikely to have that much in savings outside the IRA. You agree to take repayment of the $10,000 over 10 years at 8 percent interest. Monthly payments are $121.32. After 10 more years, your children are debt free and you've got all your money back.

If the IRA earns a 12 percent compound rate of return and your children never contribute another cent after age 35, the IRA will grow into a retirement fund worth more than $1.5 million at age 65. Thus, for a total lifetime cost of $14,558.40, including interest at 8 percent, your children will have established a retirement fund that could pay them $184,000 each year for life without ever diminishing the principal if the 12 percent earning rate continues. The effective purchasing power of the $200,000 annual return (depending on how many years is chosen to deplete the account) would be diminished by 40 years of inflation. If the index of inflation were to be about 5.0 over 40 years, the $184,000 per year at age 65 could buy the equivalent of $26,286 worth of goods and services at today's prices.

I can't think of a more satisfying investment for you or any parent.

CONCLUSION

IRAs are widely recognized as a way to reduce income taxes for those who are eligible. Far more important than the tax-saving benefits are the tax-deferred rates for compounding investment returns. Every right-thinking investor should recognize the benefits available from the many innovative uses of IRAs. Maximizing the use of IRAs for retirement and capital accumulation should become a major component of your plans for lifetime investing.

CHAPTER 11

STRATEGIES FOR ACHIEVING YOUR PERSONAL FINANCIAL OBJECTIVES

(ACTION PLANS YOU CAN LIVE WITH)

Reaching your financial objectives—having enough money to retire without worry, accumulating funds to start your own business, paying for your children's college expenses, taking a sabbatical for two or three years while you're young enough to enjoy the adventure, or achieving any of the goals many of us aspire to—is the financial bottom-line. And now we're down to the ways and means. Many financial solutions are available, but we are also looking for emotional solutions. Here's why.

I could lay out an odds-on plan for solving your financial problems, but the risks might keep you tossing and turning at night. Many financial plans with highly probable chances of success fail to take into account your personal and emotional responses to risks. So what happens? Nothing. Individuals seldom take actions they are not comfortable with. I have worked with people who have been paralyzed by fear. Those brilliant plans for reaching your goals are worthless if you don't take action to implement them. Thus, in this action plan we are looking to answer both needs—a solid, proven plan to help you achieve your financial goals without losing sleep over the risks. I call this your "sleep-easy" action plan.

Remember our goal is to provide the highest return, with the lowest risk, with the highest liquidity at the least cost. We are not really concerned about short-term goals, such as saving money for a vacation trip this year. You can use the money-saving techniques detailed in Chapter 9 for accumulating cash to pay for a trip to Europe, a new car, or similar goals. The plans I am concerned with here are intended for long term growth of assets, the ones that should eventually involve hundreds of thousands or millions of dollars.

BASIC ACTION PLAN

I call our basic action plan the "12 percent solution." It aims to earn a conservative, low-risk return of 12 percent each year. If you have been burned reaching for lofty 20 percent-plus annual returns, relate these differences in returns to the fable of the tortoise and the hare. Consistent, steady evenhanded returns will get you farther over the long term than attempts to reach lofty goals in a few bold leaps.

The most common multiyear goal is the accumulation of assets that will generate income to supplement Social Security benefits and pension plan payouts to support your retirement. Additional income will help you achieve a satisfying lifestyle during your golden years. Other specific goals, such as funding children's college, accumulating cash reserves to finance a new business startup, or other objectives, call for minor deviations from the basic action plan. These deviations are detailed later.

For years I studied numerous options for positioning a person's portfolio to meet long-term goals that would be financially acceptable and emotionally satisfying. I want you not only to feel comfortable with this plan but also to enjoy the process. The plan involves dividing your portfolio into four parts:

Part 1

A quarter of your portfolio is to be invested in a riskless to extremely low-risk financial instrument—certificates of deposit, Treasury bills, or money market funds. These short-term investments incur little or no credit risk. Their exposure to interest-rate risk is so slight, it can be ignored. We covered the debt investments in Chapter 2.

Other possibilities are available to improve the return from this 25 percent portion. They involve some interest-rate risk; that is, the capital value of your funds could vary slightly up or down depending on the direction of interest rates.

One is the extended money market account. Neuberger & Berman's PLUS account is similar to a money market fund except it invests in instruments with longer maturities than the usual money market fund. Under the new rules issued by the Securities and Exchange Commission in early 1991, N&B cannot continue to classify its PLUS mutual fund as a money market fund. So N&B renamed it the Ultra Short Bond Fund (USB Fund). Investments in the USB Fund are exposed to a bit more interest rate risk, and the fund does not maintain a constant $1 value for shares. However, the return from the USB Fund is considerably better than typical money market funds, in the range of 100 to 130 basis points higher. For a bit higher return along with a bit higher risk, look at intermediate-term bond mutual funds, those with maturities in the range of three to five years. The long-term record of intermediate bond funds is detailed in Chapter 2, as it provides one of the most consistent returns with less volatility than longer term bond funds.

Another possibility is a high-grade tax-exempt bond fund, applicable to individuals with marginal income in the 31 percent tax bracket. Here again, some interest-rate risk may apply, but overall returns, considering the effect of taxes at the highest rates, would make these minimal additional risks acceptable. Using state-specific tax-exempt bond funds for this 25 percent portfolio position could be particularly desirable for investors living in states with high state income taxes. State specific means the tax-exempt bond fund includes municipal bonds issued by authorities within that state to avoid state as well as federal income taxes.

GNMA (Government National Mortgage Association) certificates and investment-grade corporate bond funds are both low risk and more productive than government T-bills or T-notes. GNMA certificates are guaranteed by the full faith and credit of the U.S. government, but they are available only in $25,000 minimum amounts at original issue. Further, as individual mortgagees pay off the principal in the pool, small amounts of capital are returned to certificate owners. Buying shares in a GNMA fund begins at a $1,000 minimum, and the payments of principal by mortgagees are reinvested by the fund managers in new certificates. GNMA funds pay 1 to 1 1/2 percent more than T-bills. Investment-grade corporate bond funds carry little credit risk. However, both GNMA and corporate bond funds are exposed to interest-rate risk. When interest rates are declining, total return exceeds dividend payouts because the certificates or bonds rise in price. When interest rates are rising, reductions in the capital value of the GNMA certificates or corporate bonds will offset some of the dividend return to show a lower total return.

These alternatives need evaluation on a case-by-case basis. One group of investors could be conservative. It would stick to totally risk-free investments. A second group could be more aggressive. It could invest the 25 percent in ultra-short or intermediate-term bond funds or tax-exempt bond funds, depending on the tax situation. For most investors, our basic action plan calls for 25 percent of your portfolio to be invested in riskless to near-riskless instruments (Group 1). Table 11A details returns for Group 1 investments.

Part 2

A second quarter of your portfolio is to be invested in an index or index-like no-load mutual fund. This portion of your portfolio may be invested in an index fund, such as the Vanguard 500 Index Trust that is structured to mimic the Standard & Poor's 500 index. Or this portion could be invested in any of several fully invested funds with good track records, including one or more international funds (Group 2). If you are many years away from retirement, your Part 2 investments may be comprised of

TABLE 11A
Group 1—Riskless or Low-Risk Investment Performance

Instrument	Annualized Performance		
	1990	5 Years	10 Years
Treasury bills—3-month	7.75 %	6.83 %	8.55 %
Money market mutual funds	8.38	7.34	9.10
Treasury notes—intermediate term	9.73	9.34	12.52
Treasury bonds—long term	8.11	10.75	13.75
Corporate bonds—AAA	8.88	10.43	14.07
Municipal bonds	6.71	9.0	10.95

aggressive growth funds, such as 20th Century Ultra or 20th Century Vista. Table 11B shows returns of Group 2 investments.

The 25 percent of your portfolio invested in index-like or fully invested funds aims to help you feel good during bull markets—to hold a winning ticket in a bull market. I connect this with my experience at our local racetrack. I have been going to the racetrack about once a year since 1963. I consider the experience to be an advanced course in human nature. I pick horses that have a record in the racing form of breaking quickly from the gate and leading the pack during the early going. I like to hold a ticket on a front-runner. I like to bet on a horse that allows me to feel like a winner for at least part of the race. I should tell you, however, that I have had only one winning day since 1963, so the front-running picks seldom endure the distance. Fortunately, I know the difference between investing and gambling and limit my bets to $2.

The fully invested portion helps you to feel exuberant when the market is rising. Excitement reigns during bull markets, as individuals whether invested or not watch what happens on Wall Street. You can participate in all this excitement with your holding of shares in an index or fully-invested mutual fund.

During a bear market, you may be hurt temporarily. But if you hold on, the S&P index has grown at about 13 percent annually with dividends and gains reinvested since World War

TABLE 11B
Group 2—Index and Fully Invested Mutual Funds

Name	Annualized Performance		
	1990	5 Years	10 Years
Columbia Special	−12.4%	14.4%	N/A
Twentieth Century Growth	−3.9	13.7	11.2%
Twentieth Century Select	−0.4	13.3	15.7
Twentieth Century Ultra	9.4	14.8	N/A
Twentieth Century Vista	−15.7	12.0	N/A
Vanguard 500 Portfolio	−3.9	12.7	N/A
Vanguard Extended Index Trust	−13.9	N/A	N/A
Ivy International	−12.9	N/A	N/A
T. Rowe Price International	−8.9	18.3	15.6
Scudder International	−8.9	15.9	14.7
Vanguard World International	−12.0	16.7	N/A

II. Mutual funds that maintain a fully invested position in small-capitalization companies should have produced an average yearly gain of about 12 to 16 percent with dividends and gains reinvested. Thus, although you can benefit from the emotional thrust of being in a winning fund during bull markets, you must also be patient through those inevitable bear markets.

Part 3

A third quarter of your portfolio is to be invested in funds that practice defensive stock selection. These funds (Group 3) select stocks for their portfolio based on value analysis. If the market is languishing in a bear phase, bargains are readily available, and the fund may be fully invested. These managers consider stocks under bear market conditions to be undervalued. During bull markets, stocks may no longer be good values according to the criteria of the funds' managers. When the market is bullish and particularly frothy, value-oriented funds are allowed to and may choose to be largely in cash. At times, such funds may be totally out of the market with their assets invested in T-bills or other risk-free short-term instruments.

    While not viewed as market-timed funds, the value-oriented funds in Group 3 may be mostly out of the market when

TABLE 11C
Group 3—Bottom-Up (Stock Selection) Defensive Mutual Funds

Name	Annualized Performance		
	1990	5 Years	10 Years
Gabelli Growth	-2.0%	N/A	N/A
Gabelli Asset	-5.0	N/A	N/A
Janus Fund	-0.7	14.4%	15.7%
Janus Twenty	0.6	12.3	N/A
Janus Venture	-0.4	15.9	N/A
Mathers	10.4	14.9	11.8
Mutual Beacon	-8.2	12.6	10.5
Lindner Fund	-11.3	9.9	16.5

it reaches vulnerable cyclical high levels and heavily invested during bear market valleys. I refer to this approach as bottom-up timing where the emphasis is on stock selection rather than a technical analysis of the market's trend. Mutual funds in this group have successfully captured a large part of upward market moves and avoided large portions of market declines. In this sense, they practice a form of market timing. Because they spend a portion of time in a defensive posture, their betas are low, indicating a low level of risk.

Investing in bottom-up funds should satisfy both of our objectives—a better than 12 percent return plus lower risks for emotional calm. Mathers, one of the Group 3 funds, has reported an almost 15 percent average total return for 25 years. Its most recent record is shown in Table 11C. Note the consistency—few big gainers but few losers either from 1986 through 1990. Group 3 funds tend to be less risky because they are not fully invested at all times.

The effect of the defensive strategy of holding value-oriented stocks at times and of being largely in cash at other times is unique to only a few stock mutual funds. Fidelity funds make up almost one third of all stock funds, and they take no responsibility for market risk. At times, some of their funds may be as much as 10 percent in cash, but such small positions are not enough to provide a serious defense against declining values in bear markets.

TABLE 11D
Group 4—Top-Down (Internally Timed) Defensive Mutual Funds

Name	Annualized Performance		
	1990	*5 Years*	*10 Years*
Flex-Fund Muirfield	2.3 %	N/A	N/A
Flex-Fund Growth	4.3	5.4 %	N/A
Merriman Timed Blue Chip	3.8	N/A	N/A
Merriman Timed Capital Appreciation	3.1	N/A	N/A
Merriman Timed Asset Allocation	1.0	N/A	N/A

Part 4

A final quarter of your portfolio is to be invested in timing funds, those that are internally market-timed or managed from the top down. Only a few of these funds are available on a no-load basis and they are named in Group 4 in Table 11D. In contrast to the funds in Group 3, internally timed funds may be as much as 100 percent in the market or out of the market in cash according to signals generated by technical analysis. The decision is not one of stock selection but rather one of market selection.

Internally timed mutual funds came into being to solve two problems:

1. Newsletter writers and market gurus continue to supply information for switching from an invested position into a money market fund or other cash equivalent as markets change direction. The record of these market analysts varies from brilliant to disastrous, but many good, consistent, and reliable market timing systems exist. But investors confound analysts by not following directions. Market timing systems work, but only if the individual investor follows directions promptly.

2. Every switch from an equity position to a cash position counts as a sale. Even two to four switches in a year can compound record-keeping and tax reporting problems. Each fund investment's cost basis must be calculated, including the reinvestment of dividends and capital gains. The book work of tracking costs and figuring profits was such a headache for many investors they gave up on the system—even if it was producing profits. Some believed their profits were flowing to the CPA who figured their taxes instead of into their pockets.

Internally timed funds solved both problems. Professional managers analyze the market and follow through with a discipline few individuals can match. If the timing indicators called for switching out of equities into cash, the manager switches that day. Timing systems allow little latitude for "feel" or intuition. They rely strictly on discipline. Because the fund managers make the switches from equities to cash and vice versa, shareholders do not have to track costs and profits on each switch. They don't agonize over switch signals and market direction. Switching out of a fund at one price and buying back in at a higher price can be unsettling, but reversals happen occasionally. Professional managers are better equipped to handle the emotional trauma of the switches. Shareholders receive a single Form 1099 at the end of the year showing income and recognized capital gains. Only if investors sell shares must they calculate their own capital gain tax liability.

Internally timed funds are highly defensive. They aim to garner 75 to 85 percent of any upward market move, but they do their best work in declining markets. By moving from equity or bond positions into cash, they avoid the major losses fully invested funds incur. Timed funds typically invest in aggressive issues because they are confident they can get out of major market declines. Thus, internally timed funds become far more conservative than they would be without timing. Betas, as an indication of risk, are considerably lower for timed funds than for untimed, fully invested funds.

ACTION PLAN SUMMARY

Your basic plan calls for the following:

• 25 percent of your portfolio invested in CDs, bond funds, T-bills, or government money market funds. Note the alternatives listed for Group 1 in Table 11A.

• 25 percent invested in index-type or fully invested equity funds. Pick one or more of the mutual funds listed in Group 2 in Table 11B.

• 25 percent invested in bottom-up funds, those that practice a defensive strategy through stock selection. Pick one or more of the mutual funds listed in Group 3 in Table 11C.

• 25 percent invested in top-down, internally timed mutual funds. Pick one or more of the mutual funds listed in Group 4 in Table 11D.

Whether you select one, two, or more of the funds or fixed-income investments from any single group depends mainly on the size of your portfolio. If your investable portfolio totals $5,000, pick only one of the funds or investments from each group. If your investable portfolio totals $100,000, you would likely diversify your money into two or three alternatives from each group.

What does this basic plan do for you?

In a bull market, three of the four alternatives should be highly profitable. You can relate comfortably to the total profit picture and feel good about your investments, because only one quarter of the portfolio is disappointing. The money invested in CDs, bond funds, T-bills, or money market funds will yield a return, but the return will likely be considerably lower than the total return of the three mutual fund groups. Movements of the index or fully invested funds without timing can be a joy in a rising market. Both of the defensive strategies are expected to underperform the index funds. With your investments fully diversified, you deserve the emotional lift you get from being on the right side of the market with at least most of your portfolio.

In a bear market, three of your four investments should be doing better than the overall market. Your Group 1 investments continue to produce a profit. The two defensive groups (Group 3 and 4) will probably have retreated to cash and will continue to produce profits. Only the index or fully invested funds from Group 2 will be declining along with the overall market. Still, the chance that three out of four groups are producing profits is not bad. Further, you need take no additional action because the fund managers will be looking after your interests.

Once you watch the total action of the four groups through a complete up-and-down market cycle, you may be motivated to reduce the size of the Group 2 investments. The thrill of participating in the exhilarating up market may be defeated by the losses incurred by mutual funds without defensive protection in a declining market.

You can use the basic plan for retirement investing, first in your IRA and 401(k) plans, if you are eligible. Any of the funds noted in Groups 1, 2, 3, and 4 provide IRA, Keogh, 401(k), and profit-sharing plans to defer taxes on earnings until retirement. Only after these plans are fully funded should you engage in long-term investing outside of a tax-deferred plan. Until about age 40, you may prefer to select more aggressive alternatives in Groups 2, 3, and 4. But don't neglect investments in Group 1; keep your basic plan balanced.

Closer to retirement, you may move to more conservative mutual funds. Switching to income-oriented mutual funds may be desirable when you are within three to five years of retirement. Included in Group 1 are GNMA and high-quality bond funds. Switching from equity funds, particularly any you may still have in Group 2, to GNMA or investment-grade, intermediate-term bond funds can protect your income sources. Hang onto your holdings from Groups 3 and 4 to provide growth as a hedge against inflation. In a downturn, these two groups of funds will assume a defensive posture.

COUPON UPDATE

Mutual funds listed in Groups 2, 3, and 4 represent my picks at the time this book went to press. But times change. Managers move. Funds may grow to sizes that preclude the same level of growth as when they were smaller and more flexible. No-load funds become load funds and vice versa. These and other as yet unknown hazards affect mutual fund performance. To keep you updated and to provide new mutual funds for your portfolio, you are invited to send in the coupon you will find on the back flap of the book jacket. Your name will be entered on our permanent list to receive annual updates on the funds in Groups 1, 2, 3, and 4. You will also receive a free issue of *Fund Exchange*. No photo or facsimile copies of the coupon please.

INVESTING FOR SHORT-TERM GOALS

Suppose you plan to start your own business in five or six years. Your planning has already made it clear that startup capital must come from your own resources. Later, to help expand a successful business, you may borrow from the bank or sell shares to friends. But in the beginning, you must commit your own savings. Other short-term goals might include buying some big toy, such as a boat big enough to cruise the oceans; taking a two- or three-year sabbatical from your job to travel, to return to college for an advanced degree, to write a book; or doing something special only a reserve of cash will permit.

Achieving short-term goals calls for two changes in the basic plan:

1. Save more of your earnings from work to increase the rate of investing. Obviously, the more cash you can invest in the four groups, the quicker you can achieve your capital goal. Review the techniques in Chapter 9 for spending less in order to save more after-tax cash from your job earnings. A committed goal usually helps you say no to marginal spending opportunities—and motivates you to increase contributions to the four groups. Accumulating cash to meet a short-term goal is a cumulative process. You are adding new cash to your investment pool, and your pool of assets is growing from your investments. Make sure both parts of this process contribute their share.

2. Investments in Group 2 funds depend on having long periods for the ups and downs of market action to offset and gain the long-term benefits of index or fully invested fund investing. Investing in equity funds or other aggressive funds is a mistake many investors make when they need cash in a few years. If time is limited, as it would be for short-term goals, I suggest eliminating investments in Group 2 index or other fully invested funds.

FUNDING COLLEGE EDUCATION FOR CHILDREN

Positioned midway between short-term goals of 5 to 10 years and long-term retirement income goals is the plan for accumulating assets to pay the escalating costs projected for college. One answer to the question, "How much money will I need to pay for my children's college education?" is—lots. College education costs are escalating at annual rates higher than inflation. The usual rate of cost escalation is 8 to 9 percent. Any way you approach it, the problem of college costs can be sobering, but examine these alternatives.

Start Early

The longer your savings can generate income on their own, the fewer dollars you must come up with at college registration time. Compound interest needs time to work its magic. The day a child is born is not too soon to begin a saving and investment plan for his or her college education. If your figures indicate you need $20,000 each year for four years and you follow my "12 percent solution," expect to contribute about $2,000 each year for 18 years. Your 12 percent gross return will produce 8.42 percent after an annual 28 percent federal income tax bite. If your state also levies a state income tax, reduce the annual rate of growth accordingly. If you wait until the fall your first child enters college, the full $20,000 will be payable in installments over nine months from current income or from loans. Saving and investing ahead can be less costly than waiting until your son or daughter says, "Please write me a check for $20,000 by tomorrow." If you wait until six years before a child is ready to attend college, your annual contributions to a fund that will provide $20,000 for four years escalate to $10,790 per year. And this is for only one child. Waiting can be costly.

Financial Aid

As the cost of attending college escalates beyond the capability of all but the wealthiest families, government and private financial aid has become increasingly available. Scholarships, grants, and low-interest loans may be available to soften the financial requirements for attending universities. At some private institutions, as many as 80 percent of the students receive some financial aid.

Exploring the many sources of financial aid is beyond the scope of this chapter and this book. The key sources for specific information are high school counselors who work with college-bound seniors and the financial aid office at the university of choice. Once a student has been accepted at a university, the financial aid office at that university, and they all have one, can be a big help. Students may be able to borrow at less cost than parents due to available student help programs. One note of caution—incurring a large debt to attend college puts a somber damper on career and personal progress after graduation as payments take a chunk out of income.

For general information, look to your library for annually updated books on scholarships and aid programs available. While most scholarships are needs dependent, many others are available to members of special groups or individuals at specific colleges or universities.

Taxes

Accumulating funds for college can be affected by income tax considerations. A variety of abuses by innovative parents hoping to escape the tax bite on asset accumulations to pay for college led to massive changes in the tax code affecting minors. These changes are affectionately referred to as the "kiddie tax." Basically, the regulations affecting children's taxes are as follows:

• Children under the age of 14 may earn investment income of $500 per year and pay no taxes. Earnings from $501 to $1,000 are taxed at the child's own rate, 15 percent under the current tax code. Any income over $1,000 per year earned by the child is subject to tax at the parent's marginal (highest) tax rate. Gone are the opportunities for switching income to children by interest-free loans, short-term trusts, and gifts.

• Children over the age of 14 pay taxes on their income as if they were adults. Unearned income and earned income may be subject to different deduction limits. Unfortunately, only four years elapse between this emancipation and the time they ordinarily attend college.

The difference in age-related tax liabilities can change investment strategies. Until a child reaches 14, investments can be aimed at minimizing income. Buying Series EE savings bonds, for example, permits deferring all income until redemption. If a child buys EE bonds, they grow in redemption value with no taxable income. EE bonds must be held for at least five years to earn the market interest that changes twice yearly. After holding for five years and reaching age 14, a child can redeem the EE bonds and switch the accumulated cash into an investment likely to generate more growth than income. Investing in mutual funds with growth objectives would also reduce annual income subject to a minor's taxes, as growth funds typically produce little income. Taxes would be limited to the child's personal liability without throwing excess income into parents' income for tax purposes. Unfortunately, growth funds, without a defensive strategy in place, represent high risk during the final years before college. For that reason, I recommend limiting growth investments to funds in Groups 3 and 4.

To UGMA or Not to UGMA

Minors may not own assets in their own name for reasons noted in Chapter 10. The remarks above on the "kiddie tax" reflect income earned by the child, usually from funds given to the child in a Uniform Gifts to Minors Act trust (UGMA). The UGMA permits a parent or other adult to manage the funds in the child's trust account for the benefit of the child. These UGMA trusts are readily available and easy to set up. Banks and mutual funds have forms for the asking. Recognize, however, that money given to a child in a UGMA trust is an irrevocable gift; the money belongs to the child. At age 18 or 21, when the child reaches majority (age varies by state), all of the money in the UGMA trust belongs to the child with no strings attached. This freedom of the young adult to use the money that was in the UGMA trust at his or her own discretion, poses a dilemma.

If you give money to a minor in a UGMA trust, it will likely grow faster than if you invest it on your own because the minor's tax liability will be less. You can mentally set aside these funds for the minor's education. But, if the child reaches majority and declines to use the money to pay for his or her college education, there is little you can legally do. You can coax and advise, but you cannot withhold the money if the young adult decides to take the money and travel around the world with it. So there is a risk. You may accumulate money faster in a UGMA trust, but you lose control when your child reaches majority.

Parents may choose to collect money earmarked for the payment of college expenses in their own name. Annual earnings will likely be subject to higher tax liabilities, but the money is theirs. If the child chooses not to attend college or is scholastically ineligible, parents still have the money. This plan permits parents to begin a growth-oriented asset accumulation program without considering the advantage of the kiddie tax. Accumulating assets for college is another short-term variation of the basic plan. My advice—invest savings intended for a college fund in one or more of the Group 3 or Group 4 funds for growth with defenses in place and pay taxes yearly. It's important to contribute to the fund regularly, following a dollar-cost averaging strategy using one or more of the funds in Groups 3 and 4. The growth potential from defensively oriented mutual funds is almost sure to exceed the tax-advantaged investments that are limited to fixed-income instruments.

Zero-Coupon Bonds

Zero-coupon bonds, or zeros, are sometimes cited as ideal for use in accumulating capital to pay for children's college. Their one advantage is their known value at a future date. Their main disadvantage is that you must pay taxes on the imputed interest each year even though no interest is paid in cash. Paying the taxes from other resources could be a form of forced savings. Or you could select tax-exempt zeros. If the maturity of zeros is the same as projected college registration, you have the security of knowing that a specific amount of money will be available on that date. You do not have the security of knowing how much college will cost. With college costs rising at a faster rate than inflation and generally faster than after-tax returns on bonds, of which zeros are one type, achieving your goals of collecting the needed cash for college is not likely to happen with zeros or any of the other Group 1 instruments.

Using an IRA

Using an IRA is one of the most innovative solutions to the problem of accumulating college funds. An IRA accumulates money faster because money in the fund grows at tax-deferred rates. Also, if the child chooses not to attend college, you have a huge head start on your own retirement program.

IRAs are intended to be retirement funds, right? That is the reason early withdrawals before age 59 1/2 are penalized. True, but you CAN get money out of an IRA if you need to by paying a penalty and taxes. Suppose you were to start an IRA to accumulate a tax-deferred sum and withdrew some or all of the funds in the account well before you were 59 1/2 to help finance your children's education. What would the alternatives look like compared to a simple saving and investment program outside an IRA?

Table 11E examines the trade-offs between accumulating a sum for college expenses without the benefit of an IRA and a similar sum invested under the IRA umbrella after paying a penalty and taxes on withdrawals. When you contribute $2,000 each year to an IRA, your taxes are reduced by an assumed 28 percent or $560. After investment in an IRA, your earnings will grow tax-deferred. Offsetting this benefit are the 10 percent penalty and normal income taxes on any withdrawals before you reach 59 1/2.

For this example, assume a 12 percent earnings rate. After each year, the amount you could withdraw after paying a 10 percent penalty and taxes on the full amount of the withdrawal at 28 percent is shown in the column labeled "Total after Penalty & Tax @ 28%." Compare this amount to the non-IRA account in the column "Net Total." Each year $1,440 is invested in the non-IRA account, as $1,440 is the after-tax amount left from a $2,000 before-tax amount and is equivalent to a deductible $2,000 for the IRA. Earnings rate on the non-IRA account is figured at 8.64 percent, the after-28-percent-tax compounding rate equivalent to a tax-deferred 12 percent. During the

TABLE 11E
IRA for College Fund

Year Number	Beginning Balance	Amount Added Yearly	New Total	Interest Earned at 12%	Net Total
1	0	$2,000	$2,000	$240	$2,240
2	$2,240	2,000	4,240	509	4,749
3	4,749	2,000	6,749	810	7,559
4	7,559	2,000	9,559	1,147	10,706
5	10,706	2,000	12,706	1,525	14,230
6	14,230	2,000	16,230	1,948	18,178
7	18,178	2,000	20,178	2,421	22,599
8	22,599	2,000	24,599	2,952	27,551
9	27,551	2,000	29,551	3,546	33,097
10	33,097	2,000	35,097	4,212	39,309
11	39,309	2,000	41,309	4,957	46,266
12	46,266	2,000	48,266	5,792	54,058
13	54,058	2,000	56,058	6,727	62,785
14	62,785	2,000	64,785	7,774	72,559
15	72,559	2,000	74,559	8,947	83,507
16	83,507	2,000	85,507	10,261	95,767
17	95,767	2,000	97,767	11,732	109,499
18	109,499	2,000	111,499	13,380	124,879

ninth year the after-penalty, after-tax amount in the IRA reaches and exceeds the net total from the non-IRA investment. Each additional year increases the gain of the IRA fund over the non-IRA alternative.

The big gain comes when funds are withdrawn to pay for tuition and other college expenses. Note the figures in Table 11F. Begin with the gross total from the column, "Total in IRA Fund," of $124,879. Assume you need $20,000 for one year's college expenses. To have $20,000 net after 28 percent federal income taxes plus the 10 percent penalty, you must withdraw $32,258 ($20,000 divided by 1.00 − [.28 + .10] = $32,258) and pay $12,258 in taxes and penalties. After deducting $32,258, the balance remaining in the IRA is $92,621, which continues to earn 12 percent for another year. After the fourth year of similar deductions, the total remaining is $21,274, and after earnings of $2,553, the total is $23,827.

Compare the total remaining after paying $80,000 in college expenses from the IRA with the total remaining after simi-

TABLE 11E *(continued)*

Total after Penalty and Tax @ 28%	Beginning Balance	Amount Invested	New Total	Interest Earned at 8.64%	Non-IRA Net Total
$1,389	0	$1,440	$1,440	$124	$1,564
2,944	$1,564	1,440	3,004	260	3,264
4,686	3,264	1,440	4,704	406	5,110
6,638	5,110	1,440	6,550	566	7,116
8,823	7,116	1,440	8,556	739	9,296
11,270	9,296	1,440	10,736	928	11,663
14,012	11,663	1,440	13,103	1,132	14,235
17,082	14,235	1,440	15,675	1,354	17,030
20,520	17,030	1,440	18,470	1,596	20,065
24,372	20,065	1,440	21,505	1,858	23,364
28,685	23,364	1,440	24,804	2,143	26,947
33,516	26,947	1,440	28,387	2,453	30,839
38,927	30,839	1,440	32,279	2,789	35,068
44,987	35,068	1,440	36,508	3,154	39,662
51,774	39,662	1,440	41,102	3,551	44,654
59,376	44,654	1,440	46,094	3,982	50,076
67,890	50,076	1,440	51,516	4,451	55,967
77,425	55,967	1,440	57,407	4,960	62,367

lar deductions of $20,000 per year from the non-IRA account—a negative $10,752. Total difference equals $23,827 less tax and penalty of $9,054 or $14,773 plus negative $10,752 for a total of $25,525.

If you should not spend IRA capital to send your children to college, you have accumulated a tidy nest egg—a great start on your retirement plan or maybe an earlier retirement. Even if you spent half of the accumulated capital to supplement contributions from current income to finance your children's college education, you would be ahead of never starting. You could choose the option of not withdrawing capital funds in the IRA if:

• You could afford to send your children to college from current earnings. During the time your children are growing, your career could be advancing fast enough to be able to finance college for the children from your earnings.

• Your children qualify for athletic or other scholarships. If scholarships do not provide all of the money needed, the differ-

TABLE 11F
Withdrawal Plan—IRA for College Fund

Total in IRA Fund	After Withdrawal of $20,000 after Penalty and 28% Tax	Interest at 12%	Total in Non-IRA Fund	After Withdrawal of $20,000	Interest at 8.64$
$124,879	$92,621	$11,115	$62,567	$42,567	$3,678
103,735	71,477	8,577	46,245	26,245	2,268
80,055	47,797	5,736	28,512	8,512	735
53,532	21,274	2,553	9,248	-10,752	-929
23,827			-10,752		

ence between the full cost of college and the amount after a scholarship might be affordable from current earnings.

• Loans at subsidized rates again become available. The cost of borrowing could be less than spending capital accumulated within an IRA if you would be penalized, as noted in Table 11F. Here is where a compatible working relationship with your banker could pay off. You cannot put up the assets in your IRA as collateral for a loan, but if the banker knows you have the capital, even if withdrawals would be subject to the 10 percent penalty and taxes, he or she might make the loan on your signature only.

• Your children choose not to attend college. Or they might not be scholastically acceptable. Your accumulated capital within the IRA remains under your control.

• Congress changes the law to permit withdrawals without penalty to finance children's education. Congress continues to tinker with IRA legislation, and it is anybody's guess how the law may be changed. Some liberalization of withdrawal conditions will probably be enacted to permit use of IRA funds for college education and/or to buy a first house. You will likely still have to pay taxes on the withdrawals, but not having to pay the penalty would make saving via an IRA even more desirable. If your contributions to an IRA for children's education are not deductible, the benefits are less but still positive with or without a congressional change to permit withdrawals for education without penalty.

SPENDING IN RETIREMENT

Financial publications speak volubly to investments designed to build assets to be used in retirement. Advisors may recommend switching assets from growth funds to income funds in the mistaken idea that these are more conservative and offer fewer risks. To gain the most spendable cash, that is, cash you can spend after deductions for taxes, I suggest the following two approaches. If you expect to spend only income from assets and to leave the capital to your estate, follow Program No. 1. If you need to spend portions of your capital or simply wish to expand your spending rate by drawing some of your capital, follow Program No. 2.

Program No. 1

This program involves spending income only, including interest, dividends, and distributed capital gains. Assume you arrive at age 65 and retire. Income to support your retirement lifestyle will come from Social Security benefits, pension payouts, if you are eligible, and income from assets you have put aside during your working years. Social Security benefits are seldom enough to support your lifestyle. For planning purposes, you can assume Social Security benefits of $12,000 to $15,000 per year for a couple or call the Social Security Administration at its national information number (1-800-234-5772). Medicare payments will be taken out of the total. Social Security benefits are subject to income tax if a couple's adjusted gross income (AGI) exceeds $32,000 and single person's AGI exceeds $25,000. Benefits are partially indexed for inflation.

Benefits from company or government organization pension and profit-sharing plans vary widely. You will need to add these income figures, if any, to your plan.

I suggest studying your income requirements first. Once you decide you need a specific sum of after-tax income to support your lifestyle, compare your income requirements to your three sources—Social Security, pension, and investment income. If your income exceeds your income requirements, consider yourself fortunate. Retirees, on average, live on 65 to 70 percent of the income they earned when working. If your house or condominium is fully paid for, you can live on 65 percent of working income with a minimum of adjustments. However, if you expect to travel widely, as many retirees do once they have the time, the 65 to 70 percent figure could be limiting.

How do you handle this situation when you need a combination of growth and income? A client recently approached me with this problem. He had $220,000 in assets. Of the total, $40,000 was in an IRA and $180,000 was in money market funds. Since he was 63, he was not required to begin withdrawing the IRA funds. He figured he needed $14,000 in additional income beyond Social Security and a pension to support his lifestyle. I suggested he invest the $180,000 in GNMA and investment-grade bond funds. He needed a total return of 7.77 percent from the $180,000 to provide the $14,000 income, and these funds typically produce returns above 8 percent. I suggested he invest the $40,000 in his IRA in Group 3 and 4 funds for tax-deferred growth as a hedge against inflation. I always try to arrange clients' investments so that their daily cash needs are more or less guaranteed with the excess positioned for growth.

You might consider spending some of your capital, as noted in Program No. 2 below.

Program No. 2

If your spendable income exceeds your requirements, you can continue to invest the difference as a hedge against future price increases due to inflation. Following are specific steps to increase your spending:

1. Spend all of your Social Security benefits first. The Social Security Administration (SSA) will deposit monthly payments directly into your bank's checking account. Simply fill out a request for direct deposit and send it to the SSA.

2. Spend all or most of your pension benefits, if you are eligible. Ask your former employer to deposit pension payments directly into your checking account as well.

3. List all nontax-deferred investments and how much income they produce. Plan to spend this income next. Nontax-deferred income includes interest from CDs, T-bills, bonds owned directly, and distributions from mutual funds. If you directed the mutual funds to reinvest income and capital gain distributions in additional shares, write to the funds and ask for income to be sent to you in cash. You may wish to set up a distribution plan from one or more mutual funds. You can file a request for the fund to send you a set amount of cash each month or quarter. The fund will send you dividend and capital gain distributions first, but if these total less than the amount you requested, the fund will liquidate shares to make up the difference. If liquidations continue to exceed the income, you will use up the fund's capital in time. If the amount requested is less than dividends and capital gain distributions, the excess will be reinvested in additional shares.

4. List all of your tax-deferred investments. These include your personal IRA, regardless of whether contributions were deductible or nondeductible; any rollover IRAs from qualified plans with your employers or other organization; tax-deferred annuities, if any; and a Keogh plan, if you were self-employed. If you are retired from your own self-employed activity and will not be continuing contributions to your Keogh plan to age 70 1/2, you may prefer to roll all of those assets over into an IRA to simplify annual IRS reporting requirements. Plan to spend income from these tax-deferred investments last, particularly if your income exceeds current spending requirements.

5. Only if the nontax-deferred investments fail to provide enough income should you begin withdrawing cash from the tax-deferred investments listed in No. 4 above. The longer your assets continue to compound at tax-deferred rates, the more you benefit. When you reach 70 1/2, you are required to begin withdrawals from IRAs, Keoghs, 401(k)s, and other qualified plans at a rate that will exhaust the accounts over your expected lifetime or the expected lifetime of you and your spouse or another person. If you set up a joint life expectancy withdrawal plan with a younger person, the age difference is limited to 10 years. You may refigure your life expectancy each year because the longer you live, the longer you can expect to live.

6. Restructuring your investment portfolio may be desir-

able, as you begin withdrawing interest and dividends. I suggest moving any investments in Group 2 mutual funds into Group 1 instruments. I advise buying shares in one or more GNMA, investment-grade bond, and/or intermediate-term bond mutual funds. You may also keep a portion of Group 1 funds in a money market fund that offers check writing. United Services Treasury Securities Fund permits any number of checks to be written with no minimum balance. Other funds may pay slightly more income but limit checks to $100 or $500 minimums. Depending on your cash needs, more of your investments in Group 3 and Group 4 funds may also be switched to GNMA or investment-grade bond mutual funds for income and security.

7. If income alone will not satisfy your lifestyle requirements, you may wish to draw down portions of your capital rather than cut back on your spending. Using up capital is no longer a no-no in retirement planning unless one of your goals is to leave a large estate for your children or charities. An annuity you might purchase from an insurance company uses capital to buy the annuity. The insurance company agrees to provide you with a fixed monthly income for life or a minimum number of years. But at the end, no residue remains. If you elect a do-it-yourself annuitization (not with an insurance policy) of a portion of your capital instead, it could work like this:

Suppose you elect to spend half of your capital—investments in any of the four groups. The other half remains to continue producing income and growth. If that sum should equal $100,000, you can figure the amount you can withdraw each month from two additional facts:

• Your age and life expectancy. If your life expectancy is 12 years, you could elect to use 24 years as an annuity period—or some other number that would avoid all but the remote chance of outliving the capital.

• Average earning rate expected. If your assets were to earn 10 percent, for example, monthly withdrawals would be less than if your assets earned 12 percent. For example, over a 24-year period with $100,000 of capital invested at an average 10 percent, you could withdraw $888 each month. At the end of 24 years or 288 months, all of the $100,000 would be gone. If your $100,000 could earn an average of 12 percent, your monthly withdrawals would increase to $1,016 each month for 24 years. These numbers are from the Capital Withdrawal Chart referenced in Resources. The Capital Withdrawal Chart includes monthly amounts over periods from 1 through 50 years at interest rates from 5 to 25 percent to enable you to plan your own program.

Running your own annuity program to spend some capital at a preprogrammed rate provides two benefits you do not get with an annuity purchased from an insurance company:

• You have access to the capital at any time in case of emergency. A large medical expense or the need for extra custodial care at some time might call for more cash, and it would be available because you control the money.

• Any remaining capital that is not used up remains in your estate. If you should die after 14 years instead of the 24, the remaining capital would not go to the insurance company but would be available for distribution to your heirs or to charities.

LEVERAGING FOR SUPERCHARGED PROFITS

I have saved the most exciting investment opportunity for last. Investing in no-load mutual funds on margin with market timing offers the possibility of dramatic profits with surprisingly moderate risks. Buying shares on margin, a process known as leveraging, simply means borrowing money from a brokerage house to buy additional mutual fund shares, using the shares as security for the loan.

But isn't buying shares on margin speculative?

Some people think so, but some of these thoughts are relics of the Great Depression. As it was practiced before the stock market crash of 1929, margin rates as high as 90 percent encouraged speculation. Investing on margin under those conditions was risky—no question about that. After thousands of margin speculators went broke in the 1929 crash, investing on margin was viewed as little more than legalized gambling.

The maximum allowable margin ratio is now 50 percent, a much safer level. You may choose to use less than 50 percent margin, thereby cutting risk and still earning higher profits. There are aggressive and conservative ways of using margin, as we'll see.

Borrowing up to 50 percent of the value of your mutual fund portfolio greatly enhances its earning ability. For example, if you have $10,000 to invest, your broker will lend you another $10,000, enabling you to buy $20,000 of your favorite mutual funds. If the market moves up 20 percent, you'll make $4,000 instead of the $2,000 you would have made with an unmargined portfolio. Of course, if the market drops 20 percent, you would lose $4,000 instead of $2,000.

In either case, assuming an interest rate of 10 percent on the margin loan, you would owe $1,000 in interest for one year. Net earnings on your $20,000 portfolio when the market was up 20 percent would be 30 percent after paying interest, for a profit of $3,000. In a year when the market declines 20 percent, your loss, including interest, would be a whopping 50 percent of the $10,000 you invested from your own funds, leaving a total of $5,000.

The potential for big losses is the reason I never recommend buying mutual funds on margin unless you buy funds that use internal market timing or you market-time the funds yourself using our systems or others you are comfortable with. Market timing really does cut risks dramatically. You can also use funds that are defensively managed based on stock selection, such as those in Group 3.

Simulated performance data in Table 11G show what happened to Fidelity Magellan and Value Line Special Situations Fund from 1970 through 1990 with and without market timing. The big losses in 1973 and 1974 without market timing are particularly worth noting.

Table 11H shows how essential market timing is if you plan to invest with margin. It assumes an investment of $20,000, half borrowed on margin, invested in the averaged returns of Magellan and Value Line Special Situations for 1970 through 1990. The average of the two funds' returns combined results from a top fund and a less productive fund to avoid biasing the results. Interest on the margin loan was paid annually.

Without market timing, this investment was a disaster.

TABLE 11G
Performance Results of Fidelity Magellan and Value Line Special Situations with and without Timing

	Buy and Hold			Market Timing		
Year	Magellan	Special Situations	Average	Magellan	Special Situations	Average
1970	-15.70	-34.40	-25.10	24.50	10.50	17.50
1971	35.10	17.60	26.40	31.70	35.90	33.80
1972	30.10	-11.00	9.60	28.90	-4.50	12.20
1973	-42.10	-45.50	-43.80	-7.50	-1.60	-4.60
1974	-28.30	-29.50	-28.90	7.90	7.90	7.90
1975	44.40	47.00	45.70	23.50	34.00	28.80
1976	35.50	52.70	44.10	32.40	57.80	45.10
1977	16.30	12.30	14.30	4.40	3.50	4.00
1978	31.70	21.20	26.50	26.40	17.00	21.70
1979	51.70	43.60	47.70	26.90	26.00	26.50
1980	69.90	54.40	62.20	74.30	78.40	76.40
1981	16.40	-2.20	7.10	20.40	8.50	14.50
1982	48.10	23.10	35.60	43.10	30.70	36.90
1983	38.60	19.40	29.00	35.80	21.40	28.60
1984	2.00	-25.50	-11.80	10.30	-5.70	2.30
1985	43.10	-21.10	11.00	40.50	19.30	29.90
1986	23.70	5.10	14.40	16.50	-7.50	4.50
1987	1.00	-9.10	-4.10	23.80	19.40	21.60
1988	22.70	3.30	13.00	8.70	-7.60	0.60
1989	34.60	21.70	28.20	34.60	21.70	28.20
1990	-4.60	-4.50	-4.60	-3.30	-0.90	-2.10

After 21 years, the investment was worth $25,932, and the $10,000 principal of the margin loan was still due to be repaid. A bank passbook savings account would have been more profitable over the same period.

But look what happens with market timing! The $20,000 margined investment grew to nearly $751,000. Table 11H includes deductions for annual interest payments but does not deduct for taxes. The striking difference in bottom-line results lies in market timing's ability to cut losses dramatically. The market timing system applied was my own PM&A equity timing model. Since my system is the least effective of the four systems we use, our four-timer system applied to these funds would have produced still better results.

TABLE 11H
Average of Fidelity Magellan and Value Line Special Situations (Invest
$10,000 and Borrow $10,000; Invest at 12 Percent)

Year	Without Market Timing		With Market Timing	
1970	-25.10	$13,780	17.50	$22,300
1971	26.40	16,218	33.80	28,637
1972	9.60	16,575	12.20	30,931
1973	-43.80	8,115	-4.60	28,308
1974	-28.90	4,510	7.90	29,344
1975	45.70	5,458	28.50	36,595
1976	44.10	6,665	45.10	51,900
1977	14.30	6,419	4.00	52,776
1978	26.50	6,920	21.70	63,028
1979	47.70	9,021	26.50	78,530
1980	62.20	15,832	76.40	137,328
1981	7.10	15,756	14.50	156,040
1982	35.60	20,165	36.90	212,419
1983	29.00	24,813	28.60	271,971
1984	11.80	20,685	2.30	277,026
1985	11.00	21,760	29.90	358,657
1986	14.40	23,694	4.50	373,597
1987	-4.10	21,522	21.60	453,094
1988	13.00	23,120	0.60	454,012
1989	28.20	28,440	28.20	768,323
1990	-4.60	25,932	-2.10	750,988
	1 Year in 4 Loses		1 Year in 10 Loses	
	Average loss -21.3		Average loss -3.4	
	Average Gain 26.7		Average gain 32.2	
			CRR = 23%	

Tables 11J and 11K detail the two hypothetical margin
investments during the 21-year period using the same two funds
and the single market timing system. These tables detail deductions for margin interest and taxes paid at a 31 percent
rate. Tax impacts are included because margin investments are
not permitted in tax-advantaged programs, such as IRAs or
401(k)s. In some cases, margin can be used in profit-sharing
plans if the plan allows it.

If you are a bit nervous about borrowing to buy fund shares,
let me point out that most of us use margin. Your home mortgage is a common example. When you put 10 percent down on
your dream home and borrow the other 90 percent from the
bank, you're buying a home on margin. Buying a house is more
satisfying to many of us than renting, and houses are recom-

mended as good investments. But, frankly, borrowing 90 percent of the purchase price of a house over 30 years makes me nervous as an investor. If you stay in your house for 30 years, it will likely be worth a great deal more than you paid for it. But it's also possible that it might not be worth as much as the loan balance if property values decline. This happens often enough that owners sometimes simply walk away from their house because they can't sell it for enough to pay off the balance. They lose all they have paid up to that point. Yet most of us don't even blink when we sign those mortgage loan documents.

In contrast, I am comfortable using 50 percent margin to buy mutual fund shares. Charles Schwab & Co., Jack White Co., Freeman-Welwood & Co., and Waterhouse Securities are discount brokers that will lend you the money to buy mutual funds on margin.

You can decide when to pay off the margin loan, but I recommend paying off a margin loan with regular monthly installments, just as you pay off the mortgage on your house. For example, you can put up $10,000, borrow $10,000, and pay it off at $150 per month. In about eight years, your account will be paid off and the balance could be worth $40,000 to $50,000 after taxes. If you are young enough at that point, you could decide to take the same approach again and turn your $40,000 into $120,000, paying it off at $600 per month. If you paid that off over eight more years, you might have an extra $120,000 to $150,000 retirement account.

LEVERAGING UP

Instead of paying off a margin loan, Tables 11J and 11K show the effect of leveraging up, similar to the way a business increases its borrowing as it grows.

In Table 11J, your initial investment was $10,000 and the initial margin loan was $5,000, or one third of the total investment. After seven years, your equity would have grown enough to allow you to almost double your margin loan while maintaining the same margin-to-equity ratio. By continuing to increase your margin loan, you boost your earning potential.

Table 11K shows how your $10,000 would grow if you bor-

TABLE 11J
Results of Leverage Program Using 33 Percent Margin

Year	Beginning Balance	Loan Amount	Total Investment	Percent Gain or Loss	Gross Gain
1970	$10,000	$5,000	$15,000	17.50	$2,625
1971	11,466	5,000	16,466	33.80	5,566
1972	14,962	5,000	19,962	12.20	2,435
1973	16,297	5,000	21,297	-4.60	-980
1974	14,817	5,000	19,817	7.90	1,566
1975	15,552	5,000	20,552	28.80	5,919
1976	19,292	5,000	24,292	45.10	10,956
1977	26,506	13,253	39,759	4.00	1,590
1978	26,689	13,253	39,942	21.70	8,667
1979	31,755	13,253	45,008	26.50	11,927
1980	39,070	19,535	58,605	74.60	43,719
1981	67,889	13,197	81,086	14.50	11,757
1982	75,091	37,545	112,636	36.90	41,563
1983	101,178	50,589	151,767	28.60	43,405
1984	127,637	63,819	191,456	2.30	4,403
1985	125,659	63,819	189,478	29.90	56,654
1986	160,347	80,173	240,520	4.50	10,823
1987	162,283	80,173	242,456	21.60	52,371
1988	192,886	96,443	289,330	0.60	1,736
1989	184,978	96,443	281,421	28.20	79,361
1990	233,083	116,541	349,624	-2.10	-7,342

rowed $10,000 for a 50 percent margin. Both tables assume a 31 percent income tax rate on realized and unrealized profits, even though in most cases, unrealized profits would not be taxed until they are paid. Margin interest at 10 percent is also paid at the end of each year. The column labeled "Net Year-End Value" in Tables 11J and 11K indicates how much you would have left if you decided to withdraw from the program at any point during the 21 years after paying off the margin loan principal and taxes on any gains.

For the one-third margin program detailed in Table 11J, you would have had $214,086 at the end of 1990. The 50-percent margin program, Table 11K, produced $250,259. In both cases, the initial $10,000 is the only investment you ever make; increases in margin based on asset growth fuel investment growth.

TABLE 11J *(continued)*

Margin Interest at 10%	Taxes at 31%	Net Gain	Gross Year-End Value	Net Year-End Value	Borrowing Capacity
$500	$659	$1,466	$16,466	$11,466	$489
500	1,570	3,495	19,962	14,962	1,654
500	600	1,335	21,297	16,297	2,099
500		-1,480	19,817	14,817	1,606
500	330	735	20,552	15,552	1,851
500	1,680	3,739	24,292	19,292	3,097
500	3,241	7,214	31,506	26,506	5,502
1,325	82	183	39,942	26,689	61
1,325	2,276	5,066	45,008	31,755	1,750
1,325	3,287	7,315	52,323	39,070	4,188
1,954	12,947	28,818	87,424	67,889	9,606
1,320	3,236	7,202	88,288	75,091	16,232
3,755	11,721	26,088	138,724	101,178	8,696
5,059	11,887	26,459	178,226	127,637	8,820
6,382		-1,978	189,478	125,659	-659
6,382	15,584	34,688	224,165	160,347	10,903
8,017	870	1,936	242,456	162,283	645
8,017	13,749	30,604	273,060	192,886	10,847
9,644		-7,908	281,421	184,978	-2,636
9,644	21,612	48,104	329,526	233,083	13,399
11,654		-18,996	330,628	214,086	-6,332

If you elect to invest in a long-term leveraged program using margin, these are the steps you would take. The figures are from Table 11J with 33-percent margin.

1. Open a margin account with one of the discount brokers noted earlier. You will need to deposit at least $2,000.

2. I recommend investing at least $10,000 in the account and leveraging to $15,000 or $20,000, depending on how much leverage you apply. Invest the total in an aggressive no-load mutual fund.

3. Monitor performance of the fund and switch out of the equity fund into a money market fund when your timing indicator flashes a defensive signal. When your timing indicator flashes a signal to switch back into the equity fund, move the total amount from the money market fund into the equity fund. Continue this market timing activity throughout the year. Or

TABLE 11K
Results of Leverage Program Using 50 Percent Margin

Year	Beginning Balance	Loan Amount	Total Investment	Percent Gain or Loss	Gross Gain
1970	$10,000	$10,000	$20,000	17.50	$3,500
1971	11,725	10,000	21,725	33.80	7,343
1972	16,102	10,000	26,102	12.20	3,184
1973	17,609	17,609	35,218	-4.60	-1,620
1974	14,228	17,609	31,837	7.90	2,515
1975	14,748	17,609	32,357	28.80	9,319
1976	19,963	17,609	37,572	45.10	16,945
1977	30,441	30,441	60,881	4.00	2,435
1978	30,021	30,441	60,461	21.70	13,120
1979	36,973	30,441	67,414	26.50	17,865
1980	47,199	47,199	94,398	74.60	70,421
1981	92,533	92,533	185,066	14.50	26,835
1982	104,664	104,664	209,328	36.90	77,242
1983	150,739	150,739	301,479	28.60	86,223
1984	199,832	199,832	399,664	2.30	9,192
1985	189,041	199,832	388,873	29.90	116,273
1986	255,481	255,481	510,963	4.50	22,993
1987	253,719	255,481	509,200	21.60	109,987
1988	311,981	311,981	623,963	0.60	3,744
1989	284,527	311,981	596,509	28.20	168,215
1990	379,069	379,069	758,138	-2.10	-15,921

you could invest in one of the defensively managed funds in Group 3 or 4.

4. On the last business day of each year, pay the interest due on your margin loan. Calculate your income tax liability, federal and state, and withdraw that amount from the margin account. You will want to keep the money withdrawn for taxes in a separate money market account to earn interest until you actually pay the taxes. If the program should produce a loss, you need not remove any money from the margin account for taxes, but use the loss to offset other investment gains or ordinary income up to $3,000.

5. Examine the column labeled "Borrowing Capacity." This figure results from dividing the gross year-end value by three to find the amount of margin that could be used and subtract-

TABLE 11K *(continued)*

Margin Interest at 10%	Taxes at 31%	Net Gain	Gross Year-End Value	Net Year-End Value	Borrowing Capacity
1,000	$775	$1,725	$21,725	$11,725	$863
1,000	1,966	4,377	26,102	16,102	3,051
1,000	677	1,507	27,609	17,609	3,804
1,761		-3,381	31,837	14,228	-1,690
1,761	234	520	32,357	14,748	-1,430
1,761	2,343	5,215	37,572	19,963	1,177
1,761	4,707	10,477	48,050	30,441	6,416
3,044	-189	-420	60,461	30,021	-210
3,044	3,124	6,952	67,414	36,973	3,266
3,044	4,594	10,226	77,640	47,199	8,379
4,720	20,367	45,334	139,732	92,533	22,667
9,253	5,450	12,131	197,197	104,664	6,066
10,466	20,700	46,075	255,404	150,739	23,038
15,074	22,056	49,093	350,572	199,832	24,546
19,983		-10,791	388,873	189,041	-5,395
19,983	29,850	66,440	455,314	255,481	27,825
25,548	-792	-1,763	509,200	253,719	-881
25,548	26,176	58,263	567,463	311,981	28,250
31,198		-27,454	596,509	284,527	-13,727
31,198	42,475	94,542	691,050	379,069	33,544
37,907		-53,828	704,310	325,241	-26,914

ing the amount of margin actually being used. The net result is the amount of borrowing capacity available. On the line for 1970, note that the gross year-end value is $16,466. One third of that ($5,489) exceeds the actual loan amount by $489. To keep margin loan increases to a practical amount, this program assumes the margin loan will not be increased until it can be increased by at least $3,500. On this basis, the margin loan remains at $5,000 until 1977 following an increase in the borrowing capacity of $5,502 for 1976.

6. When the rules permit following the minimum gain of $3,500 in year-end value, increase the loan amount to one third of the total investment. At the beginning of 1977, following the gain from 1976, you would increase the loan amount by $13,253, which is half of the beginning balance. Increasing the loan amount by $13,253 reestablishes the 33 percent margin position in the account.

7. Continue monitoring your program to switch into and out of your equity fund on cue from your market timing system. When additional borrowing capacity is available, increase the loan amount to maintain the 33-percent margin position.

What happens if the market tanks? The traditional bogeyman of margin investing is the margin call—that dreaded day when your broker calls and demands that you put more cash into your account. Clearly, a margin call is an unpleasant prospect. Our back-tested data indicate, just as clearly, that if you stick to market timing principles, you are not likely to suffer a setback severe enough to encounter a margin call. During the 21-year period covered in Tables 11J and 11K, when market timing was applied, no decline was big enough to trigger a margin call.

But let's assume the worst; the market nose-dives. How bad must it get before you receive a margin call? Most discount brokers require you to maintain an equity of at least 35 percent of the value of your securities in your account at all times, but they will not make a margin call until your equity falls to 30 percent. Your equity is the total value of cash and fund shares priced at the close in the account minus your margin loan.

Thus, if you had invested $10,000 and borrowed $10,000, the value of your account would have to fall to $14,286—a loss of $5,714 or 28.6 percent—before your Schwab broker would call to ask for more money. At that point, you would be required to bring your equity back up to 35 percent, a deposit of at least $714 in cash or securities.

If you had invested $10,000 and borrowed $5,000, your account value would have to tumble to $7,143—a loss of 52.4 percent—before you would receive a margin call. Losses of these magnitudes were not experienced in our testing, and we doubt you would encounter similar losses in reality with market timing defenses in place. But there are no guarantees.

One more advantage of margin borrowing is the low rates brokers charge for margin loans. Margin rates at the time this book was written were typically 10 percent for a margin loan up to $25,000, 9 percent for $25,000 to $50,000, and 8.5 percent

TABLE 11L
Mutual Fund Purchase Commissions (Fees)

Discount Broker	Fee for $20,000 Purchase	Rates
Charles Schwab	$100	.006 of 1st $15,000
		.002 $15,000-$100,000
Jack White & Co.	60	$20 + .002
Freeman-Welwood	79	$39 + .002
Waterhouse Securities	100	.006 of 1st $15,000
		.002 over $15,000

for loans above $50,000. Interest rates for margin loans change often; ask about the current rate.

One drawback with margin investing is you must do it through a brokerage, and that means fees. Schwab, Jack White, Waterhouse, and Freeman-Welwood charge moderate fees (see Table 11L). On a $2,000 investment, the minimum to establish a margin account, Schwab's transaction fees would amount to $34 or 1.7 percent. On the purchase of $20,000 of mutual funds, the fee would drop to 0.4 percent.

For all of these reasons,

- The power of leverage
- The moderate risk possible with market timing
- The flexibility of margin borrowing and
- The low interest rates charged on the borrowed funds

Margin makes sense as a way to supercharge your earning potential.

CONCLUSION

The action plans are provided in specific detail to help you fulfill your financial objectives. Whether you are a conservative or aggressive investor, the key to success is to find an action plan or plans that will allow you emotional stability along with the financial rewards you expect to meet your objectives. The challenge is moving to action. Don't procrastinate. Do it! Just remember, as you look at those tempting high-risk investments, it's not what you make that counts, it's what you keep.

EXTRA HELP AVAILABLE

The purpose of this book is to motivate you to action—to help yourself. If you are still stuck or are hesitant to take action after reading this book, please call me at 1-206-285-8877. Ask for Paul Merriman. I will be glad to answer any question or to help you apply any disciplines described in my book.

APPENDIX

Risks and Benefits—Ratings of Investment Opportunities

Investment	Risk	Yield	Appre-ciation	Cost	Liquidity	Score
			Characteristic			
Bank/S&L savings account	1	3	5	1	1	11
Certificate of Deposit	1	2	5	1	3	12
EE bond	1	3	5	1	2	12
U.S. Treasury bond	2	2	4	2	2	12
Corporate bonds	3	2	2	3	3	13
Common stocks—listed	3	3	2	3	2	13
Common stocks—OTC	4	4	3	3	3	17
Preferred stocks	3	2	4	3	2	14
Real estate	5	4	1	5	5	20
Stock options	5	5	1	3	2	16
Futures options	5	5	1	3	2	16
Commodities	5	5	1	3	2	16
Mutual funds, Load	2	3	3	3	2	13
Mutual funds, no-load	2	2	3	1	2	10
Mutual funds, no-load with timing	2	2	2	1	2	9
Gold	4	5	2	3	3	17
Limited partnerships	5	4	2	5	5	21
Insurance, cash value	2	4	5	4	5	20
Insurance, tax deferred annuity	2	3	5	4	5	19

RESOURCES

PERIODICALS

Forbes
Forbes, Inc., 60 Fifth Ave.
New York, NY 10011

Money
Time-Life, Inc.
Time & Life Bldg.
Rockefeller Center
New York, NY 10020

Kiplinger Personal Finance Magazine
The Kiplinger Washington Editors, Inc.
1729 H Street, N.W.
Washington, DC 20006

The Wall Street Journal
200 Liberty St.
New York, NY 10281

Investor's Daily
1941 Armacost Ave.
Los Angeles, CA 90028

Barron's
200 Liberty St.
New York, NY 10281

NEWSLETTERS

NoLoad Fund X, DAL Investment Co.
235 Montgomery St.
San Francisco, CA 94104

The No-Load Fund Investor
Box 283
Hastings-on-Hudson, NY 10706

Fund Exchange
Paul A. Merriman & Associates
1200 Westlake Ave. N., Suite 700
Seattle, WA 98109

IBC/Donoghue's Moneyletter
Box 8008
Holliston, MA 01746

Personal Finance
1101 King St., Suite 400
Alexandria, VA 22314

Mutual Fund Advisor
One Sarasota Tower, Suite 602
Sarasota, FL 34236

Mutual Fund Investing
7811 Montrose Rd.
Potomac, MD 20854

Growth Stock Outlook
Box 15381
Chevy Chase, MD 20825

Bob Nurock's Advisory
Box 988
Paoli, PA 19301

The Volume Reversal Survey
Box 1451
Sedona, AZ 86336

Professional Tape Reader
Box 2407
Hollywood, FL 33022

Dessauer's Journal of Financial Markets
Box 1718
Orleans, MA 02653

Standard & Poor's Outlook
25 Broadway
New York, NY 10004

Investment Quality Trends
7440 Girard Ave., Suite 4
La Jolla, CA 02037

Hulbert Financial Digest
643 S. Carolina Ave., S.E.
Washington, DC 20006

Dow Theory Forecasts
7412 Calumet Ave.
Hammond, IN 46324

The Zweig Forecast
Box 360
Bellmore, NY 11710

BOOKS

Analysis of Financial Statements, 3rd ed., by Leopold Bernstein
Business One Irwin
1818 Ridge Rd.
Homewood, IL 60430

The Donoghue Strategies, by William E. Donoghue
Bantam Books
666 Fifth Ave., New York, NY 10103

Donoghue's Money Fund Directory, annual editions
The Donoghue Organization
P.O. Box 6640, Holliston, MA 01746

Donoghue's Mutual Funds Directory, annual editions., ibid.

Dow Jones Investor's Handbook, by Phyllis Pierce
Dow Jones-Irwin, 1818 Ridge Rd.,
Homewood, IL 60430

Guide to Mutual Funds, annual editions
Investment Company Institute
1600 M Street, N.W.
Washington, DC 20036

The Handbook of Financial Market Indexes, Averages, and Indicators, by Howard M. Berlin
Dow Jones-Irwin, 1818 Ridge Rd.,
Homewood, IL 60430

Individual Investor's Guide to No-Load Mutual Funds, annual editions
American Association of Individual Investors
625 N. Michigan Ave.
Chicago, IL 60611

Standard and Poor's Stock Reports (Separate volumes for NYSE, AMEX, and OTC Market)—at your library

Stock Market Trading Systems, by Gerald Appel and Fred Hitschler
Dow Jones-Irwin
1818 Ridge Rd.
Homewood, IL 60430

Stocks, Bonds, Bills and Inflation, annual editions
Ibbotson Associates
8 South Michigan Ave.
Chicago, IL 60603

The Wall Street Journal Guide to Understanding Money & Markets, by Richard Saul Wurman, Alan Siegel, Kenneth M. Morris
Access Press, Ltd.
133 Spring St.
New York, NY 10022

Why the Best-Laid Investment Plans Usually Go Wrong & How You Can Find Safety and Profit in an Uncertain World, by Harry Browne
William Morrow & Co.
105 Madison Ave.
New York, NY 10016

ADDRESSES

The American College
Bryn Mawr, PA 19010

College of Financial Planning
9725 E. Hampden Ave.
Denver, CO 80231

Institute of Certified Financial Planners
Two Denver Highlands
10065 E. Harvard Ave.
Denver, CO 80231

Institute of Chartered Financial Analysts
P.O. Box 3668
Charlottesville, VA 22903

International Association of Financial Planners
Two Concourse Parkway, Suite 500
Atlanta, GA 30328

DISCOUNT BROKERS

Charles Schwab & Co., Inc.
101 Montgomery St.
San Francisco, CA 94104
(415) 627-7000; 1-800-442-5111

Freeman Welwood & Co., Inc.
2800 Century Square,
501 4th Ave.
Seattle, WA 98101
(206) 382-5353; 1-800-426-1160

Jack White & Co.
La Jolla Gateway Bldg.
9191 Towne Centre Drive, Suite 220
San Diego, CA 92122
(619) 587-2000; 1-800-233-4411

Waterhouse Securities, Inc.
44 Wall St.
New York, NY 10005
(212) 344-7500; 1-800-327-7500

MISCELLANEOUS

Capital Withdrawal Chart
Merle E. Dowd & Associates
7438 S.E. 40th St.
Mercer Island, WA 98040
Available only by mail, $3 postpaid

IRS Publication 590
Free from Internal Revenue Service offices

Standard & Poor's Stock Guide, monthly editions
Standard & Poor's Corp.
25 Broadway
New York, NY 10004

Your Personal Money Plan
Merle E. Dowd & Associates,
7438 S.E. 40th St.
Mercer Island, WA 98040
Available only by mail, $4.50 postpaid

INDEX

Also Available from
Business One Irwin:

RAGING BULL
How to Invest in the Growth Stocks of the '90s
David Alger

After several years of disappointing performance, small capitalization stocks are now outperforming the S&P 500 and offer individual investors a multitude of profit opportunities. This is your guide to making the move from stable, slow-growing blue chips to smaller stocks with potentially higher growth. (200 pages)

ISBN: 1-55623-462-7

STAN WEINSTEIN'S SECRETS FOR PROFITING IN BULL AND BEAR MARKETS
Stan Weinstein

From the editor/publisher of *The Professional Tape Reader*! Weinstein reveals his successful methods for timing investments to produce consistently profitable results. An essential guide for every investor using technical analysis to pick the winners. (348 pages)

ISBN: 1-55623-079-6

THE HANDBOOK FOR NO-LOAD FUND INVESTORS
11th Edition
Edited by Sheldon Jacobs

The complete book on mutual fund investing to help you make the most profitable decisions! A complete directory that includes advice on choosing the right fund for your situation, performance data, and more. (530 pages, 8½ x 11, paper)

ISBN: 1-55623-528-3

THE BUSINESS ONE IRWIN BUSINESS AND INVESTMENT ALMANAC, 1992
Edited by Sumner N. Levine

This classic reference tool is the most comprehensive fact book available today to help you make the best business and investment decisions. Includes major and group stock market averages, pricing/earnings ratios, reviews of the major futures markets, and more! (725 pages)

ISBN: 1-55623-532-1